W9-DFA-150

U.S.

AMERICA'S

BIRTHDAY

A Planning and Activity Guide for Citizens' Participation During the Bicentennial Years

by Peoples Bicentennial Commission

SIMON AND SCHUSTER NEW YORK

Major writers and contributors to the book:

TED HOWARD
CHARLIE JONES

General contributors:

BILL CALLAHAN—The TEA Party
KATHY JOHNSON
BOB LEONARD
CICELY NICHOLS
LOU REDDIN
JEREMY RIFKIN
SHEILA ROLLINS
JANE SCHULL
ED SCHWARTZ

Graphic sources:

Catchpenny Prints, originally published by Bowles and Carrer. New York: Dover Publications, Inc., 1970.

Edmund V. Gillon, Jr., *Early Illustrations and Views of American Architecture.* Dover Publications, Inc., 1971.

The Library of Congress

The National Archives

Posters:

Terry Dale, copyright 1973.

 Published by Simon and Schuster
Rockefeller Center, 630 Fifth Avenue, New York, New York 10020

SBN 671-21713-5 Casebound
SBN 671-21714-3 Paperback
Library of Congress Catalog Card Number: 74-371
Manufactured in the United States of America

1 2 3 4 5 6 7 8 9 10

DESIGNED BY JACK JAGET

To
SAM ADAMS
and
TOM PAINE.
They dared
to be free!

Contents

I Introduction

In the 1770's, there was a Revolution in this country.

In the 1970's, the White House and Corporate America are planning to sell us a program of plastic Liberty Bells, red-white-and-blue cars and a "Love It or Leave It" political program.

The Peoples Bicentennial Commission believes that the forthcoming two-hundredth anniversary of the American Revolution does not have to fit these commercial, Tory expectations—that it can, and must, be channeled into a new movement to reclaim the democratic ideals upon which this nation was founded.

We will be celebrating radical heroes like Jefferson, Paine and Adams, and radical events like the Boston Tea Party and the sessions of the Continental Congress. All the while, modern-day Tories will attempt to present themselves and the institutions they control—the corporations, the White House—as the true heirs and defenders of the struggle waged by the first American revolutionaries.

The forces about to be unleashed in America's Bicentennial Era are ours to take hold of. We must reassert the ideals that have driven Americans throughout our history to struggle for justice, equality and popular control of social institutions. Our revolutionary principles must be used to challenge existing institutions and those in power by constantly focusing public attention on the New Tories' inability to translate our Revolutionary dreams into reality.

A Peoples Bicentennial can inspire a new social, energetic commitment for millions of disillusioned Americans. The Bicentennial Era presents us with a unique opportunity to address the two major issues of the 1970's: the arrogant, kinglike usurpation and concentration of power within the Executive Branch—in gross violation of the Constitution—and the rise of a corporate aristocracy unresponsive to the needs of the people and the ideals of a democracy. The year 1976 can also provide a strategic target date toward which issue-oriented groups can plan. Fulfilling the promise of '76 is already being taken up as a banner by groups across the country. The Bicentennial can provide a common language and psychology that can unite individuals and groups into a force for real change during the Bicentennial decade.

The crucial task facing those of us engaged in programs for change is to prepare the psychological groundwork for a new movement, based on the fulfillment of the revolutionary promise of America.

In the past, many Americans have based their personal self-confidence on the mere fact that they were Americans: the nation's greatness was their greatness too. Today, after a decade of disastrous war, race riots, political assassinations, pollution and urban decay, political corruption, unemployment and a host of other critical problems threatening our very survival, many Americans feel bewildered and confused. Many are be-

PAUL REVERE'S RIDE

ginning to question the very values and institutions that they have held sacred all their lives. The pervasive, precipitous decline in national morale has been traced in a number of public-opinion polls; one Gallup survey concluded, typically, that "over half of the American people no longer trust the Federal Government. Traditional optimism about the nation's steady progress has faltered. The average American feels that the United States has slid back over the past few years."

A new Populist sentiment is emerging from this crisis of confidence—and the big business interests, the people who control America's wealth and power, are acutely aware of the escalating Populist mood. They realize that the economic and political institutions they control are vulnerable to intensive questioning; they realize that their own power could be exposed to serious challenge. In an attempt to cope with these gathering threats, corporate America has conceived a Bicentennial plan to manipulate the mass psychology of an entire nation back into conformity with his vision of what the American way of life should be. The strategy will be to speak of the greatness of America to those who feel insignificant; to speak of confidence in the American reality to those who feel weak; to speak of patriotic commitment to those who feel isolated and confused. The long-range goal is to convince people that the problems facing America can be solved by existing institutions; that the root of the unease and the threat to our well-being lie not in the inequality that has swollen into a rich corporate/government elite, but rather in subversive forces determined to undermine the will and resolve of a great nation and the vitality of a great people. If there are Americans who are disaffected, who are angry, who are disappointed by their nation's failure to meet the promises of the American dream at home and sickened by its murderous adventures abroad, then it is the purpose of the Bicentennial to set those people straight—or, if that fails, to isolate them from the nation's mainstream. "My fellow Americans," President Nixon declared in his 1971 Independence Day Address, "we share tonight a great moment, the beginning of the Bicentennial Era. . . . To look at America with clear eyes today is to see every reason for gratitude and little for regret, strong grounds for hope and none at all for despair. The crucial challenge now is to hold the high ground of confidence, courage and faith that is rightly ours, and to avoid the quicksand of fear and doubt."

Building a Democratic Bicentennial Movement

In the 1970's, millions of Americans are aware that many of our economic, social and political institutions operate in ways that are not consistent with the demo-

WHAT ARE WE CELEBRATING ON JULY 4TH?

cratic ideals and principles to which the nation was dedicated. Men and women from one end of the spectrum of American society to the other have lost confidence in government institutions and the political leadership. Disaffection is sweeping through the country. The frustrations do not substantially vary from group to group—the grievances are at root common grievances, the disaffection is widespread disaffection; yet with all of this shared frustration, diverse groups find it almost impossible to work together as a unified political force for fundamental change.

Land of opportunity, the family, women in their place, college as a stepping-stone to the upper class, just wars, just courts—the list of American beliefs that once seemed sturdy and are shaky now could go on and on. One immediate effect of the anxiety created by the tumbling of myths—by disaffection with long-held, formerly comfortable ideas—is distrust of change, a longing for structure and order and direction. In addition, this mass anxiety exacerbates frictions and tensions between diverse groups; the very differences between Irish and Italian, welfare recipients and hardhats, adults and youth, counterculture and silent majority, whites and blacks become reasons for distrust. Of course, it is in the interests of America's elite to perpetuate this distrust. As a start toward a truly popular movement—a movement of the people—at the least it is imperative that a common language be developed that will allow diverse groups to begin to discuss their common interests.

The Bicentennial Era provides a setting within which we can develop that common language; it is the language of the Declaration of Independence—which is demonstrated, defined and exemplified in every great movement for social justice in the past two hundred years. The language of America's Revolution can help bring Americans together now in a shared vision of our Revolutionary promise and a renewed dedication to the fulfillment of that promise. The first step is to look back at our own past, with an eye to what is relevant to today. We need to reexamine the social base laid down before and during the Revolution of 1776 and its re-

FRANCIS MARION—"THE SWAMP FOX"—CROSSING THE PEE DEE RIVER, 1778

newal in the successive dramas of change that characterize the most affirmative periods of American history: The day-to-day issues and debates that were of such significance to the people of 1776 may have passed from our memory, but the ideals and principles forged within the course of those debates remain supremely important—and there is a residue of dedication to those principles still remaining in every American, in spite of the contradictions. The Revolution of 1776 struck the established oligarchic institutions with terrible force—ending the feudal inheritance code, awarding land to settlers instead of speculators, breaking the monopolies of the state churches, confiscating the properties of the wealthy Tories. Legislatures previously limited to a few families became open to ever-larger numbers. The abominable Tea Tax gave way to the hated Whiskey Tax of the Federalist Era and then to the soak-the-rich Consumption Tax. Liberties such as the one that protects this book were woven into the political fabric.

There are many basic freedoms which the founders of our country did not deal with, or dealt with only in passing; the status of women and the status of blacks are glaring examples. A distinction must be drawn, however, between the ideals of the first Revolution and the people who pronounced them. The founders were mortal and need not be thought of as anything more. That they often failed to live up to their own principles is a fact not merely of history, but of human nature.

Humanism, it should be obvious, is created by humans, not demigods. All of us live within the narrow confines of our times. Thomas Jefferson held slaves; Benjamin Franklin was a womanizer; but we learn more about the real importance of historical figures by observing their conflict with their own world than by measuring their closeness to ours. Using this approach to examine America's past, we can begin to explore the social psychology that has historically given form and definition to our attitudes and behavior as a people.

THE DRAFTING OF THE DECLARATION OF INDEPENDENCE:
left to right: TOM JEFFERSON, ROGER SHERMAN, BEN FRANKLIN, ROBERT LIVINGSTON, JOHN ADAMS

An accurate analysis of the American spirit must take into account the fact that the American legacy is at once both authoritarian and democratic.

Our democratic beliefs—popularized through the words and deeds of such great Americans as Thomas Paine, Samuel Adams, Benjamin Franklin, Thomas Jefferson, Henry Thoreau, Abraham Lincoln, William Lloyd Garrison, Davy Crockett, John Brown, Sojourner Truth, Horace Mann, Lucy Stone, Mark Twain, Eugene V. Debs, W. E. B. Du Bois and A. J. Muste—derive from the principle of the inherent unity and amity of all mankind. These aspirations have led to a set of beliefs that forms the democratic aspect of the American experience: human equality; respect for the judgment of the common people; distrust of those who occupy positions of power and privilege. The believers in democracy advocated freedom of expression and the right to self-determination; cooperative enterprise; government of the people, by the people, for the people; conscience above property and institutions. They maintained an interest in the new, the untried, the unexplored; they kept confidence in the ability of the people to create a more just and humane world.

Our authoritarian beliefs—popularized through the words and deeds of such Americans as Alexander Hamilton, Jay Gould, John D. Rockefeller and H. L. Hunt—come from the principle that hostility and war and the survival of the fittest constitute the natural condition of man. This principle is the basis of a set of beliefs that forms the authoritarian aspect of the American experience; that promotes private property as a value more sacred than human rights, a ruthlessly competitive spirit as the means for self-fulfillment and material accumulation as a measure of man's achievement on earth.

It is important for us to challenge these authoritarian beliefs by commiting ourselves to the democratic values of the American legacy. By reasserting the democratic promise of our heritage, we can establish a sense of security and continuity with the most positive aspects of our American tradition.

JOHN NIXON "RENDS THE WELKIN"—THE FIRST PUBLIC READING OF THE DECLARATION, PHILADELPHIA, JULY 8, 1776

Using Our Own Experience

The American heritage embodies a set of principles or ideals which provides the great mass of people with a unique social identity. It is a statement of our beliefs—what we stand for and what we dedicate ourselves to as a people. We should explore our humanist tradition, which grew up side by side with oppression and which often brought the Colonists into conflict with their oppressors. We should trace the development of that tradition into the stated ideals of the American Revolution and look at the way those ideals found their way into political practice.

Understanding the democratic currents and movements that have influenced American life can help those of us already involved in political struggle to develop a revolutionary perspective that is germane to America. Past struggles against authoritarianism in America, such as the abolitionist and woman's-suffrage movements and the farmer and labor insurgencies, cannot be expected to provide a blueprint for revolution in the 1970's, but they can tell us much about American behavior and the American character. We cannot build a contemporary revolution without an acute awareness of ourselves as a people, as citizens of a nation born in revolution.

A genuine understanding of American democratic ideals is what links the American people with the struggles of all oppressed people in the world. Indeed, the American Revolution has stood as an example for the

THE CALL TO ARMS

revolutions of the Third World. Not until the majority of Americans begin to reidentify with our democratic principles and develop our own revolutionary struggle will we be able to form a real bond of fraternalism and solidarity with the struggles of all oppressed people. Solidarity comes from understanding the collective nature of our separate struggles and the cry for humanity that is shared by all.

Confidence in our ability to sustain a political movement and to develop a long-range democratic perspective that is neither rigid nor authoritarian must come from an understanding of who we are; and much of what we are has to do with our unique American heritage. Such an understanding will help bring together the existing factions and groupings within the activist community itself.

Without confidence in our democratic heritage, deteriorating economic and social conditions are liable to lead America to an increased sense of hopelessness and fear and a successful defense by Nixon's Administration of the most authoritarian aspects of the American ideology—with appeals to national honor, duty, courage and vigilance in protection of the Mother Country —as the American people make a desperate attempt to hold on to what is familiar in their everyday life.

The Bicentennial Era provides us with a unique strategic timetable around which to organize, beginning with the two-hundredth anniversary of the Boston Tea Party in 1973 and building to the anniversary of the signing of the Declaration of Independence and the Presidential election of 1976. We must begin now to prepare ourselves. The Peoples Bicentennial Commission is beginning to propagate our Revolutionary principles through every forum of communication at our disposal: radio, television, community newspapers, magazines, books, theater, music, art. We are encouraging activist organizations to integrate the principles of our revolutionary heritage into every political activity.

Revolutionary movements develop when people begin to raise their own expectations of what the promise of their society should be. It is time to expect the fulfillment of the promise set forth two hundred years ago in our own Declaration of Independence. It is time to assert our rights against those Tories who, like Nixon, would commercialize, trivialize and vandalize that promise. In 1976, we, the American people, will celebrate the two-hundredth anniversary of the signing of the Declaration of Independence. It must be our goal in the next years of struggle to recapture our promise and to build on it a society worthy of our legacy.

II

The American Revolutionary Perspective

Issues of the American Revolution

Much of what you find in history depends on what you're looking for. It's pretty generally agreed that the history of ideas in America divides into two camps, with Roger Williams, Benjamin Franklin and Thomas Jefferson the major early figures in one camp and John Cotton, Joseph Gallaway and Alexander Hamilton the leading lights in the other. The Peoples Bicentennial Commission is more interested in the first of those two camps, and in exploring the relevance of that temper of thought to our own times, than in the second camp's philosophy. After all, the first camp is the ground of revolution—of radical break with the Old World social order, of what made the New World new and inspired revolutionaries from the French Jacobins to Gandhi's nonviolent movement. The second camp—Cotton, Hamilton and their like—were merely intellectual embroiderers of the old fabric. Those who are determined to view the United States as a dog-eat-dog society, and to view the American Revolution as nothing but a transfer of power from a British aristocracy to an American aristocracy, have never been in short supply. But if there was a revolution of thought, of social order, of family life, of economic system—and there are reputable historians who say there was; and if immigrants came to America in search of new freedoms as well as economic opportunity—and that is what vast numbers of immigrants said they were doing; then the New World was more than just new land.

POWER TO THE PEOPLE

From the start, America debated and fought over what the Revolution would and should be. An unsympathetic observer of a rally, two years before the Declaration of Independence, reported:

> I beheld my fellow citizens very accurately counting all their chickens, not only before they were hatched, but before above one half of the eggs were laid. In short, they fairly contended about the future forms of our government, whether it should be founded upon aristocratic or democratic principles.

The controversy did not end with the issuance of the Declaration of Independence; many supporters of the Revolution wanted it to be only a break with England, not a break with old ways, and worked hard to limit the

Revolution to just that; on the other hand were radical democrats who expected far more. Four months after the Declaration was signed, when North Carolina got down to writing a state constitution, Mecklenburg County instructed its delegates to seek "a simple democracy, or as near it as possible." The delegates were not given a treatise on political theory, but a maxim:

> Oppose everything that leans to aristocracy of power in the hands of the rich and chief men exercised to the oppression of the poor.

In New Hampshire, when the eastern Establishment announced an electoral plan that neglected any representation of the working people in the west, the people of Grafton County, led by professors at a small college, went on strike and refused to hold elections. They said that when the Assembly acted contrary to the Declaration of Independence, the Assembly had made itself illegitimate. Therefore, they announced:

> We conceive that the powers of government reverted to the people at large, and of course annihilated the political existence of the assembly.

The new state constitutions reflected the demand for power to the people: governors were to be elected now, and furthermore, the office was stripped of all but a vestige of power; under England's rule, of course, the Royal Governors were appointees, chosen by England's rulers, and the office of governor had been a miniature version of the monarchy itself, with sweeping authority. Now the legislatures had the authority—and in the legislatures, the lower houses were the dominant force. The upper houses, erected to represent the propertied interests, had only a shadow of the power that upper houses had before the Revolution, when they had been appointed by the Royal Governors. Places on state supreme courts were to be filled by the vote of the legislature or by appointment by the elected governor—again, a radical change from the pre-Revolutionary system of appointment by the appointed governor. The new state constitutions made the will of the citizenry—though it might be delayed—in the final analysis supreme, as long as there were no private, unelected governments such as business corporations to abort that will.

Issue: Feudal Taxes and Inheritance Codes

Many aspects of the old feudal code were still intact at the time of the Revolution, though they had been steadily weakened with the landing of every shipful of new immigrants. One of the most hateful—to small farmers—was still in operation, enforced by the aristocracy: the system of "quitrents," traditional payments that peasants had to make to nobles in order to be released from the duty to perform labor for the lord of the manor. The feudal taxes were extremely oppressive in the middle states; when the Revolution got under way, the farmers immediately stopped paying.

The most notable of the holdovers from feudal times was the inheritance code, which had descended from Norman England. The code rested upon the devices of primogeniture and entail: primogeniture ensured that a man's estate would be inherited by his eldest son; entail prohibited the division of an estate, even if the debts against it were greater than its value. The rationale was clear: the British system depended on the existence of an aristocratic class that would support governmental authority and supply the personnel of government from its own membership. An English aristocrat, whether he took a political office and used it for profit or remained in his castle and gathered the profits generated by his friends in government, was both support for and beneficiary of the system. That system made his life possible, and he could be counted on to bring his power to the defense of a government that gave him ample opportunities for profit.

BEN FRANKLIN GETS THE THIRD DEGREE FROM KING GEORGE'S CABINET

The inheritance code had never really thrived in America, but American democrats knew it was the soul of the old order. In England, the inheritance code continued through the 19th century. In America, the democrats launched a full-scale assault on it before the ink had dried on the Declaration. Small farmers of western Virginia arrayed themselves against the old-line gentry of Williamsburg; when they defeated the gentry in politics, they flaunted their victory by transferring the capital from chic Williamsburg to the west, where they could keep an eye on it.

Issue: Representation

In 1765, radicals had fought to stop the government from imposing a stamp tax on, among other things, newspapers. Against the taxation ideas of George III, the Revolutionaries posed a new set of principles. They insisted on "no taxation without representation," but Samuel Adams pointed out that the slogan by no means implied a desire to have members in Parliament:

> We are far from desiring any representation there, because we think the colonies cannot be equally and fully represented, and if not equally then in effect not at all.

The truth was, the Americans didn't want any taxes at all, and they were not interested in any political theory that could lead to them. When the federalists took charge, they imposed a whiskey tax, and the people of western Pennsylvania literally rose in arms against this unjust taxation of the common man's drink. When the democrats seized control of the Treasury Department in 1801, they pushed through a consumption tax, which Jefferson praised:

> The farmer will see his government supported, his children educated, and the face of the country made a paradise by the contributions of the rich alone, without his being called on to spare a cent from his earnings.

America had come a great distance—the breadth of a Revolution—from the regressive taxation of the old regime to the egalitarian attitude of the democratic movement.

THE DECLARATION OF INDEPENDENCE, THE CONSTITUTION AND FUNDAMENTAL INDIVIDUAL PROTECTIONS

The Revolution was fought on the basis of the ideas that had been growing in the New World—and for one of the few times in the history of revolutions, the ideas were explicitly formulated, written and distributed. Thus, the purposes of the American Revolutionary War were set forth in a written Declaration of Independence which spoke of men's rights against the state and foreign control. When the country constituted itself, it drew together first with the Articles of Confederation; then later with a written Constitution, eventually amended with the Bill of Rights.

To have a written Declaration of Independence was an important act of revolution, carrying out the American spirit and reflecting the democratic ideal that all men have certain inalienable rights. These rights were considered to be self-evident. Since people, equal by nature, and born with certain worth and capacity, had rights, it was clear that they could insist upon them against any ruler. Tom Paine wrote:

> While all men could be persuaded they had no rights, or that rights appertained only to a certain class of men, or that government was a thing existing in right of itself, it was not difficult to govern them authoritatively. . . . But when the ignorance is gone and the superstition with it, when they perceive that imposition that has been acted upon them, when they reflect that the cultivator and the manufacturer are the primary means of all the wealth that exists in the world beyond what nature spontaneously produces, when they begin to feel their consequences by their usefulness and their right as members of society, it is then no longer possible to govern them as before. The fraud once detected cannot be retracted. To attempt it is to provoke derision and to invite destruction.

From the 1770's to the democratic electoral victory of 1800, a new society was built. Tom Paine called it "the birth of a world."

Making sure that these rights would be recognized became an important goal in the writing of a Constitution. The English had what they called an "unwritten constitution," which relied on judges to follow principles enunciated by other judges and thereby reflect, hopefully, some concern for human value and rights. The Americans would have none of this tradition; they wanted to ensure that people's rights against the government were clear and certain. A written document was required, specifying power, authority, duties, rights and procedures, reflecting the values declared by the Revolution.

> Let me add that a bill of rights is what the people are entitled to against every government on earth, general or particular, and what no just government should refuse, or rest on inference. —THOMAS JEFFERSON, 1787

The Constitution was not enough; certain basic rights were deemed so basic that they too must be written out explicitly. And so the Bill of Rights, initially twelve Amendments, was circulated for passage. Ten passed—of which the last two are particularly notable. The Ninth and Tenth Amendments state that all rights not specifically taken from the people are the people's. This was a new idea: people did not receive their rights and power from the state as a gift, but rather surrendered certain specific rights to a governing body in order to secure "a more perfect union." Rights flowed from the people, rights were inherent in people; the Constitution was the written embodiment, and the Ninth and Tenth Amendments make clear the source of rights. (Ironically, they have very rarely been invoked, until recently, when Justice Arthur Goldberg, for example, used the Ninth to discuss the Constitutional right to privacy.)

Considered as fundamental, the Amendments that constitute the Bill of Rights are to be read broadly. Justice Hugo Black referred to them as Commands, to be given the maximum sweep. Thus, no censorship of speech, according to him, could ever be tolerated. Others, particularly Justice Potter Stewart and Justice William O. Douglas, have found other rights that come from a reading of the first ten Amendments as one unified basic statement of rights. Thus we have a Right to Travel into and out of the United States; thus we have a Right to Privacy, even to excluding the agents of the law from our homes in most circumstances and being free in the matter of birth control.

Many of these rights today seem almost clichés—such as the freedom to assemble and to have a due-process trial. But with some of them even now under attack, it is important to remember that their written statement as the foundation of a government by "We the People" was the culmination of the Revolutionary idea of people's having inalienable rights as individuals—equal in the sight of anything or anyone. And these written expressions of this basic democratic concept have, when implemented by courts to integrate schools, invalidate convictions, guarantee the right to speak in public and due process for the accused, often caused basic rethinking about current social problems.

Issue: The Rights of Man

By and large, history is written by men and for men. It is not surprising, therefore, that the history of America's Revolution frequently mentions the Founding Fathers and the Sons of Liberty—all white, all male—when in fact it took women as well as men to make a Revolution. The personification of the idea of Liberty—whose sons the Founding Fathers were—is female; but that is only a symbolic role for women, comfortable for men to contemplate and easy to dismiss.

A SOLDIER'S WIFE AT FORT NIAGARA

Women's role in the Revolutionary War was not only symbolic, however, and nothing but the inclinations of historians justifies the dismissal of women from the history books. In spite of such inclinations, we do know that women led boycotts of British goods; that the women of Boston crashed into the warehouse of a profiteering businessman, dumped him into a cart and divided up his goods; that when battle was joined, there were not a few women firing shots at the British, from houses and on the battlefields. Women fed and clothed the patriot troops, and women who stayed on the farm or at home in towns often had the chance—and took it—to spy out British plans and pass them to the patriots.

Perhaps the most far-reaching change the New World fostered was the change in the structure of the family. The Independents and the Congregationalists among the Puritans, who were the immigrants with the greatest effect on the new society, began with the principle that each individual was responsible for the fate of his—and her—own soul; therefore, each person must learn to read, in order to understand and form an opinion of the Bible for him- and herself. Such an idea! It was much denounced at the time, by those who had a glimmering of the consequences; the consequences were that the American family, right from the start, was more egalitarian and more democratic than the family in the Old World. This more democratic family structure naturally had a dramatic—and continuing—effect on the place of children and the place of women in society.

Still, we have only hints, in current textbooks, of the fate of the family—and of the thoughts and actions of women—in the American heritage. We know that Deborah Moody, a large landowner in Salem, left there in

A MINUTE MAN PREPARING FOR WAR

1643 with a group of dissenters and founded Gravesend, Long Island, a community which she planned and managed on the principle of religious toleration for all faiths. We know that Eliza Lucas Pinckney managed an enormous estate in the Carolinas and devoted considerable time and talent to agricultural experimentation; she introduced indigo, for one instance, which became the second-largest export crop of the Carolinas. We know that Sally St. Clair of South Carolina and Deborah Sampson of New England dressed in men's clothes and fought in the Revolutionary War. The first best-selling novel by an American was by an American woman—and the second-most-popular novelist was an advocate of women's rights, as was Tom Paine. Women voted equally with men in the State of New Jersey after the Declaration of Independence—until 1807, when the right was taken away.

And we know that Abigail Adams foreshadowed the demands and philosophy of the women's movement two hundred years later, when she wrote her husband, John, as he prepared to vote on the Declaration of Independence:

> If particular care and attention is not paid to the ladies, we are determined to foment a rebellion, and will not hold ourselves bound by any laws in which we have no voice or representation.

Issue: The Right to Life, Liberty and the Pursuit of Happiness

Black emancipation was not furthered during the war against the King, and the denunciation of the slave trade that was in the original draft of the Declaration was voted out—as the denunciation of slavery was from the Constitution—but the Revolutionary mentality went to work against slavery. The Revolutionary leaders maneuvered to seal off the institution south of the Ohio River. The Constitutional Convention compromised on the slave-trade issue and forbade Congress to end it before 1807; at that time, Congress promptly ended it. Indeed, Article 1, Section 2 of the Constitution counts a slave as three-fifths of a person for purposes of representation. But the ending of the slave trade and the restriction of the slavocracy to the South cramped and eroded its power until the free states would be strong enough to force the issue. Benjamin Rush, a signer of the Declaration, and Thaddeus Kosciusko, who followed up his Revolutionary work in America with two insurrections in Poland, were among the founders of the abolition movement, which continued until Emancipation to speak the language of the First American Revolution in urging another. On March 8, 1775, Tom Paine had called for abolition in his first published article, "African Slavery in America."

The Continuing Revolutionary Tradition

The Revolutionary War was a dramatic, decisive and crucial moment in the Revolution. Embodying all the thinking and ideals that precipitated it, it unleashed forces that had again more revolutionary impact. To talk about inalienable rights leads logically to the consideration of the plight of slaves, women, Indians and other "second-class citizens." To challenge rulers' right to rule is to recognize that the government rests upon the consent of the governed—who still retain their dignity and certain fundamental rights. The events of war, the logic of the ideas, the expression of the principles that justified the Revolutionary War—all these led inevitably to the Revolution's culminating in a new and basic democratic viewpoint, embodying the worth of individuals and their right to be free of oppression.

The people did not capture voting rights and other elements of democratic government simply by overthrowing the British colonial government, but struggle against King George opened the way for them to assert their rights—and having seen the greatest military power on earth defeated by men like themselves, the small farmers and tradesmen felt able to deal with the aristocrats who held power in America. The theory of inalienable and equal rights implied democracy; those who fought for democratic control of legislatures and other institutions consistently voiced their demands in the language of the Declaration and the Revolutionary movement of 1776.

Not long after the King's troops were gone, the

Liberty

Freedom

wealthy merchants consolidated their power over the new government. In the 1790's, working people responded to this usurpation of the Revolution by organizing themselves into "democratic-republican" societies. The circular of the Pennsylvania Democratic Society complained in 1793:

> The seeds of luxury appear to have taken root in our domestic soil, and the jealous eye of patriotism already regards the spirit of freedom and equality as eclipsed by the pride of wealth and the arrogance of power.

The rich men who had taken control of the nation were believed to have been either Tories or neutrals during the war against the King. "Where are *your* scars?" the Democratic Society of Chittenden County, Vermont, asked the conservative businessmen.

Societies in every state—many of which considered themselves as Sons of Liberty clubs—met to discuss politics and also to hold social events. But there was far more to them than that. The spirit of the Revolution was still very much alive. They set up their own law system and provided for arbitration between members, for the legal process was unfair to working people. One of the most popular leaders of the democrats was William Keteltas of the New York Society, who fought all his life against imprisonment for debt, unfair punishments and corruption in government. Crowds often followed him shouting, "The Spirit of Seventy-six, the Spirit of Seventy-six!"

In the Presidential election of 1800, John Adams' bid for reelection was defeated by Thomas Jefferson, and the democratic-republican societies, which had banded around Jefferson, became the Democratic-Republican

Party, the ancestor of the present Democratic Party. Its formation had been illegal and immoral in the eyes of Washington, Adams and other Federalists; but to the radical democrats, this overthrow of government was the reasonable continuation of the Revolution.

Tom Paine wrote:

> America was turning her back on her own glory, and making hasty strides in the retrograde path of oblivion. But a spark from the altar of *Seventy Six,* unextinguished and unextinguishable through the long night of error, is again lighting up, in every part of the union, the genuine name of rational liberty.

Respectable Englishmen considered the American example of people's demanding rights foolish and dangerous. England, they felt, was a "mature" nation, whereas

> America is a young nation, and her institutions are still younger; they have been formed on speculative notions of the individual independence and inherent rights of man, without much reference to the experience of the ancient modes of government, or the social principle which combines and merges the rights of man in the duties of society. The experience of Europe was rejected in America.

On the other hand, there were the English radicals; one of their papers boasted that "America is a thorn in the bosoms of the despots of Europe. She may proudly bid them defiance." For generations, America was not only the land European working people dreamed of moving to, but also the home of the Revolution that was expected to sweep across the seas. And American leaders encouraged fellow revolutionaries in England, Ireland, France, Latin America and Poland.

The Revolutionary theory of democracy reached its zenith in the theory Thomas Jefferson first announced in a letter to James Madison in 1787. "The Earth," he said, "belongs to the living and the dead have neither rights nor powers over it." From this basic concept, Jefferson struck upon the idea that laws should expire when half the people alive at their enactment had died. Mortal men and women should not make immortal laws. This was the theory of democracy pushed to its limits: it meant that laws and institutions were, in a sense, illegitimate unless they had been created by human beings, and the dead, as Jefferson remarked, were not human beings.

Tom Paine also argued that the earth belongs to the living. When Edmund Burke published his *Reflections on the Revolution in France,* a counterrevolutionary book which George III said every respectable gentleman should read, Paine countered it in turn with his great work *The Rights of Man,* in which he wrote:

> I am contending for the rights of the living, and against their being led away, and controlled and contracted for by the manuscript-assumed authority of the dead; and Mister Burke is contending for the authority of the dead over the rights and freedom of the living.
>
> There never did, there never will, and there never can exist a Parliament, or any description of men, in any country, possessed of the right or the power of binding and controlling posterity to the end of time, or of commanding forever how the world shall be governed, or who shall govern it; and therefore all such clauses, acts or declarations by which the makers of them attempt to do what they have neither the right nor the power to do, nor the power to execute, are in themselves null and void.

The conflict between those who worked for a living and those who lived on the inheritances from their ancestors was also a warfare between the living and the dead. Working people felt that their struggle to democratize the inheritance code was a continuation of the battle against the aristocracy. The dead should not be allowed to control vast fortunes through the laws. A perceptive French visitor, Alexis de Tocqueville, discussed the effects of the Revolution in his *Democracy in America* (1830):

> The law of inheritance was the last step to equality. I am surprised that ancient and modern jurists have not attributed to this law a greater influence on human affairs. It is true that these laws belong to civil affairs, but they ought, nevertheless, to be placed at the head of all political institutions, for they exercise an incredible influence upon the social state of a people, while political laws show only what this state already is. They have, moreover, a sure and uniform manner of operating upon society, affecting, as it were, generations yet unborn. Through their means man acquires a kind of preternatural power over the future lot of his fellow creatures. When the legislator has once regulated the law of inheritance, he may rest from his labor; the machine once put in motion will go on for ages, and advance as if self-guided, towards a point indicated beforehand. When framed in a particular manner, this law unites, draws together, and vests property and power into a few hands: it causes an aristocracy, so to speak, to spring out of the ground. If formed on opposite principles, its action is still more rapid: it divides, distributes and disperses both property and power. Alarmed by the rapidity of its progress, those who despair of arresting its motion endeavor at least to obstruct it by difficulties and impediments. They vainly seek to counteract it by contrary efforts, but it shatters and reduces to powder every obstacle, until we can no longer see anything but a moving and impalpable cloud of dust, which signals the coming of the Democracy.

But as the feudal inheritance code was eliminated, a new type of hereditary privilege was being developed: corporations were being chartered and their duration was made perpetual. Democrats viewed this development as illegal and based their arguments against it upon Jefferson's theory. THE EARTH BELONGS TO THE LIVING proclaimed the banners carried by angry marchers.

DEFENSE OF THE LIBERTY POLE IN NEW YORK

To wealthy merchants and well-heeled reformers alike, the hatred of inherited inequality was an old-fashioned, naive attitude; sophisticates called such notions Agrarianism.

And Agrarianism was the epithet thrown at the Workingmen's Party which organized itself in New York in 1829. Its first leader was a machinist named Thomas Skidmore, who had just written a book titled *The Rights of Man to Property,* in which he asserted that since property was such a good thing, everybody should have a decent share of it.

Skidmore denounced the hereditary transmission of wealth and proposed a plan for its equal transmission "to every individual of each succeeding generation on arriving at the age of maturity." He soon found himself outmaneuvered and cast out of his party, and those who took control of the Workingmen's Party congratulated themselves on "wiping away the stigma of Agrarianism."

Jefferson had said the Declaration was "common sense," and so did working men and women. Seth Luther, a mechanic, spoke to a meeting in 1832 this way:

> Our business is with facts. *Indisputable facts.* Facts of the highest moment to us as individuals, and as citizens of a *nominally* free country, for we cannot admit that any country is, or any people can be, free, where distinctions in society exist, in opposition to that self evident truth—ALL MEN ARE CREATED EQUAL.

Speaking of the repeated attempts of working people to form unions, and the charge of conspiracy the authorities made against those who tried to unionize, he said:

> Men of property find no fault with combinations to extinguish fires and protect their precious persons from danger. But if poor men ask justice, it is a most horrible combination. The Declaration of Independence was the work of a combination, and was as hateful to the traitors and tories of those days as combinations among workingmen are now to the avaricious monopolist and purse-proud aristocrat.

A FARMER HEARS THE NEWS OF LEXINGTON AND CONCORD

COUNT KOSCIUSKO—POLISH REVOLUTIONARY WHO FOUGHT FOR AMERICA

Much of the spirit of the Workingmen's Party found its way into the Jacksonian movement. The mechanics were cool toward Jackson until he announced that he was vetoing the National Bank. Hearing this, Workingmen surged into the streets to support Jackson and, as their newspaper said, "to follow up the victory over the now prostrate United States Bank by a war of extermination against the smaller engines of fraud and corruption. Anti-Jackson forces called upon merchants to organize to defeat the 'spirit of Agrarianism.' "

To Southern aristocrats as well as their peers in the North, the Jeffersonian theory was dangerous and evil. Even though Jefferson himself was a slaveholder, his ideas were winds of Revolution; his name was reviled by slavemasters. Black people and their allies, however, found inspiration in the words and deeds of 1776. Often, they castigated the Founding Fathers for backing down from their own principles. A black who signed his name "Othello" asked in a pamphlet in 1778:

> When America opposed the pretensions of England, she declared that all men have the same rights. After having manifested her hatred of tyranny, ought she to have abandoned her principles?

Decades later, William Lloyd Garrison wrote in the same vein:

> It required a conflict of seven years to maintain the self-evident truths that all men are created equal, and endowed by their Creator with an inalienable right to liberty. That a people who made such sacrifices, and suffered their blood to be so lavishly shed in the cause of HUMAN RIGHTS might degenerate even to servility within half a century, was deemed a possible though not a very probable occurrence. That, on achieving their independence, they would immediately begin to doubt the soundness of their doctrines for which they had contended, who would have ventured to predict?

Even those Founding Fathers who held slaves sometimes spoke in the same tone. Patrick Henry remarked of slavery:

> Is it not amazing that at a time when the rights of humanity are defined and understood with precision, in a country above all others fond of liberty, that in such a time and such a country we find men . . . adopting a principle . . . repugnant to humanity and destructive of liberty? I will not, I cannot justify it.

Thomas Jefferson gloomily warned that if a great slave rebellion should break out, God might well intervene on the side of the slaves.

But the Revolutionary tradition was more important than the lives of the men who created it. If they were only human—if they failed in their own lives to carry out their own ideals, and failed to inspire Revolutionary deeds and labors in their successors—still the ideals of 1776 kept abolitionists going through the darkest days of the antislavery movement. Wendell Phillips, perhaps the first professional, full-time agitator for justice in the United States of America, was a living embodiment of the spirit of '76. He insisted that if Sam Adams and Jefferson and John Hancock could see how little had been accomplished in half a century, they would have renounced and disowned those who had assumed the mantle of leadership in America. Blacks saw the promise of 1776 as a hope for the future. A meeting of black abolitionists in New York proclaimed in 1831 that

> We do not believe that things will always continue the same. The time must come when the Declaration of Independence will be felt in the hearts as well as uttered from the mouth, and when the rights of all people shall be properly acknowledged and appreciated. God hasten that time. This is our home, and this is our country. Beneath its sod lie the bones of our fathers; for it some of them fought, bled and died. Here we are born and here we will die.

Wendell Phillips entered politics because a Boston man defended the murder of an abolitionist by comparing it to the Boston Tea Party. Phillips, who had never spoken to a crowd before, threw off his coat, dashed to the stage and called this comparison "revolutionary history turned upside down." He told the audience that the abolitionists were the real heirs of Sam Adams and the other patriots of 1776. "For the sentiments he has uttered," said Phillips of the speaker, "on soil consecrated by the prayers of Puritans and the blood of patriots, the earth should have yawned and swallowed him up!" The mood of the meeting was suddenly changed: those who hated slavery became aware that they, and not the defenders of inequality, were the true patriots. When a motion was offered to adjourn the disordered meeting, an abolitionist yelled, "Did your forefathers adjourn at Bunker Hill when fired on by the enemies of freedom?" From that day on Wendell Phillips became a spokesman for abolitionism, defending the precious heritage of the

THE BATTLE OF BUNKER HILL

THE BATTLE ON LEXINGTON GREEN

Revolution and calling upon others to listen to its words and live by its ideals. He chided his listeners:

> The men of our generation are hucksters, they speak today and take it back tomorrow . . . [they show] none of the broad, intelligent, earnest, practical, devoted—in one sense, reckless—enthusiasm of the Revolutionary day, except in those whom the anti-slavery struggle has stirred into life.

When the abolitionists circulated petitions to take New England out of the union with the slave states, he defended them:

> These petitions are called revolutionary. We accept the description. They are intended to be. We hope they are in another sense also Revolutionary—that is, akin to the measures and principles of our 1776. The right of the people to alter their form of government has never been denied here. It is upon that right we stand, the sacred right of Revolution.

The famous publisher and agitator William Lloyd Garrison also deeply felt the Revolutionary tradition. Imprisoned in Baltimore early in his stormy career, he wrote on the wall of his cell:

> William Lloyd Garrison was put into this cell on Wednesday afternoon, October 21, 1835, to save him from the violence of a "respectable and influential" mob who sought to destroy him for preaching the abominable and dangerous doctrine that "all men are created equal, and that all oppression is odious in the sight of God."

His momentous decision to go to Boston and found his radical paper, the *Liberator,* was made with the Revolutionary tradition very much in mind:

> I was determined, at every hazard, to lift up the standard of emancipation in the eyes of the nation, *within sight of Bunker Hill and the birthplace of liberty* . . . The apathy of the people is enough to make every statue leap from its pedestal, and hasten the resurrection of the dead.

Garrison, like other patriots from 1776 on, believed the American Revolution to be the fountainhead of all the tumult in the world, all the assaults on privilege and inequality that were troubling the aristocratic orders.

> The spirit of liberty is no longer young and feeble—it is no longer to make an abortive struggle and then be passive for years. It is abroad with power, thundering at castle gates and prison doors! From revolutionizing neighborhoods, it is going on to revolutionize nations; instead of agitating a kingdom as formerly, it is now shaking the world.

John Brown also felt himself to be squarely in the tradition of the First American Revolution. His Provisional Constitution for the republic of freed slaves he hoped to create announced in its opening lines:

> Slavery, throughout its entire existence in the United States, is none other than a most barbarous, unprovoked and unjustifiable war of one portion of its citizens upon another portion . . . in utter disregard and violation of those eternal and self evident truths set forth in our Declaration of Independence.

From his prison cell, as he awaited execution, he wrote to a kinsman:

> So far as my knowledge goes as to our mutual kindred, I suppose I am the first since the landing of Peter Brown from the Mayflower that has been either sen-

tenced to imprisonment or to the gallows. But, my dear old friend, let not that fact alone grieve you. You cannot have forgotten how and where our grandfather [Captain John Brown] fell in 1776, and that he too might have perished on the scaffold had circumstances been but very little different.

Garrison defended Brown on Revolutionary grounds:

Was John Brown justified in his attempt? Yes, if Washington was in his; Warren and Hancock were in theirs . . . Was John Brown justified in interfering in behalf of the slave population of Virginia, to secure their freedom and independence? Yes, if Lafayette was justified in interfering to help our Revolutionary fathers. If Kosciusko, if Pulaski, if Steuben, if De Kalb, if all who joined from a road were justified in that act, then John Brown was incomparably more so . . . I am for trying him by the American standard; and I hesitate not to say, with all deliberation, that those who are attempting to decry him are dangerous members of the community; they are those in whom the love of liberty has died out; they are the lineal descendants of the tories of the Revolution, only a great deal worse. If the spirit of '76 prevailed today, as it did at that period, it would make the soil of the Commonwealth too hot to hold them.

Proslavery men were well aware of the inflammatory nature of the Declaration, and they bitterly resented the radicals' constant harping on it. Their resentment found its way into a marching song of the Confederacy:

I hates the Yankee nation and everything they do
I hates the Declaration of Independence too!

Union troops, who called themselves "patriots," sang:

Away down South where grows the cotton,
Seventy-six seems quite forgotten.

Alexander Hamilton Stephens, Vice President of the Confederate States, voiced the plantation owners' view of the Revolutionary tradition:

LAFAYETTE WOUNDED

The prevailing ideas entertained by Jefferson and most of the leading statesmen at the time of the formation of the old constitution were that the enslavement of the African was in violation of the laws of nature, that it was wrong in principle, socially, morally and politically. It was an evil they knew not well how to deal with; but the general opinion of the men of that day was that, somehow or other, in the order of Providence, the institution would be evanescent and pass away. His idea, though not incorporated in the constitution, was the prevailing idea at that time . . . Those ideas, however, were fundamentally wrong. They rested upon the assumption of the equality of races. This was an error. It was a sandy foundation and the government built upon it fell when the storm came and the wind blew. Our new government is founded upon exactly the opposite idea: its foundations are laid, its cornerstone rests, upon the great truth that the negro is not equal to the white man, that slavery —subordination to the superior race—is his natural and normal condition . . . The errors of the past generation still clung to many as late as twenty years ago. Those . . . who still cling to these errors with a zeal above knowledge, we justly denominate *fanatics.*

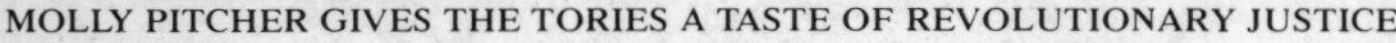

MOLLY PITCHER GIVES THE TORIES A TASTE OF REVOLUTIONARY JUSTICE

THE BOSTON MASSACRE

Abraham Lincoln clung to the "old" view:

The principles of Jefferson are the definitions and axioms of free society and yet they are denied and evaded, with no small show of success. One dashingly calls them "glittering generalities." Another bluntly calls them "self-evidentlies." And others insidiously argue that they apply to "superior races." These expressions, differing in form, are identical in object and effect—the supplanting of the principles of free government, and restoring those of classification, caste and legitimacy. They would delight a convocation of crowned heads plotting against the people. They are a vanguard, the miners and sappers of returning despotism. We must repulse them, or they will subjugate us . . . All honor to Jefferson—to the man who, in the concrete pressure of a struggle for national independence by a single people, had the coolness, forecast and sagacity to introduce into a merely revolutionary document an abstract truth, applicable to all men and all times, and embalm it there, that today and in all coming days it shall be a rebuke and a stumbling block to the very harbingers of reappearing tyranny and oppression.

During the country's Centennial celebration of 1876, militant women, led by Susan B. Anthony, demanded the fulfillment of the revolutionary promise for all *people,* not just all men. Feminists at the National Woman's Suffrage Association convention in New York City called on the women of America to publish on July 4, 1876, another Declaration of Independence:

That the women of this nation in 1876 have greater cause for discontent, rebellion, and revolution than our fathers of 1776.

That the men of this nation are political monarchs, with their wives, their sisters, and their daughters as subjects.

That a woman's head is her head, her body her body, her feet her feet, and all ownership and mastery over her are in violation of the supreme law of the land.

That the Treasury of the United States belongs to women equally with men.

That we call upon the women of the United States to meet in their respective towns and districts on the 4th of July 1876, and to declare themselves free and independent, no longer bound to obey laws in whose making they have had no voice, and in presence of the assembled nations of the world, gathered on this soil to celebrate our national Centennial, to demand justice for the women of this land.

After the Civil War, the radical Greenback movement continued the Revolutionary tradition. The Greenback Labor Party platform of 1880 demanded that "Civil government should guarantee the *divine right* of every laborer to the results of his toil." B. S. Heath, a Greenback theorist, warned:

The aim of government should be to protect man in his natural rights, "to insure domestic tranquility, to promote the general welfare," and "to insure the blessings of liberty." No one will deny that these objects have been

shamefully neglected . . . The finance legislation of the past few years has been disastrous to the general welfare; it has deprived the masses of the blessings of liberty, and, if allowed to remain in force, that blessed bond must sooner or later become erased from our inventory of inheritance, and the sons of Revolutionary sires consigned to that doom to which the same system has subjected the toilers of the old world.

"The revolution of a century ago," Heath wrote, "was the triumph of democracy over monarchy, the ballot over the scepter. The struggle now pending is between the same spirit that won the revolution . . . and that

MRS. SCHUYLER FIRING HER CORNFIELDS ON THE APPROACH OF THE BRITISH

power behind the throne, stronger and more despotic than he who sat upon it."

All phases of the powerful Populist movement felt at home with the doctrines of the early democrats. Jacob Coxey, the "general" of Coxey's Army, called for legislation to "emancipate our beloved country from financial bondage to the descendants of King George." James Baird Weaver, Greenback Presidential candidate in 1880 and Populist Presidential candidate in 1892, wrote in his *Call to Action:*

> If the master builders of our civilization one hundred years ago had been told that at the end of a single century, American society would present such melancholy contrasts of wealth and poverty, of individual happiness and widespread infelicity as are to be found today throughout the Republic, the person making the unwelcome prediction would have been looked upon as a misanthropist, and his loyalty to Democratic institutions would have been seriously called in question . . .
>
> But there is a vast difference between the generation which made the heroic struggle for self-government in colonial days, and the third generation which is now engaged in a mad rush for wealth. The first took its stand upon the inalienable rights of man and made a fight which shook the world. But the leading spirits of the latter are entrenched behind class laws and revel in special privileges. It will require another revolution to overthrow them.

William Jennings Bryan reminded the Democratic Party of the Jeffersonian heritage and asked—in language evoking the Revolutionary principle that the Earth belongs to the Living—which course the party would take: "Will it turn its face to the rising or the setting sun? Will it choose blessings or cursings? *Life or Death?* Which? Which?"

It was so typical of the men and women who fought for equality to place themselves in the Jeffersonian tradition that a conservative magazine could say, "That is the claim of every mob leader and anarchist."

America was no longer the "young nation" the British had sneered at, and opponents of change could now urge her to act her age. The Sons of Liberty Association yearbook of 1903 announced: "The past was only an era of creation. The time is now that of preservation." Mother Jones, the famed labor organizer, had other ideas about liberty, and about America. When the Liberty Bell was taken on a national tour, she responded to the event not as the showing of a relic but as the recalling of a Revolutionary dream; she gathered the children of working people to march behind the bell.

> Once that bell had sounded against tyranny. Now, many thousands of Americans were going to see it. The Liberty Bell was cracked and couldn't peal for freedom any more. But that didn't mean every free voice in America was mute. I thought maybe my children could sound off for the freedom of every worker's kid. If enough people saw them and heard them, maybe things could be changed. So I decided to tour with the youngsters, following on the heels of the Liberty Bell.

Mother Jones was a cofounder of the Industrial Workers of the World, the colorful "Wobblies." The Wobblies, like their principal spokesman and organizer, Big Bill Haywood, were Westerners who vividly remembered the freedom of the frontier and who were now being squeezed by giant corporations. Europeans

MARCH 5, 1770—FIVE PATRIOTS DIE AT THE HANDS OF GOVERNMENT TROOPS

could remember nothing but oppression, but the Wobblies of the American West knew that life had once been different—freer and more egalitarian. Haywood and Mother Jones took both inspiration and practical lessons from the founding parents. When accused of inciting to sabotage, Haywood said he never advocated direct action, only political action. Asked what the difference between the two was, he replied that the adoption of the U.S. Constitution was a political action, whereas the Revolution that had made it possible was direct action.

The Wobblies carried American flags when they picketed and demonstrated, but the commander of the troops against the Lawrence, Massachusetts, strike saw nothing sacred in it; he ordered his men not to salute the flag when carried by the striking women and men; he also commanded them to "shoot to kill."

The black freedom fighter W. E. B. Du Bois believed deeply in the legacy of 1776. "By every civilized and peaceful method," he wrote, "we must strive for the rights which the world accords to men, clinging unwaveringly to those great words which the sons of the Fathers would fain forget: 'We hold these truths to be . . .' " The Niagara Movement Principles of 1905, penned by Du Bois and others, stated:

> We note with alarm the evident retrogression in this land of sound public opinion on the subject of manhood rights, republican government and human brotherhood, and we pray God that this nation will not degenerate into a mob of boasters and oppressors, but rather will return to the faith of the fathers, that all men were created free and equal, with certain inalienable rights.

But with the corporations firmly in control, the forces of social change began to drift away from the great tradition that had moved the country forward. "The flags and symbols which once meant something to us have been seized by our employers," brooded Big Bill Haywood; "today they mean nothing to us but oppression and tyranny." In the 1930's, Huey Long said on the floor of the Senate:

> The great and grand dream of America that all men are created free and equal, endowed with the inalienable right of life and liberty and the pursuit of happiness—this great dream of America, this great light, and this great hope—has almost gone out of sight in this day and time, and everybody knows it; and there is a mere candle flicker here and yonder to take the place of what the great dream of America was supposed to be.
>
> The people of this country have fought and have struggled, trying by one process and the other, to bring about the changes that would save the American country for the ideal and purposes of America . . . We swapped the tyrant 3,000 miles away for a handful of financial slaveowning overlords who make the tyrant of Britain seem mild.

CROWD CHEERS THE FIRST PUBLIC READING OF THE DECLARATION OF INDEPENDENCE IN BOSTON

The Revolutionary tradition received new strength from the civil rights movement of the 1950's and 1960's. Martin Luther King sounded the ancient keynote:

> I have a dream that one day this nation will rise up and live out the true meaning of its creed: "We hold these truths to be . . ."

In the mid-60's, Huey Newton and Bobby Seale formed the Black Panther Party. The Party's founding document, the Ten Point Platform and Program of the Black Panther Party for Self Defense, called for freedom, food, self-determination for black people, decent education, decent housing and an end to police brutality. It concluded with the Declaration of Independence.

As minorities and majorities stirred into life once more, the Spirit of Seventy-Six became a living force

THE AMERICAN TROOPS AT VALLEY FORGE

again: Indians, proclaiming the Revolutionary Republic of Wounded Knee in 1973, recalled the arguments of the founding radicals of the United States. Politicians and functionaries found it harder and harder to pose as the heirs of the Sons of Liberty, and it became once again timely to speak of inalienable rights.

Proponents of arbitrary rule and inequality had learned not to directly challenge the American ideal, or to identify themselves as successors of the Tories. Instead, they had developed the view that arbitrary rule and inequality *are* the American ideal. Francis Wilson ("Reclaiming the American Political Tradition," *Intercollegiate Review,* Spring, 1971) complained about "the overemphasis on the idea that the Declaration is talking about individual rights, and more particularly the illegitimate use of the Declaration by Abraham Lincoln." Where defenders of privilege had formerly attacked the American tradition, their modern successors had learned to claim that that tradition *was* one of privilege. Disruptive and dangerous books, Wilson wrote,

> say that our tradition is one of freedom and equality, including the natural rights of the individual guaranteed in the Declaration of Independence and in the Bill of Rights in the national Constitution and in the state constitutions. Such a summary of doctrine has lent itself to radical, even revolutionary efforts at reform. In our time the revolutionary meaning of America has been the attainment of equality through whatever political strenuosities may be necessary. A former Justice of the Supreme Court has defended their unhistorical decisions by asking: "How else can we attain equality?"

Over the years, a succession of Tory "interpretations" of the First Revolution have been devised to prove that it didn't happen. The *National Observer* (February 17, 1973) gave a full page to the task of steeling the plutocracy against the ominous portent of the Bicentennial:

> It is frequently remarked that the United States, no less than France or Russia, has its political roots in revolution. What is sometimes overlooked by laymen is that the American uprising of the late 1770's was completely different from the revolutions that brought Napoleon and Lenin to power.
>
> The goal of the American rebels was not to overthrow the British monarchy. On the contrary, the aristocrats who engineered the break with Britain were conservatives who only wanted the same rights for the people of the Colonies that Englishmen in England enjoyed. Theirs was a conservative revolution that did not destroy the social structure.
>
> Nevertheless there are still many impatient voices in this country, particularly in the academy, in the left-liberal press, and on public television, who implicitly look forward to another revolution, one that would redesign society according to the leftist's stock ideas about egalitarianism and the redistribution of wealth.
>
> Part of the rationale is that America was born in revolution so more of the same in the 1970's would only be fitting.

PATRICK HENRY SHOUTS,
"GIVE ME LIBERTY OR GIVE ME DEATH!"

THE NEWS OF THE CAPTURE OF BRITISH GENERAL CORNWALLIS

The *Observer* takes a straightforward stance, insisting that the founders couldn't have meant what they said, and hadn't done what they said they were doing. Most anti-Americans, though, have found it tactically foolish to denounce the radical founders or call them hypocrites. For the most part, they simply try to drown out the message America announced to the world in 1776 with bass drums, or ridicule it with Bob Hope skits.

As Lincoln would say, these techniques are all alike in object and effect: the supplanting of democratic tradition with authoritarian corporate myth. Privilege, secrecy and irresponsible authority are decked out in red, white and blue. Submission to corrupt civil bureaucracies and greedy private bureaucracies is touted as Americanism. King George, of course, would have been delighted at that sort of Americanism: much more reasonable than he ever found Americans in his day! The founders of the republic, however, would raise a few eyebrows; then they would raise their voices; and then, when that failed, they would raise hell.

For those aristocrats who rest upon the swollen fortunes of their ancestors, the ideals and symbols of the First Revolution have always been a source of terror. Those same ideals have driven democrats for two centuries to take the words of the Declaration from the ancient parchment and rewrite them upon every aspect of American life. Whether the American legacy—and thereby America itself—is won by tories or patriots depends on what kind of Americans two hundred years of Revolutionary history have produced.

Millions of Americans are responding to the 200th anniversary of our Declaration of Independence with the message that the King Georges of this world have had their share—and nearly all of ours. This country, the founders understood, was to be set aside so that some corner of the Earth would belong to the people—to the living. That is the message of the First American Revolution—and the next one.

Let us disappoint the men who are raising themselves on the ruin of this country.

Samuel Adams, 1772

III

Community Programs for a Peoples Bicentennial

Introduction

The American Revolution is familiar to all of us as a series of battles, dates and Founding Fathers. But above all else, the American Revolution was a social movement—an uprising of people who launched a war for independence to secure for themselves the "inalienable rights" of "Life, Liberty and the pursuit of Happiness."

It was common people—farmers, laborers, artisans—not well-known leaders, who died in the Boston Massacre. Common folks, in communities from New Hampshire to Georgia, enforced the economic boycotts against unfairly taxed British imports. And common men and women (one out of every three, by most accounts) read Tom Paine's *Common Sense* and called for independence months before Jefferson drafted the Declaration of Independence.

As the two-hundredth anniversary of the American Revolution nears, individuals and organizations in every community in the country are presented with the opportunity to participate in a *new* social movement aimed at reaffirming our Revolutionary past; at reliving the ideals of the Spirit of '76.

In the years leading up to 1976, every American, in one way or another, will take part in the Bicentennial—the White House and its corporate buddies, by pouring hundreds of millions of dollars into "Bicentennial" programs, have made sure of that. (Indeed, one White House aide has spoken of the "Bicentennialization" of America.) The issue, clearly, is how will over two hundred million Americans participate? Through the Tory celebration of the White House and big business? Or through a program initiated *by* the people of America, *for* the people of America—in short, a Patriots' Observance?

Community organizations that wish to think clearly about our two-hundredth anniversary should distinguish between the Bicentennial as a celebration and the Bicentennial as a set of challenges. The Bicentennial as a celebration means Tom Paine postcards; red, white and blue street signs; radio and television programs extolling the virtues of America around the clock; Sara Lee Bicentennial Birthday Cake and the rest of it. The Bicentennial as a set of challenges, however, means using the occasion to raise serious questions about whether America today lives up to the principles for which the American Revolution was fought.

Nor is the opportunity a frivolous one. Today, we are besieged by commentators who tell us that we are a middle-class society that values property and security over everything else. Such questions as the gap between the rich and poor, between corporate and social wealth, between the majority and ethnic minorities, they say, might interest a few fuzzy-headed reformers, but no one else. People are too busy holding on to what they have. Therefore, the argument concludes, activists should turn the business of politics over to pragmatists in both parties who know best how to hold society together.

How curious an argument this is coming from otherwise loyal citizens! "America is the only nation in the world that is founded on a creed," G. K. Chesterton wrote many years ago. "That creed is set forth with dogmatic and even theological lucidity in the Declaration of Independence; perhaps the only piece of practical politics that is also theoretical politics and also great literature. It enunciates that all men are equal in their claim to justice, that governments exist to give them that justice, and that their authority is for that reason just." Yet there are those who, in the name of patriotism, would undermine this creed and the documents that define it. These people surely do need a Bicentennial—or some comparable occasion—to refresh their memory about what the Founding Fathers and Mothers said this country was supposed to represent. Here is where a community-based Peoples Bicentennial celebration can perform an enormous service.

The Bicentennial, in turn, can perform a service to community organizations. There is truth to the notion, after all, that people fight only for the familiar, not the unfamiliar. Who will take risks for something that he or she doesn't even understand? If we wish to encourage citizens to fight for high values, then we must articulate them in terms that we all understand, in language we all share and respect. What do we want, if not a renewed realization that we must take the ancient principles of liberty and justice seriously in our everyday lives? Why not then borrow precedents from the Declaration of Independence and the Constitution and the Bill of Rights—documents we were all brought up on—rather than from writers whom few people have even read? This is what the Bicentennial enables us to do, with devastating effect, if we choose to take the opportunity.

THE SPIRIT OF '76

Consider, for example, a Bicentennial celebration that merely attempted to adhere to four central principles of the American Revolution: "Life, Liberty and the Pursuit of Happiness"; "No Taxation Without Representation"; "Don't Tread on Me" and "Only Lay Down True Principles." It would be a far cry from the Bicentennial celebration that our Government is presently planning. Let's examine the possibilities.

Life, Liberty and the Pursuit of Happiness

The White House will try to use the Bicentennial to glamorize the role of individuals in pulling themselves up by their own bootstraps without assistance from unions, community organizations and the Federal Government. It will ignore the cooperation and mutual aid that were standard in the colonies and on the frontier.

Ordinary citizens should use the Bicentennial to examine the quality of life within their communities—to determine whether it fulfills the principles for which the Revolution was fought. The Declaration of Independence does not say that "life, liberty and the pursuit of happiness" are privileges, to be attained by an individual's ability to exploit other people. These are rights; governments are created to secure them. The community is the instrument through which they are to be realized.

Therefore, if a community establishes a Bicentennial Commission composed entirely of businessmen, reactionary leaders and professional socialites, citizens must create a local Peoples Bicentennial Commission, composed of labor leaders, community-control advocates and representatives of both working people and the poor. In this case, professional mavericks will not do, and prominent citizens who haven't tangible constituencies should play secondary roles. For once, a people's operation should actually represent the people.

As a start, a Peoples Bicentennial Commission should conduct both community research and community hearings. These will aid it in determining a community agenda.

COMMUNITY RESEARCH

Every community group needs information, but very few community groups have either the time or the resources to do the kind of research they need. The Bicentennial years provide an unmatched opportunity to remedy this situation. Within the framework of determining social priorities and goals, a Peoples Commission can develop and disseminate valuable information on how the community does and should operate. Who should undertake this research, however? What central questions should the researchers ask? How should it be disseminated? A Peoples Commission must pay close attention to each of these critical problems.

College students are a logical group of people to undertake research about community problems. They have free time. Many are anxious to contribute to movements for social change. Examining an issue or an institution for a Peoples Bicentennial Commission might well be a way for them to contribute to activist causes without jeopardizing their academic routine.

As its first project, the Peoples Bicentennial Commission might consider organizing a new group on area campuses—the People's Research Operation for the Bicentennial Era (PROBE). The purposes of the group would be to encourage students to undertake research into community problems, to pressure professors to give academic credit for community-research projects undertaken by students and to make community research an important priority of the campus as a whole.

One way individual students could be encouraged to undertake research for the community would be to persuade local campus editors to run public service ads in their student papers.

STAMP ACT RIOT OF 1765—
THE OPENING RESISTANCE OF THE AMERICAN REVOLUTION

THE "MINUTE MEN" OF THE REVOLUTION

THE DEATH OF CRISPUS ATTUCKS

The advertisements should attract at least a few students on campus who wish to make community research a priority. These respondents should constitute themselves as a chapter of PROBE. Undergraduates might volunteer to examine the community power structure or specific local problems. Graduate students, doubtless, will seek projects related to their fields. Wherever possible, PROBE should organize itself into research teams, since adequate investigative reporting often requires more than one person.

A valuable initial step for PROBE would be to persuade at least one professor to assign community-research projects as part of the regular curriculum for a course. By accomplishing this, PROBE would guarantee that several students would be undertaking investigative projects during a semester. Professors, moreover, could supervise and assist students in the technical aspects of research projects, thereby improving their quality. And the students themselves would begin to view community research as an integral part of their college careers.

Indeed, PROBE could have a substantial influence on the college as a whole. Even though student demonstrations have died down, the educational revolt that began in the 60's continues. Students everywhere now have enormous flexibility to develop independent study programs, interdisciplinary majors and new courses not included in the regular curriculum. Some colleges now offer a free month in January to allow students time to explore an unusual problem or issue in depth. A local Peoples Bicentennial Commission, through PROBE, can take advantage of this new opportunity by urging students to use their skills where they're needed most—in the community itself. Indirectly, the Commission will be helping the campus and the community get together.

Students are not the only ones who can undertake local research; almost anyone can. Tenants can investigate the housing conditions of the city. Welfare recipients can become as knowledgeable about social services as the people who direct them. Homemakers can expose consumer fraud in the marketplace. Retired professionals can take a broader look at the fields in which they themselves participated throughout their careers. Indeed, for many projects, community people will make better investigators than students, since they will have acquired easier access to certain institutions and they will have developed greater insight into the problems which they cause. More than one student intern has learned that a gang member on the block can tell more about the real attitudes and activities of a neighborhood than the most sophisticated sociologist in the entire uni-

TRIALS AND CONFLICTS YOU MUST, THEREFORE, ENDURE; HAZARDS AND JEOPARDIES—OF LIFE AND FORTUNE—WILL ATTEND THE STRUGGLE. SUCH IS THE FATE OF ALL NOBLE EXERTIONS FOR PUBLIC LIBERTY AND SOCIAL HAPPINESS.
—JOSIAH QUINCY, 1774

versity. If a Peoples Bicentennial Commission gives these people their opportunity, they will take it.

What kind of research is needed, however? All kinds, of course, but particularly in three areas: Community History, Community Power and Community Issues. A comment on each.

Community History

The first priority is exploring community history. People who know very little about their community usually know very little about the community's history. The history of any place as taught in school, moreover, often differs from the real history of the people. For these reasons, Peoples Bicentennial Commissions should consider undertaking projects in oral history. Oral history is more a means to action than an end in itself. It is a way of stimulating communication, particularly across age and class lines. Every generation tends to view its own problems as unique. In reality, there are innumerable parallels in experience between one generation and the next. Suggestions for compiling an oral history project appear in the Oral/Visual section, beginning on page 169.

Community Power

Research is also needed into Community Power. Ask a few simple questions. Who sits on the corporate boards of the five biggest businesses in your area? How

GENERAL PUTNAM LEAVING HIS PLOW FOR THE DEFENSE OF HIS COUNTRY

many sit on more than one board? More than two boards? How many of the individuals involved now hold elective office, or have held it in the past? Any close examination of *Moody's Industrials* can provide these answers.

Who sits on the boards of the utility companies in your area? On the five largest law firms?

Which law firm does your city use? Is your mayor a former member?

Is your city a "Social Register city"? How many of its corporate leaders are also considered social leaders? Do they intermarry, join the same clubs, attend the same meetings?

Who runs the United Fund or Community Chest

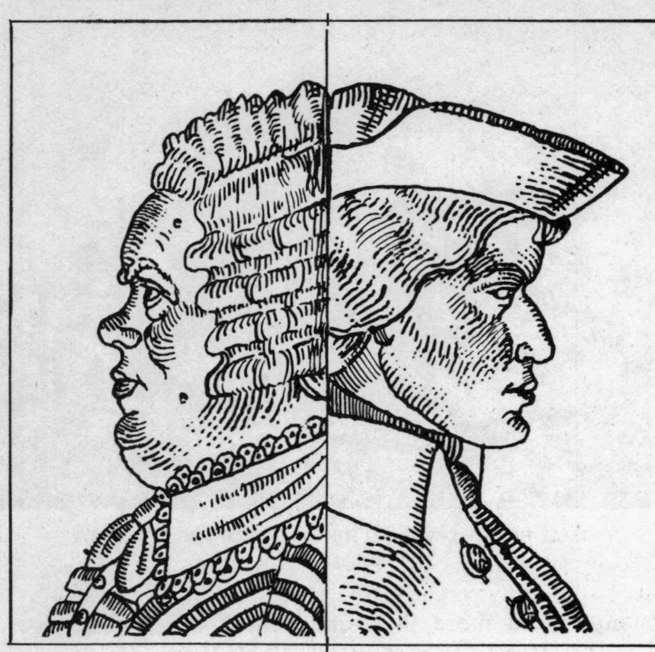

THE TORIES VS. THE PATRIOTS

drive? Is it always a corporate leader? Do the boards of the leading charities always include the same fifty or sixty corporate leaders?

Are there key decision-making groups in your community—like the Vault in Boston, a group of top industrialists, so named because they met regularly in a bank vault to make the city's key economic decisions? Can a political candidate who offends major business interests or leaders in your city get elected? Can a public agency enforce antipollution, or consumer-protection, or property-tax laws against corporations without reprisal?

Has Wright Patman's House Committee on Banking surveyed the power of banks in your community? How much power do they hold? How many bank officials are also trustees of city corporations? How much corporate stock do the leading banks own? Can researchers find out this information if the Patman report does not provide it? How do City Council representatives feel about the banks? Are they afraid to regulate them, for fear of economic retaliation? How deeply in debt is the city to the banks?

Who owns the city? Do a few landlords control large blocks of land, or are ownership patterns scattered? Do city housing authorities control the landlords, or do the landlords control the housing authorities? Can corporate leaders and landlords determine the zoning policies of the city to suit their needs?

Who runs the unions? Do they conduct regular meetings, hold democratic elections and provide regular channels for internal change? How about union pension funds? Do banks hold them in escrow, retaining the right to invest them as they please?

Who runs the community itself? Are the wards structured democratically, or are they carefully controlled by a political machine? Does an urban bureaucracy exercise most of the political power in the community, shielded from the press and the public by a complicated maze of offices and agencies? Does the City Council exercise any power? Is the Mayor more than a figurehead? Can the city itself govern its activities, or must it rely on the goodwill of the state legislature? What does the City Charter allow?

A Peoples Bicentennial Commission with a grasp of these basic facts about a community will find itself in a good position to effect needed change.

BEN FRANKLIN—SCIENTIST, STATESMAN, REVOLUTIONARY

Community Issues

Most important, research is needed into community issues.

Start with the people of the community. Can young people get quality child care, education and recreation? Are they constructive contributors to community life, or are they victimized by drugs (such as heroin, amphetamines, Quaalude) and gangs?

What about the adult citizens of the community? Are there jobs for all who want to work? Do the unemployed receive an income adequate to their needs? Does the community provide adequately for leisure time? Are the citizens generally productive, satisfied, dynamic—or are they listless and apathetic?

What about the older adults in the community? Are they treated with respect, or herded into rest homes and institutions away from public view? Is their income adequate? Are their services adequate? Are their lives enriched and productive, or are they lonely and bitter?

What about the service systems of the city—transportation, sanitation, education, police, courts, health, communication and welfare? Do they function, or are they falling apart? Are city services equally available to all—or do the rich have better roads, better schools, better hospital care and better sanitation and police protection than the working people or the poor? Do citizens take pride in city services, or is the city becoming a giant complaint department?

What about the conflicts of the city? Around what issues have community organizations already been organized? How successful have they been? What problems stand out in the minds of most people?

EVACUATION OF NEW YORK BY THE BRITISH, NOVEMBER 25, 1783

Any one of these questions would give a research team more than enough to do for months.

USING THE RESEARCH

The question of how community research can be used presumes that it has been prepared in usable form. Presently, too much research is sitting in boxes in somebody's basement or gathering dust on somebody's shelves that might have been put to good use. Unfortunately, it was not prepared with a specific community issue or movement in mind. Or it was developed by the sort of intellectuals who believed that a grandiose analysis of the entire community, divorced from the day-to-day problems people experience, somehow would raise "consciousness" in a meaningful way. Or the research was merely written badly, cluttered with technical jargon that only social scientists even pretend to understand.

A Peoples Bicentennial Commission can develop certain research guidelines to prevent many of these mistakes. It can insist, for example, that the researchers

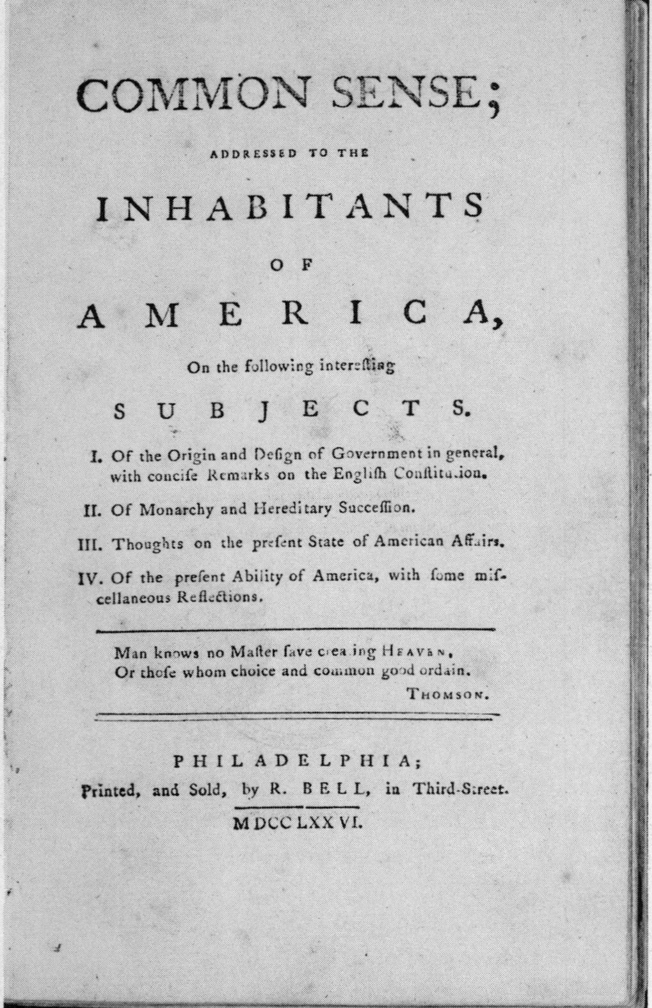

COMMON SENSE;

ADDRESSED TO THE

INHABITANTS

OF

AMERICA,

On the following interesting

SUBJECTS.

I. Of the Origin and Design of Government in general, with concise Remarks on the English Constitution.

II. Of Monarchy and Hereditary Succession.

III. Thoughts on the present State of American Affairs.

IV. Of the present Ability of America, with some miscellaneous Reflections.

Man knows no Master save creating HEAVEN,
Or those whom choice and common good ordain.

THOMSON.

PHILADELPHIA;
Printed, and Sold, by R. BELL, in Third-Street.
MDCCLXXVI.

TITLE PAGE OF FIRST EDITION OF TOM PAINE'S *Common Sense*

understand first what the citizens want to know—what a given issue means to them. Commission members can serve as editors: calling for examples to buttress assertions; replacing complicated phrases with simple ones. A Commission can even require that the designated recipients of a research report be involved in its preparation, continually forcing the researchers to think clearly about what they are trying to find out.

Even these few simple steps can prevent otherwise exciting investigative reporting from becoming just another graduate term paper.

Yet using pertinent information effectively requires additional intellectual and political skill. Here the Commission's role will be invaluable. It should choose among several possibilities:

It can merely pass the information quietly along to an individual or group that needs it. Often, no more than raw notes or interviews are necessary here. In fact, in some cases this is all a community organization really needs. Let's say, for example, that a tenants' union wants to know the background of the members of a local rent-control board. The researchers discover that all of them are connected with the largest landowners in the city—but their evidence is hearsay, not written documentation. The tenants' union would not want to issue a formal statement denouncing the rent-control board for conflicts of interest that it could not prove. Yet it would be able to predict accurately how the board would react to specific issues before it. Obviously, only a quiet discussion of this information among the researchers, the Commission and the tenants'-union officers would be appropriate.

It can translate the information into easy-to-understand leaflets. Leaflets can be overused, particularly around campaign time, but in some situations they are invaluable. If, for example, the researchers uncover a little-known activity of a public official surrounding a community issue, the Peoples Commission ought to leaflet meetings where the official speaks, to encourage the audience to question him or her about it. More than one boring meeting has been enlivened by this technique.

It can produce readable "Common Sense" pamphlets based on the material. Imagine a series like Common Sense About Taxes; Common Sense About Banks; Common Sense About Landlords; Common Sense

JOHN ADAMS

About Food Prices—all designed to explain how and why ordinary citizens are getting shafted and what they can do about it. What better way could be found to use the Bicentennial theme in community struggles for change?

It can develop slide shows, tapes, even movies based on the material. Slide shows are easiest to prepare, and can be held in anyone's living room. People can be asked to invite a few neighbors over for an evening. Although many groups will not have the necessary equipment, movies and tapes will still prove enormous educational resources to any Peoples Bicentennial Commission that can afford to make them.

It can produce a King George Exhibit to identify and explain the power structure of the city to the community. Such an exhibit would be a logical rejoinder to the various commercial exhibits that corporations will be sponsoring during the Bicentennial years. It would display photographs of the corporate leaders and bankers who exercise the most economic and political power in the city. It would explain their relationship to the various institutions of the city, and to each other. It would dramatize what the economic power of these few people means to the ordinary citizen.

It can release the information through the newspapers. If the research produces a major exposé, it can be revealed in a press conference to all papers. Usually, it is important to invite community leaders to such a conference to react—or better still, to formulate with them a plan of action before the information is released.

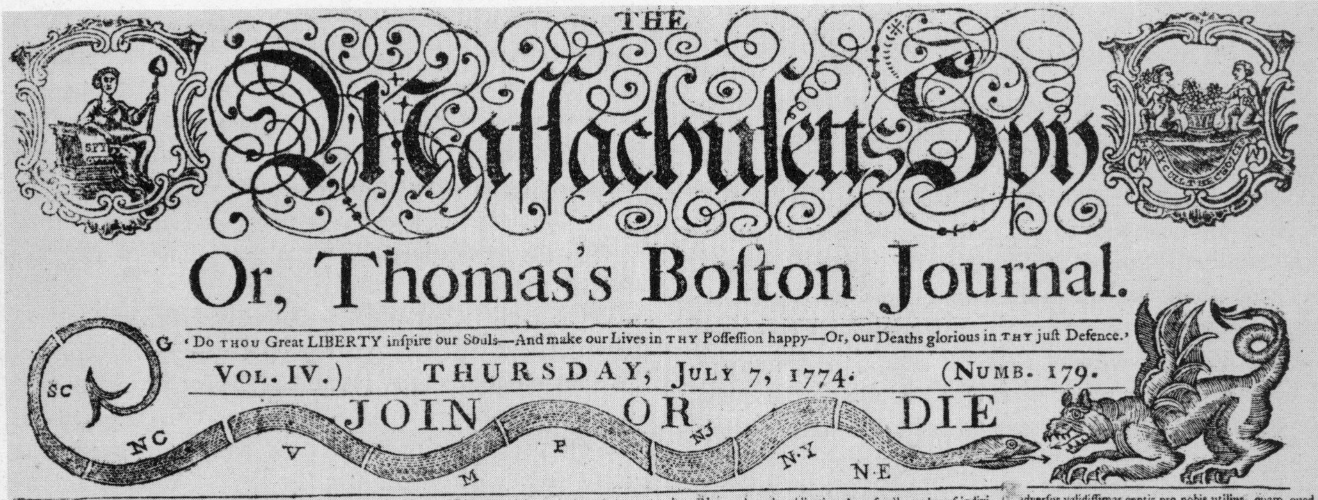

THE
Maſſachuſetts Spy,
Or, Thomas's Boſton Journal.

'Do thou Great LIBERTY inſpire our Souls—And make our Lives in THY Poſſeſſion happy—Or, our Deaths glorious in THY juſt Defence.'

VOL. IV.) THURSDAY, JULY 7, 1774. (NUMB. 179.

JOIN OR DIE

THE great demand for this paper, has often occaſioned many good cuſtomers being diſappointed, for which the publiſher is very ſorry : He will, in future, endeavour to prevent any thing of the like kind happening, ſo long as he may have the honour of being an hand-ſervant to the public.

The gloomy proſpect of public affairs, at preſent, in this devoted capital, has occaſioned ſome preſſing Demands *upon him, which with* great reluctance *he informs his cuſtomers, he can by* no means *anſwer without their* kind *aſſiſtance : He is loath to trouble them with a* 'dunning' *advertiſement, but his affairs make it neceſſary : His cuſtomers in the country towns in this province, and thoſe in the other colonies, he hopes will take* proper notice *of it, and conſider there is no poſſibility, (eſpecially for a* young beginner) *in carrying on buſineſs without* regular payments.

A work of this kind, it is well known is attended with great expence, and he begs leave to mention, that the MASSACHUSETTS SPY *is a third larger than any News-Paper publiſhed in this province, and contains as much News, as many Political Eſſays, as any in America ; and is the cheapeſt on the globe.*

I. THOMAS.

Boſton, June 9, 1774.

In the Houſe of Repreſentatives, June 14, 1774.

WHEREAS there will become due in this month, ſundry notes given by the province-treaſurer, and ſufficient proviſion having been made for the paying off the ſame, and if the poſſeſſors of ſuch notes ſhould not bring them in to the treaſurer to be paid, the province will ſuffer damage by ſuch neglect :

Therefore Reſolved, That the poſſeſſors of ſuch notes, who ſhall not bring them to the province-treaſurer, to be paid by the laſt day of *July* next, ſhall not receive any intereſt on the ſame, after that time, and the province treaſurer, is hereby directed forthwith to cauſe this order to be publiſhed in all the Boſton News-papers, three weeks ſucceſſively, that every one concerned may be notified hereof.

Sent up for concurrence. T. CUSHING, ſpeaker

In council, June 15th, Read and concurred.

JOHN COTTON, D. ſec'ry.

Conſented to, THO's. GAGE.

A true copy, atteſt. JOHN COTTON, D. ſec'ry.

*** The treaſurer of the province hereby gives public notice to the delinquent conſtables and collectors of the province taxes, that they pay the ſame into the treaſury by the 31ſt of *July* next.

Treaſury-Office, June 18, 1774.

From the PENNSYLVANIA GAZETTE.

LETTER IV.

To the Inhabitants of the Britiſh Colonies in AMERICA.

Brethren,

THE intelligence received, ſince the preceding letter was written, ſeems to render needleſs every attempt to prove from *former tranſactions*,—my firſt intention, if health had permitted—that a regular plan has been invariably purſued to inſlave theſe colonies, and that the act of

Riots and weak publications, by a ſmall number of individuals, are ſufficient reaſons with Parliament to ruin many thouſand inhabitants of a truly reſpectable town, to diſſolve charters, to aboliſh the benefits of the writ of *habeas corpus*,§ and extirpate American liberty—for the principle reaches all. But in *England* the preſs groans with publications, ſeditious, treaſonable and even blaſphemous. The diſcontented ſwarm over the kingdom, proclaiming their reſentments. Many enormous riots have diſturbed the public peace. The ſovereign has been inſulted in paſſing from his palace to the Parliament-houſe, on the buſineſs of the nation. Is it to be concluded from theſe facts, that the BODY OF THE PEOPLE is ſeditious and traiterous? can his Majeſty believe, that he is thought by his Engliſh ſubjects in *general* to be ſuch a prince, as ſome of them have repreſented him? will the two houſes of Parliament acknowledge what has been ſpoken and written and acted againſt them in *England*, expreſſes the ſentiments of the kingdom? or will they ſay, that the *people* of *England* have forfeited their liberty, becauſe *ſome of them* have run into licentiouſneſs? let a judgment be formed in *both caſes* by the *ſame* rule. Let them condemn *thoſe* or acquit us.

Pretences and reaſons are totally different. The provocations, ſaid to be given by our ſiſter colony, are but the PRETENCES for the exorbitant ſeverity exerciſed againſt her. The REASONS are theſe—the policy, deſpicable and deteſtable as it is, of ſuppreſſing the freedom of *America* by a military force, to be ſupported by money taken out of our own pockets, and the ſuppoſed conveniency of opportunity for attaining this end. Theſe REASONS are evident from the miniſter's ſpeech. The ſyſtem is formed with art, but the art is diſcoverable. Indeed, I do not believe it was expected, we ſhould have ſuch early and exact intelligence of the ſchemes agitated againſt us, as we have received. Any perſon, who examines the multitude of invectives publiſhed in pamphlets and news papers in *Great-Britain*, or the ſpeeches made in either houſe of Parliament, will find them directed *againſt the colonies in general*. The people in that kingdom have

adverſus validiſſimas gentis pro nobis utilius, quam quod in COMMUNE NONCONSULUNT. Rarus ad propulſandum *commune periculum* conventus. Ita dum *ſinguli* pugnant *omnes* vincuntur.‡

Why did the little *Swiſs* cantons, and ſeven ſmall provinces of the low countries, ſo ſucceſsfully oppoſe the tyrants, that not contended with an empire founded in humanity and mutual advantages, *unneceſſarily* and arrogantly ſtrove to "LAY" the faithful and affectionate wretches "AT THEIR FEET?" Becauſe, they wiſely regarded the intereſt of each as the intereſt of *all*.

Our own experience furniſhes a mournful additional proof of an obſervation made by a great and good man, Lord preſident *Forbes*. "It is a certain truth," ſays he, "that all ſtates and kingdoms, in proportion as they grow great, wealthy and powerful, grow wanton, wicked and oppreſſive, and the hiſtory of all ages gives evidence of the fatal cataſtrophe of *all ſuch* ſtates and kingdoms, when the cup of their iniquity is full." Another "truth" as "certain" is—that "ſuch ſtates and kingdoms" never have been, and never will be checked in the career of their "wantonneſs, wickedneſs and oppreſſion" by a people in any degree, dependant upon them, but by the prudent, virtuous and ſteady *unanimity* of that people. To employ more words to elucidate a point ſo manifeſt, would be the idle attempt of gilding gold.

Surely you cannot doubt at this time, my countrymen, but that the people of *Maſſachuſetts-Bay* are ſuffering in a cauſe‖ common to us all ; and therefore, that we ought immediately to concert the moſt prudent meaſures for their relief and our own ſafety.

Our intereſt depending on the preſent controverſy is unſpeakably valuable. We have not the leaſt proſpect of human aſſiſtance. The paſſion of deſpotiſm raging like a plague, for about ſeven years paſt, has ſpread with unuſual malignity through *Europe*. *Corſica*, *Poland*, and *Sweden*, have ſunk beneath it. The remaining ſpirit of freedom, that lingered and languiſhed in the parliaments of *France*, has lately expired, by the new modelling their parliaments. What kingdom or ſtate interpoſed for the relief of their diſ-

BANNER OF THE MASSACHUSETTS SPY, ONE OF THE MAJOR PATRIOTIC NEWSPAPERS IN THE 1770'S

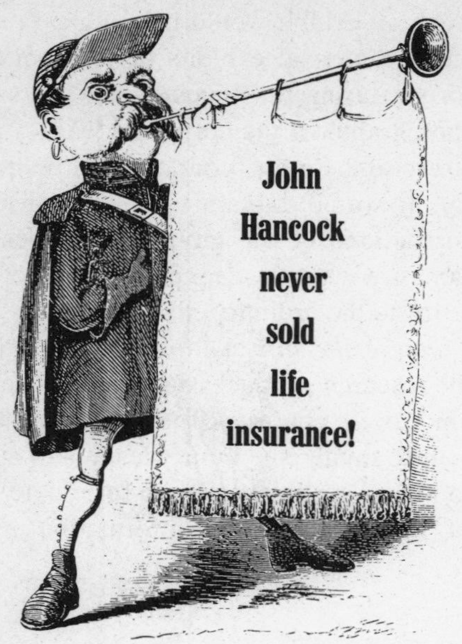
John
Hancock
never
sold
life
insurance!

Sometimes, feeding the information to one reporter for a front-page exclusive is the best strategy for handling the information, although this does run the risk of alienating the other media in the future. Without question, however, extensive newspaper and television coverage is the best way to make information available to large numbers of people simultaneously.

These, then, are the rudiments of an effective Community Research program for a Peoples Bicentennial Commission: developing PROBE chapters, composed of both students and local residents; defining the questions that ought to be asked; releasing the information in an appropriate way. If a Peoples Bicentennial Commission merely developed this sort of service during the Bicentennial years, it would already have done more for America than the combined expositions produced by all the corporations and government agencies.

Yet if research can uncover information about the community, how can the community uncover information about itself? More directly, how can people determine their own community goals during the Bicentennial years? How can a Peoples Bicentennial Commission help in developing a social agenda in the community? Here a strategy of community hearings might be the most effective.

COMMUNITY HEARINGS

In most cities, there are neighborhood councils that attempt to cope with the various problems of local areas of the metropolis. Sometimes they are organized block by block; sometimes they represent the social-service agencies in the neighborhood; sometimes they represent both. However they are structured, these councils are in a constant battle for funds to meet community needs. Their problems are growing more serious, moreover, in the wake of the Nixon Administration's resistance to federal spending programs for people.

Therefore, if a City Bicentennial Commission decides to celebrate our two-hundredth birthday with frivolous expositions and pageants, the Peoples Bicentennial Commission should persuade neighborhood councils to conduct hearings on their real priorities for the Bicentennial years. "Agenda for '76" might be a good name for the project, since the Commission would be attempting to develop a broad agenda of human-service projects around which people could organize by 1976. A tenants' union, for example, might publicize its plans to fight for low- and middle-income housing throughout the city; a social-service agency could present proposals for neighborhood child-care and recreation centers; a health clinic could outline plans to expand its operation. Whatever the specific projects, the aim should be to develop as comprehensive a statement of people's needs as possible.

The Peoples Commission can play a critical role in planning and carrying out the hearings. It can contact the relevant community organizations for proposals and pertinent testimony. It can create the citizen panels to hear the proposals, or it can serve as a panel itself. The

Commission can assemble the programs into an Agenda for '76 Booklet, for distribution throughout the city.

It is easy to see how community groups can make use of the findings of the hearings. They can use the Agenda to battle for revenue-sharing funds. They can challenge local businesses and banks to contribute to meeting the demands of the Agenda. They can demand that the local Community Chest or United Fund determine its priorities in accordance with the Agenda. Most important, the Agenda should be used to challenge the city's Bicentennial celebration itself. How could any mayor suggest a bogus celebration in the face of communitywide pressure of this sort?

Obviously, funds to solve urban and rural problems cannot come entirely from local governments. Federal funds must play a critical role. Needless to say, the federal government has resisted its responsibilities in this area. The domestic record of the past five years speaks for itself: welfare for the rich; "self-reliance" for working people and the poor. Yet serious attention to the principles of the American Revolution can offer community and citizen organizations a rallying cry against the policies of our Tory government in Washington. If the government chooses to reduce taxes on corporations and the rich by bringing hardship to millions of ordinary citizens, the people should demand, once again, "No Taxation Without Representation" in determining the priorities of the nation as a whole. Many organizers are already focusing on unjust taxation as a major issue of this era.

No Taxation Without Representation

THE BOSTON TEA PARTY

The East India Company was a monopoly corporation created by the government and sustained by the government. In 1773, its financial picture was deteriorating badly, under the influence of corrupt and incompetent officers; the value of EIC shares was plummeting, and investors were howling. In its efforts to overthrow the governments of the Indian subcontinent, the corporation had extended its resources to the breaking point; it raised armies and fleets and waged private wars in pursuit of profit and power, but its international corporate empire was profitable only to the handful of swindlers who controlled the company.

At length, the government stepped in to rescue the investors. After all, it was investors who supported the government; it was investors who could afford to finance political campaigns. In fact, many Members of Parliament were themselves EIC shareholders. So the investors, angry over the state of their company investments, called upon the government to redeem their political investments—the campaign funds and payoffs that made the system possible. The East India Act was passed, and the company, as a result, received a loan of £1,400,000.

But that was not enough to bring financial stability to the EIC: it was also awarded a monopoly of the tea trade in North America. Now losses in the Asian operations of the international corporate octopus could be relieved by a government-arranged windfall in the New World, where the company would be allowed to name

Die Americaner wiedersetzen sich der
Stempel Acte, und verbrennen das aus
England nach America gesandte Stempel-
Papier zu Boston. im August 1764.

EARLY GERMAN ENGRAVING OF TAX REBELLION

the sole agent for the sale of tea in each port. The government would collect a tax on the sales and the company would take a commission; thus both government and corporate bureaucrats—and they were interchangeable—would have revenues for the important tasks of keeping up the royal image and subduing Asia.

Americans were in no mood for a massive boondoggle; confidence in the government had been drastically eroded. A few months earlier, Benjamin Franklin had stolen some letters written by Governor Hutchinson of Massachusetts and had mailed them to the Boston radicals with the stipulation that they not be published. But when the radicals read the letters, they knew they must let the people know what the authorities were talking about behind closed doors.

Sam Adams flamboyantly informed the public that he was in possession of secret documents proving that important men were scheming to defraud and oppress the Colonists, and he promised to release the documents. The town of Boston waited with feverish anticipation for the exposé; royal politicians were silent as they waited to find out who would be exposed. Finally, Sam Adams read the pilfered letters in the Massachusetts House of Representatives. John Hancock followed the dramatic reading by stating that he had received the same letters from a different source and was therefore permitted to publish them. The publication of the documents shook the government to its roots; Hutchinson had made such remarks as "There must be an abridgement of what is called English Liberty." The people of Massachusetts were outraged, and the Hutchinson machine was never the same again. With the royal administration of Massachusetts in severe trouble, the proclamation of the tea tax and monopoly offered activists an opportunity to mobilize the community as never before. When the EIC named close associates of the Governor to administer the tea agencies, the last shred of government credibility vanished. On November 3, 1773, Sam Adams called and chaired a rally at the Liberty Tree, and the protesters circulated a demand that the Governor's cronies resign from the lucrative positions. Hutchinson, still enraged over the release of his letters, was determined to show the troublemakers who was boss, and he refused.

All over the Colonies, taxpayers were furious. The East India Company seemed to combine in itself all the hateful things so many people had left England to escape: corruption, privilege, irresponsible power . . . John Dickinson of Pennsylvania wrote of the company,

"By unparalleled barbarities, extortions and monopolies, it has stripped the miserable inhabitants of their property and reduced whole provinces to indigence and ruin."

On November 27, the ship *Dartmouth* reached Boston with a load of EIC tea, and the next day all the activists in Boston converged on Faneuil Hall to discuss the course of action patriots might take. The meeting was so large that it had to move to the Old South Church, where it resolved to firmly resist the authorities. An armed radical was sent to guard the ship and see that no tea was unloaded. On the following day, the militant *Boston Gazette* warned that any persons who tried to get the tea ashore would be "treated as wretches unworthy to live" and would be "victims of our resentment." Nobody touched the tea, and the ship remained at the pier.

Two more ships entered the harbor with tea, and they too were prevented from unloading. But the law provided that if the ships were not unloaded within a certain period of time, they would be seized by customs officials. Community leaders strongly suspected that government authorities would wait till the clamor had died and would then sell the tea as planned. The deadline was December 17, and the activists were determined to bring the confrontation to a head before the customs agents could take the ships. With lines drawn and a deep crisis approaching, the owner of the *Dartmouth* went to the Governor, asking him to allow the ship to return to England.

BRITISH GOVERNMENT OFFICIALS MOURN THE REPEAL, DUE TO WIDESPREAD AMERICAN RIOTS, OF THE STAMP TAX

On December 16, eight thousand patriots waited at the Old South Church as the Governor and the shipowner talked. At 5:45 P.M., the owner arrived with news that the chief executive had refused to back down.

Sam Adams rose and roared, "This meeting can do nothing more to save the country." A war whoop arose at the door, and soon the streets were filled with radicals dressed and painted as Indians. Off they marched to the docks, making a terrible uproar. "You'd thought the inhabitants of the infernal regions had broken loose," said a bystander. It was the sound of Revolution.

KING GEORGE III

The "Mowhawks" moved quickly and efficiently aboard the three ships, splitting into groups of about fifty each, and commenced throwing the tea overboard. Friendly spectators thronged the dock so that the authorities could neither interfere nor get a look at the "Indians." When it was over, the activists cheerfully marched away to fifes and drums.

In the morning, Paul Revere rode out to spread the tidings to Revolutionaries in other provinces, and the cities of New York and Philadelphia soon followed suit. In Philadelphia, the captain of the *Polly* was seized on arrival and taken before a committee, where he was upbraided while another eight thousand patriots jammed the State House yard. The frightened captain agreed to take the vessel back to England. In New York, the Sons of Liberty won a signal victory over Governor William Tryon, an experienced royal troubleshooter who had led troops to crush the uprising of North Carolina small farmers against oppressive corruption, taxation and privilege four years earlier.

The reaction of patriots around the Colonies was overwhelmingly favorable. John Adams observed:

> The people should never rise without doing something to be remembered—something notable and striking. This destruction of the tea is so bold, so daring, so firm, intrepid and inflexible, and it must have so important consequences, and so lasting, that I can't but consider it an epoch in history.

A Tory remarked that, from this time on,

> Many thought they could not be friends to their country, unless they trod in the same steps and imitated the example of the Bostonians.

TAX EQUITY FOR AMERICANS: A NEW TEA PARTY

Across the country, a revolt is in progress against the tax privileges of America's corporate aristocracy and the rich.

A national movement for tax justice during the Bicentennial years is not a possibility: it is a certainty. But the character of that movement—its principles, its program, how it is organized—is an open question. It is a question that ought to concern those of us who want to see democratic and egalitarian principles translated into public policy in these years.

Taxes and Power

What are taxes like for working people? Take one average city. A factory worker in Philadelphia who makes $9,000 a year (that includes a lot of overtime) will pay out over 30 percent of his salary in local, state and federal taxes during the year. Those taxes include four separate income taxes (including Social Security); nearly $500 in real estate taxes on a $10,000 house; a 5-percent sales tax on everything but food and prescription drugs and special taxes on gasoline, liquor and cigarettes. By the time all the tax men are done with him, he'll have just a little over $6,000 to feed, clothe, house, transport, insure and save for his family. That's less than the Department of Labor's standard of "minimum adequate income" for a family of four.

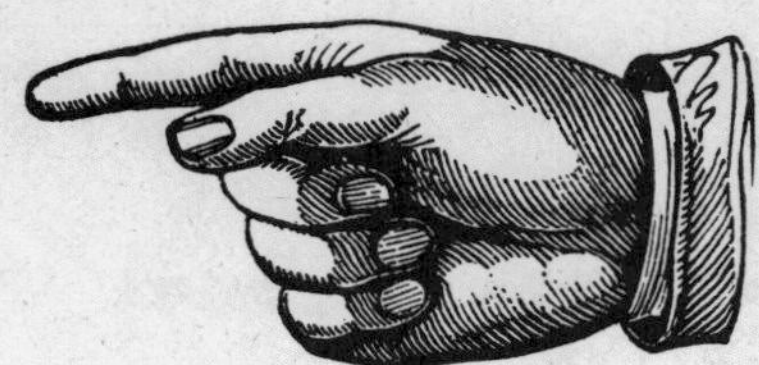

Now, our factory worker isn't the most heavily taxed citizen in the city. Both the poor and the wealthy pay higher percentages of their incomes. But he figures, with some justification, that he gets very little back in services, and what he gets is lousy; the most intimate contact he ever has with government is his tax bill. And unlike the situation with a wealthier taxpayer, his income and his house are his whole assets: he has small savings and no stocks or bonds in reserve. So 30 percent cuts to the bone. He may pay a smaller percentage than his doctor, who makes $30,000 a year. But the factory worker still ends up with less than half as much money to support his family.

The financial strain, however, is only one reason why taxes are a sore point for poor and working people. A more fundamental reason is this: the tax issue focuses a feeling of dispossession, a whole range of resentments in the lives of ordinary Americans. Politics seems to slip farther and farther from our grasp. Streets get dirtier and more dangerous; schools get crummier; unemployment and prices rise. Nobody in government seems able or willing to do anything about it. But the tax bill comes around like clockwork.

We feel more and more that we are paying for someone else's country.

Of course, this feeling has been a two-edged sword. The same outrage has been vented indiscriminately at bureaucrats and welfare mothers, hairy students and bankers; at everybody who seems more at ease with the new rules of the game. But at the core of all the resentment is an accurate perception: money is the source of power and influence in America. Taxes are a form of tribute to moneyed powers that have slipped beyond our control and understanding, powers that have no time for the values and needs of ordinary people. Taxes erode our control over our own circumstances and add to somebody else's control over us.

This is an old theme in American politics, of course; but that's because it has always been true. And never truer, one might add, than it is today.

Noah Webster warned back in 1787: "An equality of property, with a necessity of alienation constantly operating to destroy combinations of powerful families, is the very soul of a republic." We are nearly two hundred years farther along the road to inequality now.

Mr. Webster might express some consternation at these figures:

The richest 6 percent of American families own over 50 percent of the total wealth.

The poorest 50 percent of American families own only about 6 percent of the total wealth.

The poorest 25 percent own virtually nothing.

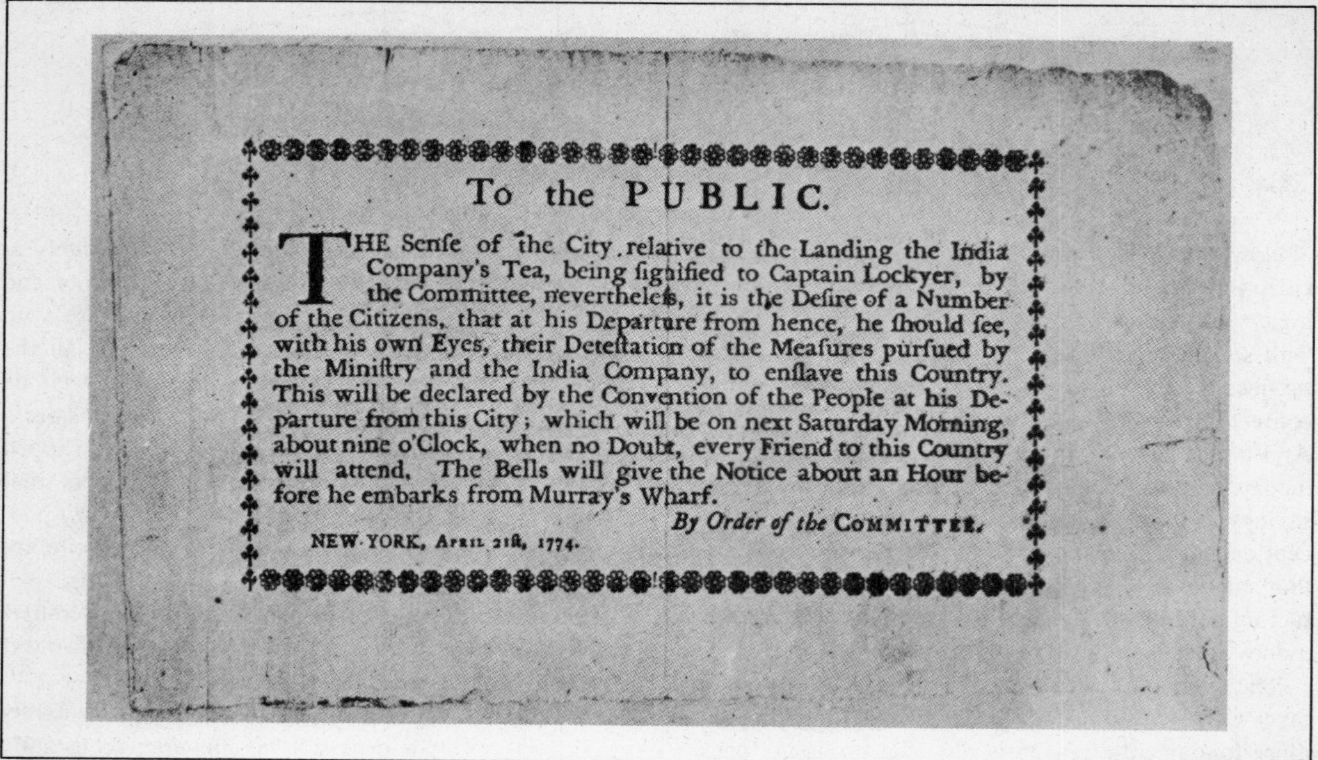

To the PUBLIC.

THE Senſe of the City relative to the Landing the India Company's Tea, being ſignified to Captain Lockyer, by the Committee, nevertheleſs, it is the Deſire of a Number of the Citizens, that at his Departure from hence, he ſhould ſee, with his own Eyes, their Deteſtation of the Meaſures purſued by the Miniſtry and the India Company, to enſlave this Country. This will be declared by the Convention of the People at his Departure from this City; which will be on next Saturday Morning, about nine o'Clock, when no Doubt, every Friend to this Country will attend. The Bells will give the Notice about an Hour before he embarks from Murray's Wharf.

By Order of the COMMITTEE.

NEW-YORK, April 21ſt, 1774.

THE PRINTED INVITATION TO THE FIRST NEW YORK TEA PARTY, APRIL 21, 1774 (FROM AN ORIGINAL BROADSHEET IN THE COLLECTION OF THE NEW-YORK HISTORICAL SOCIETY)

The American tax system is the product of two conflicting pressures arising out of this inequality. The weaker of the two has consisted of sporadic popular movements for redistribution of wealth and power in the direction of greater equality, by means of taxes that fall very heavily on the rich and very lightly on the poor. The other has been the slow, successful pressure of the rich and powerful to minimize the effect of these taxes on their further accumulation of wealth and power.

Here are some examples of how this works:

You pass a steeply graduated tax on personal income, *but* have special low rates on investment income that even out the effect on the rich.

You pass an impressive 48-percent tax on corporate income, *but* then you put in so many loopholes that the actual rate on some big companies is less than 5 percent.

You set up a Social Security system, *but* you finance it entirely out of wages and salaries—and only out of everybody's first $12,000 a year.

That's how the federal tax system works, and has worked for decades. State and local systems generally are even worse—based on property taxes, sales taxes and others that make no pretense of being progressive. And even if a state or city has a graduated personal income tax or a corporate tax, the federal system of exemptions and deductions is normally used—lock, stock and loophole.

Most working Americans have at least a hazy idea that this is going on—that while taxes scrape away at their very livelihoods and their capacities to function as citizens, vast wealth and power continue to pile up with little hindrance in a few bank accounts and stock portfolios.

Wealthy tax avoiders have the advantage of obscurity, and the comforting knowledge that each additional dollar in a tax-free bond is one more brick in their protective wall. Most working people have only the hard-won certainty that there's nothing they can do about it. As Jefferson wrote: "Those who have once got an ascendancy and possessed themselves of all the resources of the nations . . . have immense means for retaining their advantage." His words have the ring of prophecy in Bicentennial America.

Most of our tax reformers are concerned only with

plugging loopholes, or with other violations of some vague doctrine of "fairness." But there is no fairness to be had in a system of concentrated wealth and power. There is no way to construct a tax system that is "economically neutral." The taxation of ordinary citizens to support the entrenched power of an elite is inherently unfair. It is, in the most literal sense, taxation without representation.

America in its Bicentennial years needs more than a movement for closing loopholes and "distributing the burden more evenly"; we need Tax Equity for Americans—TEA—a new party, a movement that will treat tax reform as one aspect of a fight for genuine equality of property and power and against taxation without representation.

A new TEA Party should take Webster's words about the necessity of destroying combinations of powerful families quite seriously. We should not be afraid to look at taxes as a method for radical redistribution of wealth and power; and we should never feel "un-American" when we do. There is nothing un-American or treasonous about the preservation and reconstruction of real democracy; the only treason is in giving up on it.

Local Organizing for Tax Equity

The first step is to inform yourself. Local taxes can be a complicated business, and it's a good idea to be familiar with the way the whole system works. Otherwise, you'll have a hard time spotting appropriate organizing issues.

If you can read, if you can do arithmetic, you can become a local tax expert.

Find the following:

1. Your City and School Board budgets, which will list taxes by name and tell you how much they raise.

2. The local Chamber of Commerce will probably have a publication that describes each of these taxes. If not, ask at City Hall.

Already you know more than the average citizen: what taxes there are, who has to pay them, how much money they raise. With that information alone, you can watchdog any changes in the local tax structure, and you're a helpful resource person. But don't stop yet.

3. Learn some history. Was business ever taxed at a

TARRING AND FEATHERING

COERCION OF WEALTHY BUSINESSMEN...

...AND DESTRUCTION OF PRIVATE PROPERTY WERE TACTICS USED BY COLONIAL PATRIOTS TO GAIN TAX JUSTICE

higher rate than it is now? How much have small taxpayers' bills gone up? Reading old newspaper files is tedious but sometimes rewarding. Has there ever been a major assessing scandal? Seeking the company of knowledgeable tax people is more interesting, although finding such a person may be more difficult. If you're in a big city, find out if there's ever been a local business or real estate journal; ask at a library for back copies.

4. Read the newspaper. Just knowing everything the general public knows is important. Furthermore, you may find your big issue on page 49, next to the obituaries.

5. Is there a university in the area? The Economics or Urban Affairs graduate department may have papers or theses on file dealing with local taxes. These, in turn, may give you references to other sources.

Read three relevant studies, and you're a genuine expert. You may even know more than the Mayor.

The main purpose in all this is your own education. But there's an important fringe benefit: expertise is a useful organizing tool. It enables you to talk to a lot of people.

"People's experts" are a scarce commodity, and if you know what you're talking about, chances are you can find opportunities to be useful. And in the process you may establish an excellent reputation in the community—a reputation that can pay dividends in contacts and membership later on. Be knowledgeable, and be available.

It may even be a good idea to formalize your role as an expert by putting together a program on tax reform that you can present to neighborhood organizations, unions, PTA's and other groups. Again, it's important to know what you're talking about, to tailor your presentation to the concerns and the language of your audience and to make the program slick enough (e.g., with a slide show) to sell to program chairpersons.

If you have any printing money, think about putting out a series of "Common Sense" pamphlets on local tax injustices. The more topical they are, the better. Make sure they're readable. And *include a mail-back membership blank.*

You might also consider staging your own events in places with captive audiences. How about a "King George Exhibit" of tax avoiders in some public park, with pictures and charts of the loopholes they use? How about forums on Tax Day, or on the anniversary of the Boston Tea Party—in front of IRS or H. & R. Block? A little imagination will produce plenty of other ideas for getting public attention.

But remember—an important point of all this activity is to make contacts for the TEA Party as an organization. You are out to meet people who will become members, even organizers. A central part of your message must always be the importance of *organizing* for tax equity.

Have a device for getting people's names and addresses. And get back in touch with something for them to do, or at least with a newsletter and a request for membership. Here are some things to try:

Ask people to hold educational meetings in their homes and invite their neighbors—perhaps on the subject of "Why Are Our Assessments So High?"

Conduct a petition drive. Ask people to go door to door in their own neighborhoods.

If there is a public issue that folks are excited about, persuade them to go lobbying with your position on the issue—with City Councilmen, state legislators or other appropriate officials.

Remember: most people are not born meeting-goers, You should try to find ways to talk to people individually, and to let them work with you, without having to drag them across town to a citywide meeting. A TEA Party member in her own neighborhood is potentially a leader of six of her friends; at a meeting downtown, she's just another bored stranger. Citywide membership meetings should be planned only *after* you've built an active membership, so that everybody who comes is there to do business.

All this puts a lot of the burden on your organizing group. Until you're ready to pull together a citywide organization, *you're* the TEA Party. You'll have to make the same speeches seventeen different times, keep up with developing issues, keep in touch with all your active members and make decisions. The payoff comes when you decide you're ready to form an organizing committee of all your contacts, call a citywide meeting to elect officers and know—not hope, but *know*—that every one of them will be there with six friends. When that happens, you're under way. You can start thinking about major campaigns, alliances and even national strategies.

One immediate priority once you're formally established as a membership organization is to expand the number of people involved in the "expertise" part of the work: speaking in behalf of your campaigns, developing educational programs, etc. The more people who feel vital to the TEA Party, the more organizers you'll have.

LET REVENGE OR AMBITION, PRIDE, LUST, OR PROFIT TEMPT THESE MEN TO A BASE AND VILE ACTION; YOU MAY AS WELL HOPE TO BIND UP A HUNGRY TIGER WITH A COBWEB, AS TO HOLD SUCH DEBAUCHED PATRIOTS IN THE VISIONARY CHAINS OF DECENCY, OR TO CHARM THEM WITH THE INTELLECTUAL BEAUTY OF TRUTH AND REASON. —ABIGAIL ADAMS, 1775

The second priority should be to *develop a campaign* around a local issue—a campaign that can be won in a highly visible, participatory way, and that takes on the real enemy. There will be no lack of possibilities.

Local Issues

Local taxes are *the* worst for poor and working people. Thousands of American municipalities rely almost completely on real estate taxes for their local revenue. Even with the rare good fortune of honest assessing procedures and personnel, real estate taxes take a bigger bite out of lower incomes. Add in the corruption and incompetence of many assessors, and the ordinary homeowner is at an even greater disadvantage.

Many cities have additional personal taxes, which are almost always regressive—wage tax, head tax, bar and entertainment taxes, etc.

But the regressivity of city personal taxes is only one side of the situation. The other side is the decline of city tax bases and the increase in city service costs. City dwellers, who are increasingly poor and in desperate need of expensive services such as schools, are put in the position (like the parents of Philadelphia) of having to make a choice—higher regressive taxes, or reduced services.

Why are city tax bases declining? In large part, because the wealth moves outside the city limits as service costs rise. Businesses and wealthy residents who remain use the threat of departure as a club against taxes which are needed by poorer residents. What major city has not told its people, "We can't raise business taxes; we have to give tax breaks to new developments; we've got to hold the line on welfare and education expenses —or else we'll lose jobs and even more tax money"?

A local TEA Party can fight on several kinds of issues:

Are there special breaks—especially illegal breaks—going to corporate taxpayers or wealthy individuals, depriving the city or schools of funds and increasing pressure on small taxpayers?

Is there a particularly vicious tax whose repeal can be sought; or one that is about to be imposed; or a progressive tax that is under fire for reasons of "business climate"?

Is some public project, like a highway, about to reduce the city tax base by creating more exempt property? Are currently exempt properties (like college facilities, or land held by public authorities) really performing the functions for which they were given exemptions in the first place?

Is the city administration putting the squeeze on services like education because it is not willing to raise taxes on business?

It is important to remember, when choosing issues like these around which to organize, that organizations are built and sustained through victories—victories in which the members get to participate. You are trying to show people that organization works, that they have power together to make a change, however small, in the system they dislike. That is about the most complicated proposition you can put to a newly organized group. When people feel the exhilaration and responsibility of organized power, instead of the fear and futility born of their individual weakness, they will be more likely to deal with complicated analysis and strategy. In the meantime, it's a good idea to pick a fight that is simple, is vital to people and has a reasonable chance of being won. Keep the leaflets short and to the point.

The TEA Party vs. The Loophole Bank and Trust Company

Let's take an issue that many taxpayers' groups have raised—property-tax-assessment breaks—and see how it can be used to build a TEA Party.

Taxpayers' groups in dozens of communities have uncovered assessing breaks given to corporations.

For the most part, the investigations were not conducted by lawyers or appraisers. Investigating assessments is tedious but not difficult, although sometimes ingenuity is required.

Assessments are usually matters of public record. Checking their accuracy is the problem. If you can get a competent professional appraiser, use him. If the city has a transfer tax, it may require that an affidavit of "fair market value" be attached to the deed of sale; look up the deed. If a building in question is relatively new, look at local real estate or business journals from the year it was built: they may tell you its cost. If a property is closely similar to another property owned by somebody else, compare the assessments. Keep at it; you'll find something.

Now let's say you've got the goods on a thirty-story office building owned by The Loophole Bank and Trust Company. You've got an affidavit of value from the deed, and the building is assessed at 20 percent of its actual value—a revenue loss of $2.5 million to your city. What do you do about it?

THE TRUTH IS THAT ALL MEN HAVING POWER SHOULD BE DISTRUSTED. —JAMES MADISON

First, consider what you want out of a fight over this issue: You want to win it (get the assessment raised), but to win it publicly, and in a way that proves to current and potential members that organized citizens are powerful. You want to increase people's understanding of the privileges accorded to big business. And you want as many of your members as possible to feel that their participation was a necessary part of your victory. The tactics you choose should further all of these purposes.

The first step might be to dig up as much information on Loophole Bank and Trust as possible. Who's the chief executive? Where does he live? Does he have a special relationship with the Mayor? Or Assessor? How much of Loophole's business directly exploits working people—through real estate holdings, for example? Has it ever been a target of community action before? Does Loophole lend money to the city or hold tax-free city bonds? Is Loophole's president or chairman a political figure (or a well-known do-gooder)? All of these pieces of information can help you figure out tactics. And none of it will go to waste; it can all be used in speeches and other educational materials.

Next figure out what the tax break is costing small taxpayers—not just in total dollars, but in extra taxes or reduced services. Be prepared to say, "If your home cost fifteen thousand dollars, you're paying three dollars a year in real estate taxes to subsidize Loophole," or, "Loophole's unpaid taxes could pay two hundred more teachers for our school system." This is an important way of relating the actual cost of tax privilege to the people you want to organize—and provides them with a specific personal reason to be angry about it.

Both these pieces of research can ideally be done by members, but if there are students around with free time and research skills, don't be afraid to use them.

Next, pick a target. An obvious choice is the Chief Assessor, but don't be hasty: you're interested in more than bureaucratic runaround, which is what you'll get from the Assessor's office. The purpose of your initial tactic is to force the other side into reacting publicly; the best way to do this is to put him on the spot by creating news. Consider the following possible opening gambits:

1. If you have good relations with the local news media, hold a news conference. An assessing scandal *is* news. If at all possible, give the reporters an angle; for instance, hold your news conference on the steps of the Assessor's office (or that of the Mayor, or Loophole's president) and announce that you are going to visit the official immediately thereafter to demand an explanation. Bring a crowd! And make it clear that your people are organized; that this is only a first step and that you have further bad news in store for your target.

MEN WHO INJURE AND OPPRESS THE PEOPLE UNDER THEIR ADMINISTRATION PROVOKE THEM TO CRY OUT AND COMPLAIN; AND THEN MAKE THAT VERY COMPLAINT THE FOUNDATION FOR NEW OPPRESSIONS AND PROSECUTIONS.
—ANDREW HAMILTON, 1735

2. Give the story to one reporter as a scoop, with a commitment to give you credit. This probably guarantees you space, and the reporter will call the city and Loophole's president for comment. Since the paper will then have an investment in your story, you can get coverage for a follow-up demonstration, and maybe a feature on your group. But you *have* to be prepared to follow up quickly.

About demonstrations: Don't plan one if your members aren't all prepared to come and to bring other people. A small demonstration will make your people feel futile, especially if it doesn't get covered; and you'll lose credibility for the next time.

Have a gimmick. Bring a big copy of a welfare application for Loophole's president to fill out, since he's getting welfare from the taxpayers; or make a big price tag to put up on the door of the building. Be creative. Your members will enjoy it, which is important; and reporters will love it (especially those for TV).

3. If your people can't come out for a daytime news conference or demonstration, there are other ways to break your story.

a. Announce that you are filing suit against the Assessor and the Loophole Bank and Trust for recovery of all losses from the tax break (especially if you have an affidavit of value or some other really hard evidence). This can run into money, of course, especially if you haven't got a free lawyer. And if you choose this tactic, it's important to find things for the members to do: pack the courtroom, hold small auxiliary demonstrations outside, etc. Make sure your lawyer talks to the whole membership. *They* are his clients.

b. Organize small property owners to appeal their assessments en masse on the basis of Loophole's tax break. Demand open hearings; demand that all the Loophole assessing records be made public. Do everything together: file your appeals together, demand one big hearing, etc.

One or more of these opening gambits should get a response from your target. It's possible that public officials—even the Assessor when put on the spot—will get very indignant and promise to correct the situation immediately. Don't be grateful—take credit as loudly and as publicly as you can. Point out the obvious truth: that the TEA Party's work was the only reason that this secret payoff to big business was exposed and stopped. Continue to push until the change in Loophole's assessment is on the books. You might even demand a copy of its new tax bill.

It's more likely, of course, that the response will be a denial of wrongdoing. Look carefully at what the other side says. Build each response from the other side into a new action of your own. Be imaginative. Continually use the conflict as an excuse to talk to more people, to get more and more media coverage, to jam meetings. If you do your work well, and your people stick it out, eventually the heat will get too uncomfortable for whoever is on the hot seat—Loophole, the Assessor or whomever else you decide to roast. And you'll wake up one morning with your first big win.

How to Deal with Victory

Many organizations fall apart the day after they win their first big campaign. Leaders want to relax and rest; the issue they've been fighting about has taken on so much significance that people are left with a vacuum when it's no longer an issue.

Don't let people forget that Loophole Bank and Trust is just one of many local aristocrats. You haven't won the war, or even the battle—just an opening skirmish. The news conference that you call to take credit for Loophole's reassessment should also announce a bigger, better campaign—perhaps a demand that the Assessor's office, which has been proved wrong

in the Loophole case, open up its records of *all* big corporate assessments.

Organizations are built not by a series of disconnected episodes, but by gathering momentum. Don't lose yours. *Always* be prepared for the next step.

The Loophole assessment break is, of course, only one example of an issue around which to build a campaign. Other issues will call for different tactics. But the overall strategy is the same: first, gather your membership into a participatory organization using petitions, public education, small fights, etc.; second, find a simple, winnable issue, using tactics that involve as many members as possible in a public victory against a corporate or wealthy tax avoider; third, push on from that victory to another, bigger campaign.

Somebody in the TEA Party must be responsible for gathering memberships during all this. Other people should be continuing your education programs; still others should be researching new issues. The idea is not to cease involving new people as they come in. The more you're doing, the more people can be active. Don't be afraid to set up committees. On the other hand, don't set up one-member committees, either; pace your growth to coincide with the growth of active membership.

Looking Outward

As your TEA Party grows, and similar groups emerge in other communities, you'll be thinking about alliances on state and federal tax-justice issues. Local tax-equity organizing will inevitably lead your people to see the need for statewide and national organization, because some of the most critical aspects of the tax issue simply cannot be approached locally.

Local governments are increasingly dependent on state and federal funds. The problem of runaway business can probably be solved only at the federal level, insofar as corporations are less likely to run away from federal taxes, even if they object to them. Therefore, your TEA Party group will find itself looking beyond the city limits very soon.

One way to bridge the transition is to incorporate information about state and federal tax inequities into educational programs and speeches from the beginning. It's also useful to exchange information and visits with members of other taxpayer groups while building local campaigns. Apart from offering valuable insights into organizing themselves, they will give TEA Party members the sense of being part of a larger movement, a feeling that they are not alone. More than a few movements have died for want of this feeling.

State Issues

If the TEA Party is going to get involved in state issues, however, it should learn what they are. Here are some questions that may help you focus on the problems:

What are the major revenue sources? In many states, the regressive sales tax is the biggest money-maker, followed by personal income taxes and special sales taxes on gasoline, liquor, cigarettes and the like.

What is the share of state revenue produced by taxes on business vs. taxes on individuals? Is it declining?

What kind of special breaks do businesses get? Is the federal system used to determine taxable corporate income, so that all federal loopholes apply? Is there a sales-tax exemption for business purchases? How about other exemptions extended to certain parts of business property or income—such as machinery used directly in a manufacturing process?

Is there a tax on property other than real estate—stocks and bonds, for example? Property taxes in some states once affected all property, not just land and buildings, which constitute less than half the country's wealth. If such taxes were enacted today, the property-tax rate around the country could be reduced substantially.

Is there a tax on inherited wealth? Have its revenues

declined as rich people use devices like "generation-skipping" trust funds to avoid paying it?

All of these questions focus attention on ways that states offer special privileges to corporations and the rich which are denied to ordinary citizens. Even though state tax codes are long and tiresome, it's worth some trouble to know what your legislature has been doing. It will enable your organization to reach out to communities throughout the state.

Federal Issues

Tax reform has already become one of the major national issues of the Bicentennial years, and the number of bills introduced in Congress for federal action increases by the month. Indeed, one of the most comprehensive tax-reform bills introduced in the House of Representatives in 1973 was called the Tax Equity Act (T.E.A.)—hardly a coincidence in this particular period.

To review the growing volume of information about federal tax loopholes here would be quite redundant. Philip Stern's book *The Great Treasury Raid* is a good place to start. Ralph Nader's Tax Reform Research Group, located in Washington, D.C., publishes a monthly paper, *People and Taxes,* which includes up-to-date information on loopholes and efforts to close them. The TEA Party should be sure to clip all news articles on tax-reform battles in Congress, and maintain voting records of local Congresspersons and Senators on tax issues.

In addition, the TEA Party should watch developments on reform of social security and on revenue sharing. The first is *the* most regressive federal tax, and is sure to come under attack from unions and progressive Congresspersons during the Bicentennial years. The second will determine priorities for state and local spending throughout the country.

The main problem is dramatizing the relationship between these national issues and the local campaigns of the TEA Party. Usually, most people cannot go to

WASHINGTON LIBERATES NEW YORK CITY, 1783

Washington for meetings and demonstrations—at least, not regularly. Even if we were to project a major national march for Tax Reform, comparable to national Civil Rights and Peace marches, we would still need to develop ways to make complicated national issues understandable in neighborhood meetings. A number of techniques might work.

Figure out how federal tax inequities deprive local services of needed revenues. A local group might publish a leaflet reading as follows: "If municipal bonds were taxable, and the revenue were put into federal education programs, our schools could gain $________."

Figure out how much individual taxpayers are losing from unfair tax distribution.

Focus on local businessmen, banks and corporations who are benefiting from federal tax loopholes.

An organization that has learned to fight for justice in property-tax assessment in a city will have no difficulty understanding how to fight for justice in tax rates nationally. A tax-reform group that has won important victories in one city will be anxious to make coalitions to gain comparable power over arrogant corporations in the nation as a whole. It is a matter of moving from powerlessness to confidence, from despair to determination, from apathy to continued involvement in the decisions that affect people throughout their lives. It's a matter of taking seriously the slogan that prompted the American Revolution in the first place. If we demand "No Taxation Without Representation," we cannot rest until full involvement in all decisions over taxation is achieved.

"Don't Tread on Me"

Community hearings will enable a Peoples Bicentennial Commission to develop local agendas for "life, liberty and the pursuit of happiness" by 1976. The TEA Party can fight for funds for needed programs in accordance with the principle of "No Taxation Without Representation." Yet the ultimate goal of these two organizing efforts must be to secure dignity for ordinary citizens in every aspect of their lives. The Revolutionaries had a slogan that crystallized this demand: "Don't Tread on Me." It can become a watchword for Americans today.

Recall a few of the long train of "abuses and usurpations" that the Colonists leveled at King George:

DON'T TREAD ON ME

"He has refused his assent to Laws, the most wholesome and necessary for the public good.

"He has made Judges dependent on his Will alone, for the tenure of their offices, and the amount and payment of their salaries.

"He has erected a multitude of New Offices, and sent hither swarms of Officers to harass our people and eat out their substance.

"He has affected to render the military independent of and superior to the Civil Power.

"In every stage of these Oppressions, We have Petitioned for Redress in the most humble terms: Our repeated Petitions have been answered only by repeated injury."

As we see, the times change; the grievances against unresponsive and arrogant rulers do not.

A Peoples Bicentennial Commission that merely chose to reprint the Declaration of Independence and the Bill of Rights for distribution throughout the community would be making telling points about the reality of America today. A disturbing number of surveys, for example, show that millions of our citizens reject the Bill of Rights if asked questions about its provisions without knowing where they came from. Local PBC's could combat this breakdown in civic morality by sponsoring discussions on our basic rights at meetings of local fraternal and civic organizations, PTA gatherings, school assemblies, and youth forums—perhaps in cooperation with lawyers and local civil libertarians. It is important to establish the principles of our historic documents as guidelines against which to judge the reality of America today.

The arena where human dignity and civic morality

are under greatest attack today, however, is the one most frequently ignored in public discussions and debates: the workplace. Blue-collar workers languish on the assembly line, condemned to perform repetitive tasks which do little to challenge their skills and intellectual resources in a meaningful way. White-collar employees become paper-pushers, paralyzed from exercising any power over the institutions that use them. Absentee rates soar; frustration with work in general becomes a national ethic. If, therefore, the Bicentennial years are to enhance the dignity of the American people, citizens everywhere must look to changing the nature of the assembly line and the office as a major civic priority. For every issue, there is an appropriate strategy. Consider the following:

1. The Workplace Is Unsafe

How about a citywide conference that brings together trade unionists, health organizations, environmental groups and public officials to demand that local industries meet accepted standards of public health and safety? To add historical perspective, the Peoples Commission can put on a graphics exhibit dramatizing working conditions during the Revolutionary period. If there is no legislation in the community or state setting proper health and safety standards for the workplace, the conference could launch a campaign to pass some. If there is legislation, the conference could develop mechanisms to ensure its enforcement. The Peoples Commission might well develop a service designed to publicize serious industrial accidents in the media, so that these issues can reach public consciousness on a regular basis.

2. The Employees Cannot Criticize the Employers

Why not? The abridgment of freedom of speech and criticism within institutions must be held largely responsible for the breakdown of public respect for these freedoms generally. A concerned Peoples Commission should meet with union officials on these matters, encouraging them to develop employees' Bills of Rights, extending our civic principles to private institutions throughout the community.

3. The Work Is Tedious

Despite enormous hardships, the Colonists saw work in the New World as a great adventure. The reason was simple: they knew that whatever they built was in fact *theirs*. They felt a sense of involvement in the process of production.

Today, working people get no such sense of pride in the jobs they perform. Blue-collar workers are mere units on the assembly line, almost extensions of the machines; white-collar employees are trapped in bureaucracies for which no one seems to take responsibility. It is no wonder that most Americans are trying to escape their jobs rather than improve them.

A Peoples Bicentennial Commission can combat these conditions by disseminating all available information on new patterns of workplace organization throughout the country and world. Why not modular assembly lines, such as those in operation in Sweden, where a group of workers exercises collective responsibility for the manufacture of a product? Why not office teams, which assume the direction of a corporation's activities? A series of meetings on these issues throughout the Bicentennial years among unions, secretaries' associations and public officials would do much to generate new experiments in making the workplace livable for the people.

4. The Employees Exercise No Control over Working Conditions

This issue was as important to the first American Revolutionaries as questions of taxation and representation in government. Many owned their own businesses, after all, and were determined to protect them from British mercantilists and the Crown. Some modern chains have sought to recapture this spirit by allowing local people to operate their franchises on a semiautonomous basis. Unfortunately, the autonomy is quite limited, as any gasoline-station operator will attest, and offers nothing whatsoever to the millions of citizens without the capital to take advantage of it.

Every major study of work in modern America has found that employees now value influence over their jobs as highly as adequate salaries and working conditions. Peoples Bicentennial Commissions can contribute to this growing movement by developing slide shows and tapes on the struggle for democracy in work throughout American history. They should remind unionists of the early demands of farmers to protect their farms against large corporations and of the proposals of the Knights of Labor as far back as the 1880's to retain workers' control over local industries. Most important, Commissions should publicize all movements for union democracy in their city to civic and educational groups throughout the community, in order to give working people the feeling that the public is on their side. With this support, nothing can stop them.

5. The Employees Cannot Serve the Community

Can employees live up to civic values in the course of their work? Can they serve the people? Of course, the demand for socially useful work among young people and professionals has been attracting national attention. Law firms now grant part-time options for public-service practice on the part of their younger attorneys; a few doctors and nurses have given up traditional jobs in the medical profession to work in low-income areas; architects and engineers have created cooperatives to work with community organizations and social movements on neighborhood planning and rehabilitation of substandard housing.

There has been little effort, however, to duplicate this process in the blue-collar and middle-class work force. Here a Peoples Bicentennial Commission can undertake a number of projects:

a. *Sponsorship of local conferences on work and citizenship* among unionists and professional associations, focusing on opportunities for employees to live up to civic values in the course of their work. Through general presentations and informal discussions, the Commission would hope to encourage the participants to take questions of social worth, or quality, or responsibilty to the community (or however else it might be phrased) seriously as a framework for union demands of the future. Why shouldn't teachers be demanding quality education in the schools, as well as pay raises? Why shouldn't retail clerks be demanding protection for the consumer as well as for themselves? Why shouldn't auto workers be demanding detailed plans from management surrounding conversion from the car to public transportation, since the need for public transportation could not be greater? Why should any of us be forced to sell things we wouldn't buy, to deliver services we wouldn't accept, to produce commodities we feel are detrimental to the long-range health of our communities? These are the questions which the Commission might encourage participants to take seriously, as a framework for campaigns in the future.

b. A local *Vocations for Social Change* employment service. Vocations for Social Change, operating out of Canyon, California, has been encouraging socially use-

ful employment for years. Why couldn't local Commissions develop counseling centers in cities, designed to serve as a clearinghouse for jobs that perform useful services to the community? Such centers could identify not only worthwhile jobs, but unions that were fighting for social responsibility as part of their programs.

c. *Civic Responsibility Press Service* for labor press associations and professional journals and newsletters. Such a service could supply articles to pertinent journals on all efforts to perform service in the course of work and to hold institutions accountable to civic values. Perhaps a Peoples Bicentennial Commission could even sponsor meetings with local editors of labor newspapers, designed to interest them in focusing attention on these issues.

"Only Lay Down True Principles"

Despite White House intentions, the Bicentennial is not an occasion of partisan politics, but a time, as Tom Paine wrote, to "refresh our patriotism by reference to first principles." "It is by tracing things to their origin," he wrote, "that we learn to understand them, and it is by keeping that line and that origin always in view that we never forget them. An inquiry into the origin of rights will demonstrate to us that rights are not gifts from one man to another, nor from one class of men to another."

The Bicentennial presents political clubs and caucuses with the chance to raise issues of concern in the light of the Revolutionary principles of 1776. But more important, the Bicentennial can be a chance to cut through partisan issues, political parties and even the Constitution, to stand face to face with the "self-evident" truths of the Declaration of Independence.

Political clubs and caucuses, in helping to revive the Spirit of '76, can renew their own purpose. Nonpartisan educational efforts in the community will be a public service *by* your organization and also a service *for* your organization, strengthening the dedication of your club's members to the political and social goals of our founders.

> Only lay down true principles and adhere to them inflexibly. Do not be frightened into their surrender by the alarms of the timid, or the croakings of wealth against the ascendancy of the people.
>
> —THOMAS JEFFERSON

Since your political club will naturally be concerned with candidates, elections and political platforms, use these institutional *political forums* to lay down, and discuss, the true principles of the Revolution. Some questions and issues you might raise publicly:

- When voters go to the polls, are they aware of the nature of the rights they exercise, or have they been programmed, through years of political hoopla and partisanship, to simply pull a lever? If they are aware of their Revolutionary rights, are they prepared to assert them? Have your club ask that the Declaration of Independence be prominently displayed at the polling place, so that citizens may spend their time in line thinking about self-evident truths.
- The ideals of 1776 are a standard against which the positions and conduct of candidates can be measured. Ask them to discuss the Revolutionary principles; ask them to endorse these principles; ask them to justify their political views upon these principles. Do their views hold up?
- Does the candidate believe that Life is an inalienable right? If yes, does his or her position on medical care support that belief?
- Does the candidate agree with the founders that Liberty is also an inalienable right, or does he or she believe that Liberty should be "balanced" with the demands of those in power?
- Does the candidate accept the premise that we have

LAY DOWN TRUE PRINCIPLES

an inherent right to pursue Happiness, or does he or she think that govenment should regulate lives for the "general" good?

- Does the candidate accept the Bill of Rights and the absolute freedoms it guarantees, or does he or she think the radicalism of our ancestors must be tempered by "interpretation"?
- Our founders believed that democratic government is designed to be responsible to (i.e., respond to the needs and desires of) the people. The Constitution is supposed to do just that—ensure that government is responsible to the will of the people. Where does the candidate think corporations fit into the Constitution? Does he or she think corporations respond to the people? If yes, in what way does he or she think the exercise of vast, corporate power by the unelected "governments" of big business secure the rights of the people? Does he believe that *all* government should be democratic, including corporations?
- Does the candidate believe that government is today securing the rights with which it is charged? If not, does he or she accept the logical conclusion set forth by our founders that the people have the duty as well as the right to throw off "any form of government which becomes destructive of these ends"?
- Demand that the candidate (if the office carries with it a franking privilege) use his or her free postage rights, if elected, to send a copy of the Declaration of Independence to each and every constituent, along with a personal testament of belief in the Revolutionary ideals.

Beyond these general questions which should be raised publicly, political clubs and caucuses should attempt to organize their own platforms along Revolutionary lines, perhaps dividing up planks into those intended to secure Equality, Life, Liberty and Happiness. Selections from the writings and speeches of the founding radicals can be employed as preambles to planks. For instance, Patrick Henry's "Caesar had his Brutus, Charles the First his Cromwell, and George the Third may profit by their example" is a concise statement on executive power and privilege exercised against the rights of the people.

Keep in mind that the founders of this country regarded themselves as patriots and Revolutionaries. They fought for inalienable rights and self-evident truths, not for political office or personal power. Rededicating your club to the principles of the Revolution should carry that message along with it.

I AM NOT A FEDERALIST, BECAUSE I NEVER SUBMITTED THE WHOLE OF MY OPINIONS TO THE CREED OF ANY PARTY OF MEN WHATEVER IN RELIGION, IN PHILOSOPHY, IN POLITICS, OR IN ANYTHING ELSE WHERE I WAS CAPABLE OF THINKING FOR MYSELF. SUCH AN ADDICTION IS THE LAST DEGRADATION OF A FREE AND MORAL AGENT. IF I COULD NOT GO TO HEAVEN BUT WITH A PARTY, I WOULD NOT GO THERE AT ALL.
—THOMAS JEFFERSON, 1789

For this reason the internal education of club members is as important as performing nonpartisan educational activities in the community. Remember Abigail Adams' words: "We have too many high sounding words, and too few actions that correspond with them." It is easy to mouth the words of the Declaration of Independence. It is another thing to live them.

This, then, is the task which lies before us:

- To develop community agendas which fulfill the principles of "Life, Liberty and the Pursuit of Happiness" for all people.
- To campaign for funds to support human needs on the principle of "No Taxation Without Representation."

- To demand dignity in work in the spirit of the historic cry "Don't Tread on Me!"
- To dedicate ourselves to "Only Lay Down True Principles."

The ideas contained herein are only a few of the many possibilities that the Bicentennial theme provides. We have outlined programs for local Peoples Bicentennial Commissions, for community Tax Equity for Americans programs, for labor unions, churches and political clubs that aim at reaffirming the Spirit of '76. Beyond these possibilities, the Bicentennial, as a theme, can be taken up by any organization or group that is waging specific battles around economic, political or social issues in the community.

The Bicentennial dynamic offers an opportunity to reach out to larger audiences to gain support for specific issues. Community organizations can use important commemorative events leading up to July 4, 1976, as a strategic timetable for enlisting support behind specific programs and demands. The language of the campaigns can be placed within the context of the principles of '76 and the fulfillment of the Promise of America. Organizational materials, including brochures, posters, buttons and slide shows, can incorporate quotations from the Founding Fathers and Mothers and graphic illustrations from the American Revolution.

Reidentifying with the American Revolutionary principles during the Bicentennial years can provide local organizations with the beginning of a new philosophical and political focus as well as a new spirit of enthusiasm and hope.

Our suggestions are openers. The possibilities are limitless: to commit ourselves to one another; to plan a birthday the world will never forget; to become the new patriots of America.

> Stain not the glory of your worthy ancestors, but like them, resolve never to part with your birthright; be wise in your deliberations, and determined in your exertions for the preservations of your liberties. Follow not the dictates of passion, but enlist yourselves under the sacred banner of reason; use every method in your power to secure your rights . . .
>
> —JOSEPH WARREN, *oration to commemorate the Boston Massacre, March 5, 1772*

IV

The Light in the Steeple

The American continent was peopled by various types and successive waves of religious dissenters. For a century and a half they came, and they formed churches and discussed things common people hadn't been able to discuss in a long time: man's relationship to God; man's relationship to man . . .

By the 1770's the churches had become focal points for public debates, and pastors had become spokesmen for something new and exciting in human affairs. Where their ancestors had heard "Obedience" droned from the pulpit, Americans now heard, again and again, the word "Happiness." By July 4, 1776, the pursuit of happiness, and government's duty to secure it, had become part of the religious tradition.

The midnight ride of Paul Revere was set into motion by a light in the steeple of the Old North Church in Boston, warning the inhabitants that the forces of despotism were approaching in the night, imploring them to act in defense of their rights and liberties. Does that light still shine in the steeple of *your* church?

The following theme areas suggest a starting point for church sermons, convention topics and youth seminars. These general theme outlines can be explored through film and multimedia presentations, Oral/Visual Projects, articles for church publications, radio and television forums and theater productions.

The Awakening

In the 1740's, the first wave of revivals swept America; it was called the Great Awakening. In contrast with the staid, somber manner of the formal churches, evangelists poured forth a stream of emotion, and the people responded in kind. Conservative churchmen could not accept the strange new phenomenon; they castigated the revivalists. But the most brilliant theologian of the period, Jonathan Edwards, defended the Awakening:

> If it be so that true religion lies much in the affections, hence we may infer that such means are to be desired as have a tendency to move the affections. Such books, and such a way of preaching the word, and administration of ordinances, and such a way of worshipping God in prayer and singing praises, is much to be desired, as has a tendency deeply to affect the hearts of those who attend these means.

George Whitefield, the first and most popular of the evangelists, wrote after a tumultuous day at the Old South Church in Boston:

> I am verily persuaded that the Generality of preachers talk of an unknown, unfelt Christ. And the Reason why congregations have been so dead, is because dead men preach to them. O that the Lord may quicken and revive them for his own name's sake. For how can dead men beget living children?

Men and women trained from youth to take their place within the secure bastion of the congregation were called upon to take responsibility for their own souls, and it was a terrifying experience. Sarah Blanchard wrote:

> There was a great struggle between my conscience and my pride . . . for though I was convinced that this was

> the truth as it is in Jesus . . . yet I could not bear to be called a Separate and bear the flouts and scoffs of my companions . . . so I went to the meetinghouse still.

But Sarah finally chose her conscience over her pride. The churches called upon the "separates" to explain why they were leaving the fold, and replies minced no words:

> I being at a church and seeing so much want of Love and faithfulness at that time, as well as many other times . . .
>
> —JERUSHA MORSE

> Now, my dear Brethren, which of you can set to your seal that God has really founded you upon the Rock of Ages? For according to the Word of God, this church is right the reverse!
>
> —DAVID MORSE

> I went to the meetinghouse, and when I came there was nobody there; and as I set there, these words came to me: "My house is a house of prayer, but ye have made it a den of thieves." Then sudden fear came over me, so I got up and went out and walked over the burying place, and I thought I had rather lie down among the graves than go into the meetinghouse.
>
> —HANNAH CORY

The new and frightening experience of chosing between security within the fold and the dangers of individual choice transformed the American mind. For those who were called upon to break with the past, the question was not merely one of earthly alternatives: if these dirt farmers and laborers were wrong in this awful choice, they could expect eternal damnation. To women and men who had been annealed in the forge of the Great Awakening, no trial was too great, and no decision seemed too important for the people who had decided upon the fate of their own souls. Herman Husband, who had been awakened by the evangelists of the 1740's, led the Regulator movement in North Carolina in the 1760's, and his religious visions inspired the small farmers to open insurrection against the corrupt and vicious tax-gatherers of the Colonial aristocracy.

Q: *How is religion received? Through the emotions? Through the intellect?*

Q: *If religion is received through the intellect, does a computer then have a religious sense?*

Q: *If religion is received through the intellect—inasmuch as intellectual capacity varies, does capacity for religious experience then vary?*

Q: *If through the emotions, which emotions?*

Q: *If religion is received through the emotions, in what way does the education of clergymen enable them to communicate a religious sense?*

Q: *What sort of education do lay people need in order to receive religion through the "affections"?*

The Chosen People

The trip to the New World reminded people of the Israelites' flight from Egypt into the Land of Milk and Honey. John Winthrop, who led the emigration of 1630, told his flock:

> We must consider that we shall be as a city upon a hill; the eyes of all people are upon us, so that if we shall deal falsely with our God in this work we have undertaken and so cause Him to withdraw his present help from us, we shall be made a story and a byword through the world. We shall open the mouths of enemies to speak evil of the ways of God and all professors for God's sake; we shall shame the faces of many of God's worthy servants, and cause their prayers to be turned into curses upon us till we be consumed out of the good land whither we are going . . . Beloved, there is now set before us life and good, death and evil, in that we are commanded this day to love the Lord our God, and to love one another, to walk in His ways and to keep His Commandments and His Ordinance, and His laws, and the articles of our covenant with Him, that we may live and be multiplied, and that the Lord our God may bless us in the land whither we go to possess it. But if our hearts shall turn away so that we will not obey, but shall be seduced and worship other gods, our pleasures and profits, and serve them; it is propounded unto us this day, we shall purely perish out of the good land whither we pass over this vast sea to possess it.

From the beginning, Americans viewed themselves

as a new Chosen People, with a special mission in the name of all humanity. When conflict mounted between Colonists and Crown, John Adams said, "We are Joseph"—and government, of course, was Joseph's cruel family. The Chosen People must regain their freedom.

When the Revolution struck, Americans became even more strongly convinced that they had been singled out for an experiment in the name of all humanity. Liberty was seen as a special gift, enjoyed by only a few people in all of history, and now given to the masses of the New World. Tom Paine wrote of the great symbol of this gift, the Liberty Tree:

Unmindful of names or distinctions they came,
For Freemen like brothers agree.
With one spirit endued, they one friendship pursued,
And their temple was Liberty Tree.
Beneath this fair tree, like the patriarchs of old,
Their bread in contentment they eat,
Unvexed with the troubles of silver and gold,
The cares of the grand and the great.

The Revolutionaries saw America as the hope of the world and repeatedly reminded one another of their mission "in the name of all humanity." Jefferson, in his first inaugural address, called the young republic a "chosen country," and in his last testament he expressed the hope that the Fourth of July would be for all the world "a Signal of arousing men to burst the chains." Walt Whitman believed that America's First Revolution foreshadowed "a glorious dawn for downtrodden people."

Q: *Is the concept of a Chosen People chauvinistic?*

Q: *The Hebrew idea of a Chosen People implied special trials and tribulations as well as special favor. Does America's great wealth suggest special duties in the world?*

Q: *Do political leaders exhort Americans to view themselves as a Chosen People? In what way?*

Q: *Do Americans regard themselves as a Chosen People?*

Q: *Are Americans a Chosen People?*

PILGRIMS FLEEING ENGLAND IN SEARCH OF RELIGIOUS FREEDOM IN THE NEW WORLD

Passover

> The people of Israel groaned under their bondage, and cried for help, and their cry under bondage came up to God. And God heard their groaning, and God remembered His covenant with Abraham, with Isaac, and with Jacob. And God saw the people of Israel, and God knew their condition.
>
> —EXODUS 2, 23–25

God *knew* their sufferings and decided to bring them out of Egypt, saying, "I know that the king of Egypt will not let you go unless compelled by a mighty hand." (Exodus 3, 19) Far from gladly accepting divine aid, "they did not listen to Moses, because of their broken spirit." (Exodus 6, 9)

Freedom was not merely to be desired: it was something God wanted for His people, something God commanded for His people, something toward which God drove His people, even over their objections. Before the Hebrews could receive the Commandments, they must first undergo a Revolution, according to God's plan.

In the desert God had to push them every step of the way; when Moses went to the mountain, they turned to Aaron and asked for statues of gods to comfort them. Again and again God had to force them forward to the new land and to human dignity, "because of their broken spirit."

It was with this point in mind that Sam Adams noted that "a people long inured to hardships lose by degrees the very notions of liberty." Liberty was learned, and it was also unlearned. In Egypt, in England or in America, the condition of humanity determines its spirit: slaves think like slaves; freemen think like freemen. And so patriots must lose no time in opposing tyranny before it grew too strong; and God, who commands humans to be free and equal, would be expected to give aid again.

The exodus from Egypt had a powerful appeal in 1776. Men and women engaged in Revolution found the plight of the Hebrews understandable, and patriots like Sam Adams discerned a profound lesson in God's decision to make people free. The notion of divine intervention in human affairs occurs to those who win against overwhelming odds. When the little cities of ancient Greece turned back the hosts of the Persian Empire, a citizen-soldier watching the great mass of military manpower and hardware depart said, "It is not we who have done this." To the Americans, like the Hebrews and the Greeks, pitted against the greatest power on earth, success had to mean divine aid.

The example of God's aiding the oppressed in 1776 could be extended to other struggles. Jefferson said he trembled for his country when he reflected "that God is just, and that His justice cannot sleep forever." The Almighty, he suggested, might well intervene in behalf of the enslaved blacks.

The Passover tradition had also been on the minds of the Puritans who overthrew the English King in the mid-seventeenth century; one of them saluted the beheading of Charles I with the remark "Rebellion to tyrants is obedience to God." While sitting in the Continental Congress, Ben Franklin repeated that phrase to his young friend Tom Jefferson, who appreciated it so greatly that he had a seal made with the motto boldly engraved around its perimeter; in the center was a scene depicting the drowning of Pharaoh's army, while the Israelites watched from the shore and a flame roared in the sky. The seal was proposed as the official emblem of the new republic, but was voted down. The phrase, however, was used by Jefferson as his personal seal, and became so well known among those who followed in the footsteps of the founders that the leading abolitionist and feminist Henry Wright remarked, "Few axioms are more clearly established in my mind than this: resistance to tyrants is obedience to God."

Q: *Why didn't the Lord deliver the Commandments—the basis of the Hebrew faith—before making the Hebrews free?*

Q: *What similarities do you see between the Passover and the issuing of the Ten Commandments and the American Declaration of Independence and the Bill of Rights?*

Q: *Do Americans still believe that God sides with the oppressed? Should they?*

Q: *If you know of a tyrant, either great or petty, should you do something to oppose that tyrant, in obedience to God?*

Render unto Caesar

Jesus said, "Render to Caesar the things that are Caesar's, and to God the things that are God's."

The theory of Caesar's government was that Caesar *was* a god. When he died, the imperial treasury paid a respected nobleman to swear he had seen the ghost ascending to heaven to take his place among his brother and sister gods. Caligula, who butchered Christians, made his horse a god, and accordingly, it was worshiped.

Consonant with his unlimited, totalitarian power, Caesar Augustus sent out a decree that all the world should be taxed. While the aristocrats of Rome lived in luxury and devoured the goods made by conquered peoples, the peasants of the world were bled dry by the imperial revenue service.

In America, the Roman philosophy of government was never accepted; from the Pilgrims on, Americans believed in very different theories of authority and rights. In opposition to the Roman concept of arbitrary power and deification of men who believed themselves gods, Americans erected the idea of inherent and inalienable human rights, shared equally by humankind. Americans never believed that Caesar or anybody else was entitled to grab anything his thugs could steal, and in 1776 they pressed the point.

King George might fancy himself one of the heirs to Caesar, as did the Czar of Russia and later the Kaiser of Germany; but American patriots who danced around their beloved Liberty Poles on the Fourth of July wore red woolen Liberty Caps said to be of the same sort worn by *freed slaves* in ancient Rome.

Patrick Henry spoke for the Revolutionary generation when he warned, "Caesar had his Brutus, Charles the First his Cromwell, and George the Third may profit by their example!" What did Henry think was Caesar's? Not America, to be sure. To the founding Revolutionaries, it seemed that Caesar and his look-alikes had had enough of the world. Now at last there was a corner of the earth set aside for people, where human beings could live as God intended.

Q: *What is Caesar's in a democratic society?*

Q: *To say we should give unto Caesar is to suppose that we have a Caesar. Who is Caesar in America?*

Q: *Caesars tortured Christians. Do modern Caesars, if there are any, also perform this traditional role?*

The Divine Right of Kings

The divinity of rulers is an old idea, and the rulers tend to believe it more and more as they increase their power and the duration of their reigns. "I feel myself becoming a god," said a Roman emperor. Emperors claimed they were the near relatives of prominent deities and gave themselves appropriately divine subtitles, such as Diocletian's "Restorer of the World." Pharaoh was the offspring of the Sun and therefore the bringer of life and prosperity to Egypt. His spiritual authority was matched by his economic power: nearly all of Egypt was his personal possession, and nothing happened without Pharaoh's mandate.

In Christian Europe, kings ceased to be gods, but soon discovered that God had appointed them to rule. Great incomprehensible treatises were published to prove the point, and if the point was not accepted, the more persuasive power of the hangman was in reserve. In days past, Sam Adams recalled, "The divine, hereditary right of kings, and their being accountable to God alone, were doctrines generally taught, believed and practiced: But behold the sudden transition of human affairs!"

Tom Paine found kings grotesque and useless; na-

KING GEORGE III

QUEEN CHARLOTTE

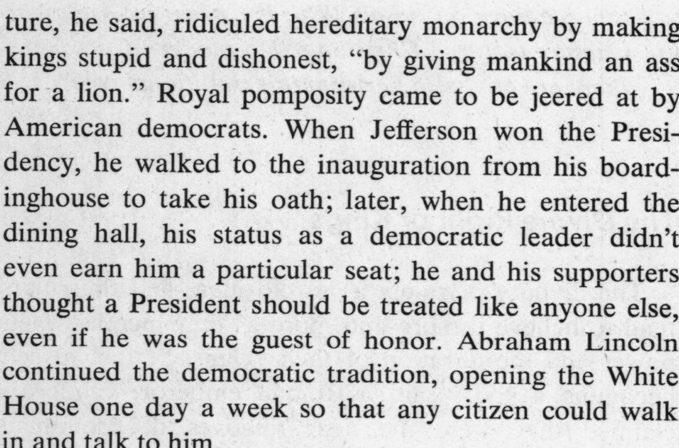

ture, he said, ridiculed hereditary monarchy by making kings stupid and dishonest, "by giving mankind an ass for a lion." Royal pomposity came to be jeered at by American democrats. When Jefferson won the Presidency, he walked to the inauguration from his boardinghouse to take his oath; later, when he entered the dining hall, his status as a democratic leader didn't even earn him a particular seat; he and his supporters thought a President should be treated like anyone else, even if he was the guest of honor. Abraham Lincoln continued the democratic tradition, opening the White House one day a week so that any citizen could walk in and talk to him.

Q: *In a democratic society, where the divine right of kings is not an article of faith, what is the duty of the church toward the President?*

Q: *What use of religious ritual and symbolism is proper for a democratic statesman? At what point does he begin to propagate antidemocratic notions of divine right?*

Q: *Has the Constitution been equipped with reminders to the President that he does not rule by divine right? Enough reminders? How about the cultural traditions? Are they sufficiently antimonarchical?*

Q: *Do we need more direct reminders, for the President and public, that divine right is not part of republican government?*

Q: *Are there provisions in the laws or customs applicable only to Presidents, which place them above ordinary mortals?*

Equality

The story of Adam and Eve has always been hard for aristocrats to explain to their subjects in a satisfactory manner. If all people had the same ancestors, how did a few become lords and many become peasants? Monarchical and aristocratic privilege was justified on the grounds of "noble" ancestry; against this ancient view, the idea of common ancestry detailed in the Adam-and-Eve story was a persistent image of equality. "Consider your origin," Dante advised. "You were not formed to live as brutes."

In the fourteenth century a "mad priest of Kent," called Mad John Ball, wandered among the hungry peasants of England saying:

> Good people, things will never go well in England so long as goods be not in common, and so long as there be villein and gentlemen. By what right are they greater folk than we? On what grounds have they deserved it? Why do they hold us in serfage? If we all came of the same father and mother, of Adam and Eve, how can they say or prove that they are better than we?—If it be not that they make us gain for them by our toil what they spend in their pride? They are clothed in velvet and warm in their furs and their ermines, while we are covered with rags. They have wine and spices and fair bread, and oatcakes and straw, and water to drink. They have leisure and fine houses; we have pain and labour, the rain and the wind in the fields. And yet it is of us and our toil that these men hold their state.

In the seventeenth century, radical Protestant sects invoked the spirit of equality of Genesis. The conservative Sir Thomas Aston warned his friends about one of these militant groups:

> Presbyterianism would be dangerous doctrine if once grounded in vulgar apprehensions. The old, seditious argument will be obvious to them, that we are all sons of Adam, born free. Some of them will say the Gospel hath made them free. And law once subverted, it will appear good equity to such Chancellors to share the earth equally. They will plead scripture for it, that we should *all* live by the sweat of our brows!

The American generation of 1776 did not find equality a "mad" idea at all. Indeed, the founding Revolutionaries, like Mad John, considered equality self-evident. The great pamphleteer of '76, Tom Paine, made this simple statement of his religious faith:

> I believe in one God and no more, and I hope for happiness beyond this life. I believe in the equality of man; and I believe that religious duties consist in doing justice, loving mercy and endeavoring to make our fellow creatures happy.

Equality was basic to the faith of the Founding Fathers. A Philadelphia militiaman of 1796 greeted the Fourth of July by toasting: "Let us never forget we are all equal."

Q: *Why did rich men and women consider equality a "mad" idea?*

Q: *How do those with excessive wealth and power today justify inequality? How would they react to the sermons of Mad John? To the Declaration of Independence?*

Q: *Franklin, Jefferson, Paine and other egalitarians were geniuses in several fields. Do leaders and spokesmen who disapprove of or evade the ideal of equality seem as gifted as the founding democrats? Match a spokesman of privilege and elitism against Ben Franklin. Which seems more sensible and convincing? Who has the better credentials?*

Q: *Have you ever heard anyone call himself a patriot and a religious person and yet sneer at the religious ideal of equality which was the faith of the Founding Fathers?*

Q: *If we are all sons and daughters of Adam and Eve, why are some of us born with immense wealth?*

WASHINGTON'S PRAYER AT VALLEY FORGE

Resistance to Authority

Rebellion against the mightiest nation on earth presents great military problems; it also presents severe ethical problems, for no one thinks of himself or herself as a criminal, even a successful one.

On July 26, 1581, the provinces of Holland declared their independence from the Spanish Empire, the Spain of the Great Armada which terrified even England. The Dutch justified their Revolution in these words:

> As it is apparent to all that a prince is constituted by God to be ruler of a people to defend them from oppression and violence as the shepherd his sheep; and whereas God did not create the people slaves to their prince, to obey his commands whether right or wrong, but rather the prince for the sake of his subjects (without which he could be no prince), to govern them according to equity, to love and support them as a father his children or a shepherd his flock, and even at the hazard of his life to defend and preserve them.
>
> And when he does not behave thus, but, on the contrary, oppresses them, seeking opportunities to infringe their ancient customs and privileges, exacting from them slavish compliance, then he is no longer a prince but a tyrant, and the subjects are to consider him in no other view.
>
> And particularly when this is done deliberately, unauthorized by the states, they may not only disallow his authority, but legally proceed to the choice of another prince for their defense. This is the only method left for subjects whose humble petitions and remonstrances could never soften their prince or dissuade him from his tyrannical proceedings; and this is what the law of nature

dictates for the defense of liberty, which we ought to transmit to posterity even at the hazard of our lives.

In 1750, the American preacher Jonathan Mayhew attacked the English doctrine of "unlimited submission to the higher powers." He had been ordered to make a speech on the anniversary of the execution of King Charles, a day of fasting and repentance for all His Majesty's subjects, for their collective guilt in killing a king. He turned the ordered sermon into a monumental statement of the rights of the people. Going beyond the *right* to resist, he said it is the *duty* of a Christian to resist corrupt, tyrannical rulers. In the Declaration of Independence, this view is written into law: "It is their right, it is their *duty,* to throw off such Government . . ."

OLD NORTH CHURCH. IN THIS STEEPLE HUNG THE LAMP THAT STARTED PAUL REVERE ON HIS FAMED RIDE

Q: *Mayhew suggested that if God sanctifies good governments and governors, he must also disapprove bad rulers. Is that reasonable?*

Q: *If God enjoins us to endure hardships (i.e., taxes, public service, war, etc.), does He also enjoin us to endure hardships in order to abolish unjust governments? If so, what kind of hardships?*

Q: *If, as Mayhew and the Revolutionary tradition insist, individuals have the duty to resist unjust government, what of churches? Should they resist unjust governments? How?*

Q: *Churches perceive a duty to support or legitimize government assumed to be just. (For instance, participation in inaugurations and other political functions.) What of the corresponding duty to oppose unjust government? Does the former imply the latter?*

Q: *When a church gives tacit support to a government, what is its duty in observing and judging the actions and policies of that government? What responsibility does a church incur toward the public when it lends legitimacy to the authorities?*

Jubilee

And you shall count seven weeks of years, seven times seven years, so that the time of the seven weeks of years shall be to you forty-nine years. Then you shall send abroad the loud trumpet on the tenth day of the seventh month; on the day of atonement you shall send abroad the trumpet throughout all your land. And you shall hallow the fiftieth year, and proclaim liberty throughout the land to all its inhabitants; it shall be a jubilee for you, when each of you shall return to his property and each of you shall return to his family. A jubilee shall that fiftieth year be to you.

—LEVITICUS 25, 8–11

The thrust of Biblical economics was that the advantages won by a few, however much they might aid the community toward prosperity in the short run, could ultimately wreck the social order. The Jubilee redistributed wealth before it became too concentrated.

The Founding Fathers and Mothers of the United States understood that point very well, and they also tried to ensure as wide as possible a distribution of wealth. Indeed, the American definition of a republic *assumes* a wide distribution of wealth. "A general and tolerably equal distribution of landed property is the

ENGRAVED by W. I. STONE for the Dept. of State by order of J. Q. ADAMS Sec. of State July 4th 1823.

IN CONGRESS, JULY 4, 1776.

The unanimous Declaration of the thirteen united States of America,

When in the Course of human events it becomes necessary for one people to dissolve the political bands which have connected them with another, and to assume among the powers of the earth, the separate and equal station to which the Laws of Nature and of Nature's God entitle them, a decent respect to the opinions of mankind requires that they should declare the causes which impel them to the separation. — We hold these truths to be self-evident, that all men are created equal, that they are endowed by their Creator with certain unalienable Rights, that among these are Life, Liberty and the pursuit of Happiness. — That to secure these rights, Governments are instituted among Men, deriving their just powers from the consent of the governed, — That whenever any Form of Government becomes destructive of these ends, it is the Right of the People to alter or to abolish it, and to institute new Government, laying its foundation on such principles and organizing its powers in such form, as to them shall seem most likely to effect their Safety and Happiness. Prudence, indeed, will dictate that Governments long established should not be changed for light and transient causes; and accordingly all experience hath shewn, that mankind are more disposed to suffer, while evils are sufferable, than to right themselves by abolishing the forms to which they are accustomed. But when a long train of abuses and usurpations, pursuing invariably the same Object evinces a design to reduce them under absolute Despotism, it is their right, it is their duty, to throw off such Government, and to provide new Guards for their future security. — Such has been the patient sufferance of these Colonies; and such is now the necessity which constrains them to alter their former Systems of Government. The history of the present King of Great Britain is a history of repeated injuries and usurpations, all having in direct object the establishment of an absolute Tyranny over these States. To prove this, let Facts be submitted to a candid world. — He has refused his Assent to Laws, the most wholesome and necessary for the public good. — He has forbidden his Governors to pass Laws of immediate and pressing importance, unless suspended in their operation till his Assent should be obtained; and when so suspended, he has utterly neglected to attend to them. — He has refused to pass other Laws for the accommodation of large districts of people, unless those people would relinquish the right of Representation in the Legislature, a right inestimable to them and formidable to tyrants only. — He has called together legislative bodies at places unusual, uncomfortable, and distant from the depository of their public Records, for the sole purpose of fatiguing them into compliance with his measures. — He has dissolved Representative Houses repeatedly, for opposing with manly firmness his invasions on the rights of the people. — He has refused for a long time, after such dissolutions, to cause others to be elected; whereby the Legislative powers, incapable of Annihilation, have returned to the People at large for their exercise; the State remaining in the mean time exposed to all the dangers of invasion from without, and convulsions within. — He has endeavoured to prevent the population of these States; for that purpose obstructing the Laws for Naturalization of Foreigners; refusing to pass others to encourage their migrations hither, and raising the conditions of new Appropriations of Lands. — He has obstructed the Administration of Justice, by refusing his Assent to Laws for establishing Judiciary powers. — He has made Judges dependent on his Will alone, for the tenure of their offices, and the amount and payment of their salaries. — He has erected a multitude of New Offices, and sent hither swarms of Officers to harrass our people, and eat out their substance. — He has kept among us, in times of peace, Standing Armies without the Consent of our legislatures. — He has affected to render the Military independent of and superior to the Civil power. — He has combined with others to subject us to a jurisdiction foreign to our constitution, and unacknowledged by our laws; giving his Assent to their Acts of pretended Legislation: — For Quartering large bodies of armed troops among us: — For protecting them, by a mock Trial, from punishment for any Murders which they should commit on the Inhabitants of these States: — For cutting off our Trade with all parts of the world: — For imposing Taxes on us without our Consent: — For depriving us in many cases, of the benefits of Trial by Jury: — For transporting us beyond Seas to be tried for pretended offences — For abolishing the free System of English Laws in a neighbouring Province, establishing therein an Arbitrary government, and enlarging its Boundaries so as to render it at once an example and fit instrument for introducing the same absolute rule into these Colonies: — For taking away our Charters, abolishing our most valuable Laws, and altering fundamentally the Forms of our Governments: — For suspending our own Legislatures, and declaring themselves invested with power to legislate for us in all cases whatsoever. — He has abdicated Government here, by declaring us out of his Protection and waging War against us. — He has plundered our seas, ravaged our Coasts, burnt our towns, and destroyed the lives of our people. — He is at this time transporting large Armies of foreign Mercenaries to compleat the works of death, desolation and tyranny, already begun with circumstances of Cruelty & perfidy scarcely paralleled in the most barbarous ages, and totally unworthy the Head of a civilized nation. — He has constrained our fellow Citizens taken Captive on the high Seas to bear Arms against their Country, to become the executioners of their friends and Brethren, or to fall themselves by their Hands. — He has excited domestic insurrections amongst us, and has endeavoured to bring on the inhabitants of our frontiers, the merciless Indian Savages, whose known rule of warfare, is an undistinguished destruction of all ages, sexes and conditions. In every stage of these Oppressions We have Petitioned for Redress in the most humble terms: Our repeated Petitions have been answered only by repeated injury. A Prince, whose character is thus marked by every act which may define a Tyrant, is unfit to be the ruler of a free people. Nor have We been wanting in attentions to our British brethren. We have warned them from time to time of attempts by their legislature to extend an unwarrantable jurisdiction over us. We have reminded them of the circumstances of our emigration and settlement here. We have appealed to their native justice and magnanimity, and we have conjured them by the ties of our common kindred to disavow these usurpations, which, would inevitably interrupt our connections and correspondence. They too have been deaf to the voice of justice and of consanguinity. We must, therefore, acquiesce in the necessity, which denounces our Separation, and hold them, as we hold the rest of mankind, Enemies in War, in Peace Friends. —

We, therefore, the Representatives of the united States of America, in General Congress, Assembled, appealing to the Supreme Judge of the world for the rectitude of our intentions, do, in the Name, and by Authority of the good People of these Colonies, solemnly publish and declare, That these United Colonies are, and of Right ought to be Free and Independent States; that they are Absolved from all Allegiance to the British Crown, and that all political connection between them and the State of Great Britain, is and ought to be totally dissolved; and that as Free and Independent States, they have full Power to levy War, conclude Peace, contract Alliances, establish Commerce, and to do all other Acts and Things which Independent States may of right do. — And for the support of this Declaration, with a firm reliance on the protection of divine Providence, we mutually pledge to each other our Lives, our Fortunes and our sacred Honor.

John Hancock

Button Gwinnett
Lyman Hall
Geo Walton.

Wm Hooper
Joseph Hewes,
John Penn

Edward Rutledge 1.

Thos Heyward Junr.
Thomas Lynch Junr.
Arthur Middleton

Samuel Chase
Wm Paca
Thos Stone
Charles Carroll of Carrollton

George Wythe
Richard Henry Lee
Th Jefferson
Benja Harrison
Thos Nelson jr.
Francis Lightfoot Lee
Carter Braxton

Robt Morris
Benjamin Rush
Benja Franklin
John Morton
Geo Clymer
Jas Smith
Geo Taylor
James Wilson
Geo Ross
Caesar Rodney
Geo Read
Tho M:Kean

Wm Floyd
Phil Livingston
Frans Lewis
Lewis Morris
Richd Stockton
Jno Witherspoon
Fras Hopkinson
John Hart
Abra Clark

Josiah Bartlett
Wm Whipple
Saml Adams
John Adams
Robt Treat Paine
Elbridge Gerry
Step Hopkins
William Ellery
Roger Sherman
Samel Huntington
Wm Williams
Oliver Wolcott
Matthew Thornton

whole basis of national freedom," wrote Noah Webster.

Wealth, then, must not be allowed to accumulate in great fortunes over endless generations. Before the ink was dry on the Declaration of Independence, radical democrats went to work against the English land system, and what resulted was a Revolutionary code which, in the words of Alexis de Tocqueville in 1830, "shatters and reduces to powder every obstacle, until we can no longer see anything but a moving and impalpable cloud of dust, which signals the coming of the Democracy."

The American work ethic included a deep distrust of sophistries that tended to support luxurious idleness, and the idle rich were figures of whom Ralph Waldo Emerson, in his "Essay on Self Reliance," wrote:

> A cultivated man becomes ashamed of his property out of new respect for his nature. Especially he hates what he has if he sees that it is accidental—came to him by inheritance, or gift, or crime. Then he feels that it is not having; it does not belong to him, has no root in him and merely lies there because no revolution or robber takes it away.

By the 20th century, wealth had congealed into the hands of a tiny handful of prominent families, and Senator Williams of Mississippi, in 1913, declared the great fortunes "a menace to the Republic" and called upon the Senate to "destroy the menaces in great fortunes transmitted from generation to generation." But the Third Jubilee of the Republic passed in 1926 without a redistribution of wealth and power. The Fourth Year of Jubilee approaches.

Q: *The commandment to redistribute wealth every fifty years, which Moses brought down from Sinai, was part of the higher law of Israel. Is the statement of original, natural human equality in the Declaration also intended as higher law? Should it be viewed as such?*

Q: *The Bible takes strong positions on economic questions. It is for redistribution of wealth and forgiving of debts, and against usury and greed. Is it proper, then, for a church or its members to be neutral on these issues?*

Q: *What is the responsibility of churches in proclaiming the Word of God in matters of the distribution of wealth and other economic questions? There are several "schools" of economic thought. What about the religious school of economic thought? Why is it not heard?*

Q: *We are approaching the two-hundredth birthday of the republic—the fourth Year of Jubilee; we have not observed even one of them. Can we discern bad effects of our ignoring the Biblical injunction?*

Q: *Should wealth be redistributed in America? In the world?*

A COUNTRY CHURCH

Covenant

HAYM SALOMON—THE MAN WHO FINANCED OUR REVOLUTION

If you walk in my statutes and observe my commandments and do them, then I will give you your rains in their season, and the land shall yield its increase, and the trees of the field shall yield their fruit. And your threshing shall last to the time of vintage, and the vintage shall last to the time of sowing; and you shall eat your bread to the full, and dwell in your land securely. And I will give peace to the land, and you shall lie down, and none shall make you afraid; and I will remove evil beasts from the land, and the sword shall not go through your land. And you shall chase your enemies, and they shall fall before you by the sword. . . . And I will have regard for you and make you fruitful and multiply you, and will confirm my covenant with you. And you shall eat old store long kept, and you shall clear out the old to make way for the new. And I will make my abode among you . . . and will be your God, and you shall be my people. I am the Lord your God, who brought you forth out of the land of Egypt, that you should not be their slaves; and I have broken the bars of your yoke and made you walk erect.

But if you will not hearken to me, and will not do all these commandments, if you spurn my statutes, and if your soul abhors my ordinances, so that you will not do all my commandments, but break my covenant, I will do this to you: I will appoint over you sudden terror . . .

—LEVITICUS 26, 3–16

The concept of the covenant between God and his people is very prominent in the Bible, but covenant theology was not revived until the 16th-century Reformation. In America, it became a basic feature of life in Congregational and Presbyterian churches, and to some extent among Baptists. In the words of John Winthrop: "We are entered into a Covenant with him for this work. We have taken out a commission."

On July 20, 1629, a year before Winthrop's new flock landed, the Pilgrims at Salem met and held the first election in America with written ballots. They elected men for the posts of pastor and teacher, but only after hours of prayer and study of Scripture and singing praises of the Lord. The candidates swore that they had been "twice called"—once by God and once by the people of Salem. On August 6, all thirty citizens met to pledge, "We Covenant with the Lord and one with another and do bind ourselves"; and newly elected pastors received their honor with the words "I take this people to be my people." The surroundings were unimpressive; but Cotton Mather shrugged off the fact that a new church was born in a barn, saying, "Our glorious Lord Jesus Christ himself was born in a stable."

The Covenant was not merely a formal agreement; it really formed a new society akin to a large family—or, as one Puritan said, "a little bundle of eternal life." Winthrop explained that "We must be knit together in this work as one man; we must entertain each other in brotherly affection." And his flock believed that deeply. Covenanters met at the Dedham church "lovingly to discourse and consult together." The Pilgrims and Puritans believed that people must cling together and support each other.

Much later, Sam Adams' Solemn League and Covenant, a term borrowed from Revolutionary Puritan tradition, helped bring the aristocracy to its knees. It also prepared the way for the signing of the Declaration of Independence—an epochal event not only for American political history but also for our religious history, for the signers, steeped in the heritage of the Pilgrim Fathers and Mothers, felt deep in their bones that they were making a new Covenant.

Q: *When people make a solemn vow and fail to keep it, do they know they have been unfaithful? Does this knowledge affect their lives?*

Q: *Have we kept the Covenant of July 4, 1776?*

Q: *The Israelites and the Puritans were terrified at the prospect of the Lord's becoming angry over the breaking of the Covenant. They expected terrible punishment. Does the breaking of the Covenant binding us to pursue Life, Liberty and Happiness bring punishment?*

Q: *Should the Covenant of the Declaration be enforced?*

Vox Populi, Vox Dei

At the end of the 8th century, an English philosopher named Alcuin made the first recorded mention of the maxim *Vox populi, vox Dei* (The voice of the people is the voice of God). The saying, by that time, had become rather well known among certain seditious subjects, and theorists, including Alcuin, were anxious to refute this democratic idea. In the process of refuting it, they publicized it, and many readers over the course of the next thousand years became familiar with the motto through the writings of intellectuals who mentioned it only in order to deny that it was true.

Conventional thinkers feared the People, and referred to them collectively as a "many-headed monster." But Tommaso Campanella, a 16th-century Dominican philosopher, spoke of the People's dumbness with frustration:

The People is a beast of muddy brain
That knows not its own force and so stands
Loaded with wood and stone; the feeble hands
Of a mere child lead it with bit and rein.
One kick would be enough to break the chain,
But the beast fears, and what the child demands
It does, nor its terror understands.

QUAKER RELIGIOUS SERVICE

Confused and stupefied by bugbears vain,
Most ridiculous! With its own hand it ties
And gags itself, gives itself death and war
For pence doled out by kings from its own store!
Its own are all beings between heaven and earth,
But this it knows not, and if one arise
To tell the truth, it kills him unforgiven.

Tommaso was involved in an insurrection in Naples and spent twenty-seven years in a dungeon. But there were other religious folk to take up the standard of Vox Populi, and the phrase got around enough to be a topic of the Harvard debates (Is the Voice of the People the Voice of God?) in the years leading up to the First American Revolution. Patrick Henry, in one of his great, treasonous speeches, blurted out the maxim. And Jeffersonian novelist Charles Brockden Brown entitled his feminist dialogue of 1798 *Alcuin*. The feeling that the People was a many-headed monster continued to show itself among Tories—both before and after the eviction of the King's army. When Jefferson expressed confidence in the sense of the People, his powerful opponent Alexander Hamilton snarled, "Your People, sir, is a great beast!"

The Voice of the People lost its direct religious connotation, but those who believed in it continued to feel religiously about it. One of the Haymarket conspirators, a hero of the early labor movement, said, as he stood on the scaffold, "Let the Voice of the People be heard!" The broadening tradition was celebrated by Carl Sandburg:

When was it long ago, the murmurings began,
And the joined murmurings became a moving wall,
Moving with the authority of the great sea,
Whose Yes and No stood in an awful script,
In a new, unheard-of handwriting?
"No longer," began the murmurings,
"Shall the king be king,
Nor the son of the king be king;
Their authority shall go,
And their thrones be swept away.
They are too far from us, the People.
They listen too little to us, the People!"

Q: *Is it more reasonable to say that God speaks through some people (i.e. clergymen, politicians, functionaries) than simply the People?*

Q: *If the Voice of the People is the Voice of God, what is the proper role of "wise men"?*

Q: *If the Voice of the People is the Voice of God, what may we say of restraints on the popular will, such as constitutional roadblocks to amendment?*

Q: Is *the Voice of the People the Voice of God?*

Natural Rights

In the 17th and 18th centuries, it was customary to draw analogies between the social order and the human body: each had a head and subordinate organs, and each was expected to operate smoothly only if the

"brain" was quickly obeyed. When a subordinate part of the human body, or of the body politic, failed to carry out the task appointed by the head, catastrophe and perhaps death was near. Such a condition of insubordination was viewed as a sickness, a "distemper." John Winthrop matter-of-factly remarked that some must be "high and eminent" and others "mean and of low degree," and that the Lord required "in the poor and inferior sort, their faith, patience, obedience, etc."

During the course of the 18th century, the concept of "natural law" was reversed and internalized. Nature, which had sanctified the social order, was now found to sanctify the rights of the individual. Instead of institutions' justifying the lives of men and women, men and women were found to be the owners of all rights, some of which were delegated to institutions. And as Sam Adams said in 1772, "Every natural right not expressly given up or, from the nature of a social compact, necessarily ceded, remains!"

When the authorities trespassed on those remaining, unceded rights, people could be expected to resist. In 1772 a pamphlet titled *An Oration upon the Beauties of Liberty* announced:

> I declare it before God, the congregation, and all the world . . . Shall a man be deemed a rebel that supports his own rights? It is the first law of nature, and he must be a rebel to God, to the laws of nature and his own conscience, who will *not* do it!

When the constitution of 1787 was circulated, those who had been activists in the struggle against the King were alarmed at the absence of ironclad guarantees of their natural rights, and so they screamed for a Bill of Rights. (One of Jefferson's suggestions was a prohibition of monopolies, but it got nowhere.) The Bill of Rights is usually referred to as a charter of *civil* liberties, but to those who worked to obtain it, it was something much more imposing—a charter of *natural,* God-given rights. Nor are the stipulated rights necessarily the only natural rights. Tom Paine pointed out that "We cannot at one stroke acquire knowledge of all our rights."

In the 19th century, in the golden age of Newtonian science, it became fashionable to deprecate the Rights of Man; a host of pseudoscientific social theories pushed the old "sentimentalism" aside. But 19th-century scientism, developed in imitation of a now outmoded concept of physical science, looks somewhat callow today. Norma Gist, an imprisoned activist supported by the Black Panthers, wrote in the Panther newspaper:

> No man or group of men, however callous or compassionate, can arbitrarily devise a code for humanity to improve upon the divine rights of man, which include Life, Liberty and Self-determination.

Q: *If Life is a natural right, why are medical care and pharmaceutical supply so profitable?*

Q: *What are the implications for society of the natural-rights doctrine?*

Q: *Do the language and actions of leaders indicate that they accept the doctrine of natural rights?*

Q: *Is it unscientific to say that human beings are born with natural, inherent rights?*

Q: *If God gives us natural rights, what does that indicate about His social views?*

Q: *Does God grant natural rights without assigning to us specific duties in securing and protecting those rights for ourselves and others?*

Reason

The Founding Fathers, especially Paine and Jefferson, wrote paeans to Reason. But their Reason was by no means the rationality of computer logic or legal arguments. When deduction brought them face to face with an unacceptable proposition, the Revolutionary thinkers dismissed it as un-Reasonable.

Reason was God's, and man was supposed to find it; thus superior intellect did not necessarily bring one

WASHINGTON BIDS FAREWELL TO HIS OFFICERS

closer to it. William Langland spoke of the same sort of Reason in the medieval poem *The Vision of Piers Plowman*:

> And I bowed my body, beholding all about,
> And saw the sun and the sea and the sand after,
> Where birds and beasts wander with their mates;
> Wild worms in the woods and wonderful fowls
> With flecked feathers of full many a color.
> Man and his mate, both might I see,
> Poverty and Plenty, peace and war;
> Bliss and bitterness, both I saw at once,
> And how that men took coin and mercy refused.
> . . .
> In sooth, I saw Reason ruling all beasts,
> Save man and his mate, and thereof I wondered.

What kind of society did Reason dictate? Tom Paine, author of *The Age of Reason,* dreamed of America's being the "Land of Love and Liberty." When the democratic movement overthrew the moneyed interests in 1800, he saw a victory for Reason:

> A spark from the altar of *Seventy-six,* unextinguished and unextinguishable through the long night of error, is again lighting up, in every part of the Union, the genuine name of rational liberty.

Jefferson, that preeminent Deist (like Paine, called an atheist in his day), suggested that God, being Reasonable, would personally intervene in behalf of the slaves. This great, irresistible force called Reason would not be confined to measurable things, or to cold calculations:

> Is Reason to be forever amused with the physical sciences, in which she is indulged merely to divert her from solid speculations on the rights of man and wrongs of his oppressors? It is impossible. The day of deliverance will come, although I will not live to see it.

Reason, thought Jefferson, was bound up with an innate sense of justice:

> Good acts give us pleasure, but how happens it that they give us pleasure? Because nature hath implanted in our breasts a love of others, a sense of duty to them, a moral instinct, in short, which prompts us irresistibly to feel and succor their distresses . . . The Creator would indeed have been a bungling artist had he intended man for a social animal without planting in him social dispositions.

John Dickinson wrote that human rights "are founded on the immutable maxims of Reason and Justice." Immutable! Reason and Justice, which were bound together, were eternal principles and did not change with a new theory or a new system. Reason was very much like Revelation, and it proceeded from the same source.

Q: *Why should a land governed by Reason be "the Land of Love and Liberty"? What is the connection between the three terms?*

Q: *Is it contradictory for a man who praises Reason to prophesy the intervention of God in behalf of the oppressed?*

Q: *Many institutions and disciplines believe they operate according to Reason. Is their Reason the same as that of the Founding Fathers?*

Q: *What is the relationship between Reason and science? Reason and technology? Reason and business systems?*

Q: *What is Reason?*

Democracy

The Greek historian Herodotus, called the "Father of History," praised democracy this way:

> A tyrant disturbs ancient laws, molests women, kills men without trial. But a Democracy—the name is so beautiful, and a people ruling does none of the things a tyrant does.

After the fall of Greek democracy, the word became ugly in the ears of aristocrats. For two thousand years, the term was one of abuse. One was not described as a democrat; one was *accused* of being a democrat.

But in America the word, by degrees, grew respectable. In 1717, John Wise, a clergyman and former indentured servant, wrote:

> A Democracy. This is a form of government which the light of nature does highly value and often directs to as most agreeable to the just and natural prerogatives of human beings . . . Upon the experience of several thousand years, after the world had been tumbled and tossed from one species of government to another, at a great expense of blood and treasure, many of the wise nations of the world have sheltered themselves under it again, or at least have blended and balanced their governments with it.

THE TORIES ARE COMING! THE TORIES ARE COMING!

He was speaking principally of the government of the church; but the practice of democracy in the churches, mounting throughout the 18th century, eventually burst into the secular sphere. The right to start one's own church implied the right to start a new government.

But even after the end of royal rule in America, Democracy was a bad word. Martha Washington scolded her daughter for consorting with "filthy democrats," and John Adams, who, on the eve of the Declaration, had criticized Paine's *Common Sense* for its "Democratical" ideas, succeeded Washington and did his best to stop America from drifting toward democracy. Adams' opponent, Jefferson, had a wide reputation as a "violent Democrat and a vulgar demagogue." It was not until after the Democrats' victory over the Federalists that the former could safely admit their beliefs; and then Jefferson stated that the world was divided into Aristocrats and Democrats.

Being a democrat would never be easy; the people sometimes made unwise choices. Walt Whitman, reacting to disaffection on the part of some activists, put the matter in perspective:

> We know well enough that the workings of Democracy are not always justifiable in every trivial point. But the great winds that purify the air, and without which nature would flag into ruin, are they to be condemned because a tree is prostrated here and there in their course?

Our public education system, the rights of a free press and many other facets of American life were installed as part of the democracy, because they were expected to create the new democratic citizen who would be able and willing to rule his own country.

Q: *How is your church governed?*

Q: *What does it teach the congregation about democracy? Equality? Human rights?*

Q: *If your church became the government, what kind of government would it be?*

Q: *Do the functionaries within the church assume less or more honor and dignity than the founder of the faith did?*

Q: *Does "the light of nature" direct us to democracy?*

Useful Quotations

These are suggested quotations to accompany topical headlines or to be used with appropriate graphics:

JULY 4, 1776: THE LIBERTY BELL RINGS OUT THE REVOLUTIONARY MESSAGE: "PROCLAIM LIBERTY THROUGHOUT ALL THE LAND, UNTO ALL THE INHABITANTS THEREOF."

The wicked draw the sword and bend their bows,
to bring down the poor and needy,
to slay those who walk uprightly;
their sword shall enter their own heart,
and their bows shall be broken.

—Psalm 37, 14

The fool will no more be called noble,
nor the knave said to be honorable.
For the fool speaks folly,
and his mind plots iniquity;
to practice ungodliness,
to utter error concerning the Lord,
to leave the craving of the hungry unsatisfied,
and to deprive the thirsty of drink.
The knaveries of the knave are evil;
he devises wicked devices
to ruin the poor with lying words,
even when the plea of the needy is right.
But he who is noble devises noble things,
and by noble things he stands.

—Isaiah 32, 5–8

Woe to those who decree iniquitous decrees,
and the writers who keep writing oppression,
to turn aside the needy from justice
and to rob the poor of my people of their right,
that widows may be their spoil,
and that they may make the fatherless their prey!
What will you do on the day of punishment,
in the storm which will come from afar?
To whom will you flee for help,
and where will you leave your wealth?

—Isaiah 10, 1–3

Woe to those who call evil good
and good evil,

who put darkness for light
 and light for darkness,
who put bitter for sweet
 and sweet for bitter!
Woe to those who are wise in their own eyes,
 and shrewd in their own sight!
Woe to those who are heroes at drinking wine,
 and valiant men in mixing strong drink,
who acquit the guilty
 and deprive the innocent of his right!

—Isaiah 5, 20–23

The Lord has taken his place to contend,
 he stands to judge his people.
The Lord enters into judgment
 with the elders and princes of his people:
"It is you who have devoured the vineyard,
 the spoil of the poor is in your houses.
What do you mean by crushing my people,
 by grinding the face of the poor?"
  says the Lord God of Hosts.

—Isaiah 3, 13–15

Bring no more vain offerings;
 incense is an abomination to me.
New moon and sabbath and the calling of assemblies—
 I cannot endure iniquity and solemn assembly.
Your new moons and appointed feasts
 my soul hates;
They have become a burden to me,
 I am weary of bearing them.
When you spread forth your hands,
 I will hide my eyes from you;
even though you make many prayers,
 I will not listen;
 your hands are full of blood.
Wash yourselves; make yourselves clean;
 remove the evil of your doings
 from before my eyes;
cease to do evil,
 learn to do good;
seek justice,
 correct oppression;
defend the fatherless,
 plead for the widow.

—Isaiah 1, 13–17

Your prophets have seen for you
 false and deceptive visions;

OLD NORTH CONGREGATIONAL CHURCH, MARBLEHEAD, MASSACHUSETTS, CIRCA 1875

they have not exposed your iniquity
 to restore your fortunes,
but have seen for you oracles
 false and misleading.

—Lamentations 2, 14

When I would restore the fortunes of my people,
 when I would heal Israel,
 the corruption of Ephraim is revealed,
 and the wicked deeds of Samaria;
for they deal falsely,
 the thief breaks in
 and the bandits raid without.
But they do not consider
 that I remember all their evil works.
Now their deeds encompass them,
 they are before my face.
By their wickedness they make the king glad,
 and the princes by their treachery.

—Hosea 7, 1–3

Hear this, you who trample upon the needy,
 and bring the poor of the land to an end,

saying "When will the new moon be over,
  that we may sell grain?
And the sabbath,
  that we may offer wheat for sale,
that we may make the ephah small and the shekel great,
  and deal deceitfully with false balances,
that we may buy the poor for silver
  and the needy for a pair of sandals,
  and sell the refuse of the wheat?"
The Lord has sworn by the pride of Jacob:
"Surely I will never forget any of their deeds."
Shall not the land tremble on this account,
  and every one mourn who dwells in it,
and all of it rise like the Nile
  and be tossed about and sink again, like the Nile of Egypt?

—Amos 8, 4–8

Woe to her that is rebellious and defiled,
  the oppressing city!
She listens to no voice,
  she accepts no correction.
She does not trust in the Lord,
  she does not draw near to her God.
Her officials within her
  are roaring lions;
her judges are evening wolves
  that leave nothing till the morning.
Her prophets are wanton,
  faithless men;
her priests profane what is sacred,
  they do violence to the law.
The Lord within her is righteous,
  he does no wrong;
every morning he shows forth his justice,
  each dawn he does not fail,
  but the unjust knows no shame.

—Zephaniah, 3, 1–5

Wail . . .
  For all the traders are no more;
  all who weigh out silver are cut off.
. . . I will search Jerusalem with lamps,
  and I will punish the men
who are thickening upon their lees . . .

—Zephaniah 1, 11–12

Thus they drivel on their dais, the Deity to know,
And know God in their gullet when their guts are full.
But the careworn may cry and complain at the gate
Both a-hungered and athirst, quaking with cold—
Is none to call him near, to help his need,
But they hew him away like a hound and order him off.
. . . . .
God is much in the mouths of these great masters,
But among poor men His mercy and works.

—PIERS PLOWMAN

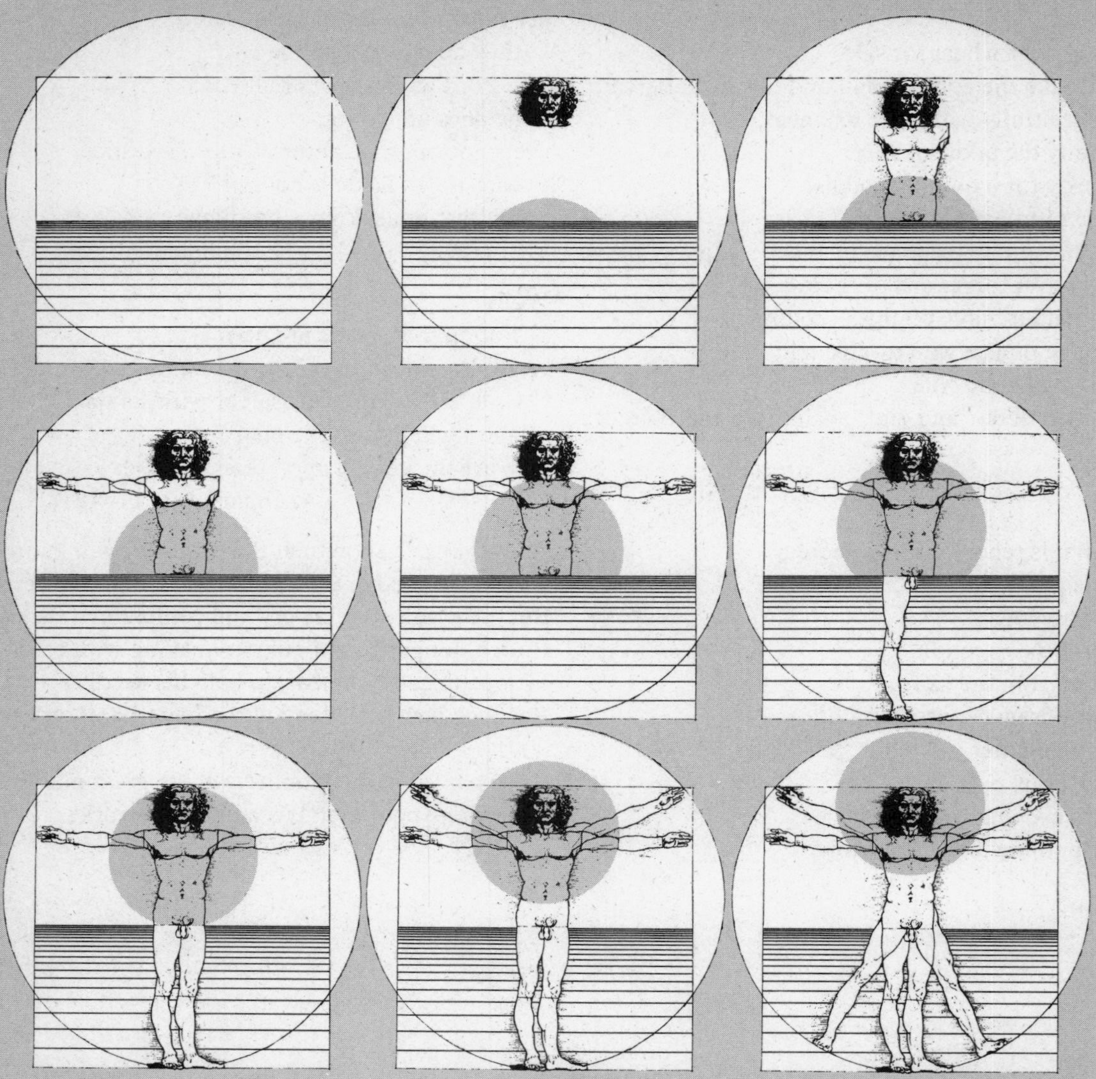

Can one generation bind another
and all others in succession forever?

I think not.

The Creator has made the Earth
for the living, not the dead.

A generation may bind itself
as long as its majority continues in life;

when that has disappeared,
another majority is in place,

holding all the powers
their predecessors once held,

and may change their laws and institutions
to suit themselves.

Nothing then is unchangeable

but the inherent and inalienable
rights of man.

Thomas Jefferson, 1781

V

Student and Teacher Programs for a Peoples Bicentennial

Introduction

Two hundred years ago, America was moving toward revolution. A decade of royal injustice and oppression —"tyranny," Colonial patriots called it—had been met, step by step, with increasingly radical resistance. Tea was destroyed; Tory merchants were tarred and feathered; stores and homes of Loyalists were sacked; Royal Governors and politicians were forced to flee to England. Finally, "embattled farmers" stood their ground and turned the government troops back from Concord at gunpoint. Soon, a full-fledged war for human rights broke out, ending seven years later in victory for the Revolutionary forces.

The America that emerged from the war was unlike any other nation on earth. The Revolution was the first successful anticolonial war, representing an uprising of an entire people against the most powerful imperial force in the world. Unlike other wars up to that time, the Revolution was more than a simple transfer of power from one set of rulers to another. The Revolution was, above all else, a struggle against an entrenched establishment, and the society that emerged from that struggle was radically different from the old regime: large land holdings were broken up and distributed among the common people; feudal inheritance laws were smashed; voting rights were greatly extended; blind allegiance was no longer due the King.

Revolutionary advances had been made, to be sure. But European monarchies, and domestic conservatives, were bent on halting the revolutionary republic and reasserting the old order. The Founding Fathers and Mothers understood, as Benjamin Rush wrote, that "the American war is over, but this is far from the case with the American Revolution. On the contrary, nothing but the first act of the great drama is closed." Revolution, our founders knew, was an ongoing process, involving far more than winning battles and seizing territory.

How to hold on to the victories won, and continue along the Revolutionary path—this was the task that lay before the patriots. To those who had lived through the Revolutionary years, the answer was obvious: the war for independence had been won through armed struggle, but the key to victory had been popular support. John Adams wrote, "The revolution was effected before the war commenced. The revolution was in the minds and hearts of the people."

To continue forward, the postwar Revolution must be the cause and life of all Americans; it must remain in the minds and hearts of the people. During the war, patriots fought for their "inalienable rights" with guns, swords and cannon; after the war, patriots believed, Americans would hold on to their freedoms, and acquire new ones, by forging a new weapon against tyranny: Education. Education, Thomas Jefferson wrote, "on a broad scale, and not that of the petty academics . . ." Education not for personal gain, or social

status, but because, James Madison declared, "A people who mean to be their own governors must arm themselves with the power which knowledge gives."

The perils of an uneducated population were apparent to those who had lived through the Revolution. David Ramsay, a Revolutionary War historian, noted in 1789:

> It is a well-known fact, that persons unfriendly to the Revolution, were always most numerous in those parts of the United States which had either never been illuminated, or but faintly warmed by the rays of science. The uninformed and the misinformed, constituted a great proportion of those Americans who preferred the leading strings of the parent state, though encroaching on their liberties, to a government of their own countrymen and fellow citizens.

So the best safeguard of the ideals and programs of the Revolution was a sound education. The founders had a simple view of education: it armed the people against tyrants. To do this, they believed, education must be available to all. It must be an education concerned with subjects that would serve to alert the people against the schemes of despots, not an education concerned with high-flung intellectual theory. Any subject that was not easily understood and meaningful to the common people was a potential tool of tyrants who would use it for their own evil purposes. Education, too, must be pertinent to daily life. Since the purpose of knowledge was to defeat the evil designs of tyrants, education should instruct toward that end. To teach courses such as Greek and Latin and to ignore relevant Revolutionary subjects was, Benjamin Rush felt, "to turn our backs upon a gold mine, in order to amuse ourselves in catching butterflies."

Finally, education was to be a training ground of democracy. The educational experience was to imitate that of society, so that students would enter the political arena as experienced patriots, aware of the intrigues and designs of politicians and the wealthy, and armed to defeat their conspiracies. *Does the educational experience of today allow students to exercise their democratic rights of full participation in the school community before gaining the vote at eighteen?*

EDUCATION TODAY: HAVE THE TORIES WON?

To look at America today is to see not a nation in keeping with the Revolutionary ideals of the founders, but a system that would make the Tories of the 1770's think they'd won after all. The same is true of education. Far from being a Revolutionary weapon against tyrants and a training ground for new patriots, our educational system seeks to pacify students and to channel them into predetermined roles in society.

From kindergarten through college, a student's fate is not his or her own. Younger students are "tracked"—that is, they are placed in different programs according to inaccurate I.Q. tests and according to sex and social and racial background. Designed to give "additional" attention to "less intelligent" students, tracking in reality is simply another form of separate and unequal education. In grammar school students are already divided into those going to college and those being readied for manual and service-oriented labor. In college, students are educated to assume roles in the corporate structure of America. Far from being armed against tyranny, America's students are educated to be slotted into society with as little fuss as possible.

Education, too, fails in its Revolutionary duty by depriving students of a chance to assert their basic "inalienable rights." Students are seldom allowed any meaningful input into decisions affecting their education. "Learning comes by doing," wrote Ben Franklin, but today's educational process provides little chance to "do"—only to obey and to parrot.

Further, our education often has little relevance to today's world and its problems. If the purpose of education is to arm ourselves against tyrants, then education must be a means toward that end. Benjamin Rush's criticisms of the "dead" subjects of Greek and Latin in his day are relevant to our system.

Subjects that can be useful in confronting the problems of today are often presented in a fashion that is hopelessly biased and irrelevant. Take history for example. Students are often taught to look at the American Revolution as a succession of battles and Founding Fathers, not as a social movement of the common people—men and women—of this country. If we are to believe the history that is taught, America's prominent people are almost always Presidents, generals and wealthy industrialists, not women, workers and poor people.

The purpose of learning history, Thomas Jefferson wrote, is that "by apprizing [students] of the past, [it] will enable them to judge of the future; it will avail them of the experiences of other times and nations; it will enable them to know ambition under every disguise it may assume; and knowing it, to defeat its views." Does Jefferson's vision bear any similarity to the way history is taught in our schools today?

THE CONTEST OF EDUCATION

Nothing was truer to the patriots of 1776 than Ben Franklin's maxim "We must all hang together, or assuredly we shall all hang separately." But this lesson of unity in the face of oppression has been lost in our education. Today's students are urged to compete (for grades, for acceptance into colleges, for jobs), not to unite for the common good. Instead of the cooperation

OLD INN TAVERN, PHILADELPHIA

that was natural to our founders, to the pioneers on the frontier, to the farmers and workers who built America, students are urged to become better than their friends in order to get ahead in life. The artificial divisions of the thirteen Colonies have been replaced by the equally false divisions of sex, race, social background and I.Q.-test results. In short, education pits students one against another. A far cry from the founders' hope of Revolutionary purpose and unity stemming from education.

Not only are students divided among themselves, but students are artificially divided from their teachers. Students are made to rely on the opinion and knowledge of their teachers over those of their fellow students. Students find themselves forced to obey rules and orders they have no part in making. They are forced to compete against their will. For their part, teachers are also the victims of our Tory system of education. Teachers too are forced to obey and to accept regulations they have no part in forming. Lesson plans must be drawn up and adhered to. Teachers are often stifled in the range of material they can use in their classes. What should be a common experience that bridges the gap of age becomes a constant battle between teacher and student.

WHAT IS TO BE DONE?

With the two-hundredth anniversary of the American Revolution approaching, the attention of Americans will turn toward an examination of our past. The President and his big-business cronies have set up systems already to market the Bicentennial as a "Love It or Leave It" spectacular. Far from reaffirming our Revolutionary past, the White House and Corporate America will attempt to reassure us that all is well; that the Revolution is over; that the America of today is right in line with the philosophies of our founders.

THE BOSTON TEA PARTY

Those in power will resurrect radical heroes like Jefferson, Paine and Adams and radical events like the Boston Tea Party and the Continental Congress. All the while, these modern-day Tories will attempt to present themselves and the institutions they control as the true heirs and defenders of the struggle waged by the first American revolutionaries.

And that's the "Catch-22." Today's rulers are opening up a Pandora's box. Corporate America and the White House will be publicizing Revolutionary principles which, if taken seriously, would undermine their very power and control over the American people.

FIRST PRINCIPLES

In demanding the fulfillment of the American Promise of democratic education for all, we should keep in mind Tom Paine's words:

> It is at all times necessary, and more particularly so during the progress of a revolution, and until right ideas confirm themselves by habit, that we frequently refresh our patriotism by reference to first principles. It is by tracing things to their origins, that we learn to understand them, and it is by keeping that line and that origin always in view that we never forget them.

The First Principles of America were set forth by the patriots of the 1770's. These principles were revolutionary for their time, and they are still revolutionary today; for while many Americans (notably government officials and corporate leaders) give lip service to them, they are far from being realized. As students and teachers raise their Bicentennial educational demands, these first principles provide a philosophy and a language which are common to all Americans, and around which effective organizing can be launched. Schools in particular, or the institutions where we all learn American history and social studies, are an obvious place for launching a Bicentennial movement for change based on America's Revolutionary promise. Consider, for example, these basic First Principles, and how they can fit into organizing for educational change:

- All people are created equal—The Declaration of Independence. We are far from this principle's fulfillment, either in society at large or in our schools in particular. Schools are notorious for the inequality they foster: between teachers and students; between male and female students; between the poor and the wealthy. Equal education for all is our goal.
- Life, liberty and the pursuit of happiness—The Declaration of Independence. This principle is a call for the basic right we should all have of determining our own fate. Yet schools, as presently constructed, are utterly opposed to this basic right of self-determination. Students are rarely allowed meaningful input into their own education, but instead are told what to do, and forced to comply.
- The right, and duty, to alter or abolish unresponsive

We hold these truths
to be self-evident...

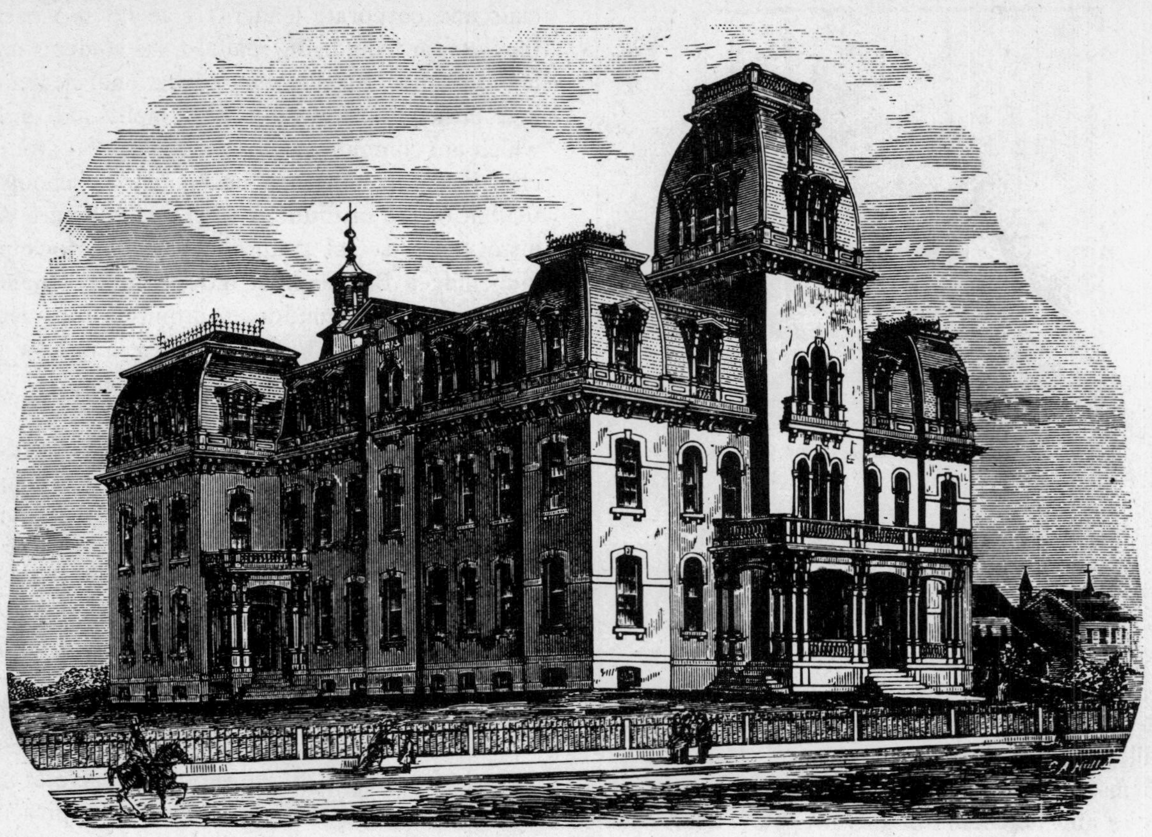

A PROVIDENCE, RHODE ISLAND, HIGH SCHOOL FROM ABOUT 1848

institutions—The Declaration of Independence. Today's schools, clearly, have strayed far from their original Revolutionary purpose. Education today is effective for fulfilling only the needs of corporate power. Students and teachers, in keeping with this basic tenet of our heritage, have not only a right, but a duty to change the current system. Nothing is more American than to fight against institutions that do not satisfy the needs of the people.

- The earth belongs to the living—Thomas Jefferson and Tom Paine. In 1781, Jefferson wrote, "Can one generation bind another and all others in succession forever? I think not. The Creator has made the Earth for the living, not the dead." This meant that the laws and rules of one generation, once that generation had passed away, could no longer hold the next. In our schools, many of the rules and regulations that govern the educational process were made decades ago. The generation concerned with education now—the students and teachers—should have the right to determine their own rules.
- Freedom of speech and of the press, and the right of the people to assemble and to petition the Government for a redress of grievances—The Bill of Rights. Students are denied many of the Constitutional guarantees and, above all else, the First Amendment guarantees which are essential to a free society and to free education.

IS THE PROBLEM IN THE SCHOOLS . . . ? OR IN SOCIETY?

To raise educational demands, divorced from launching efforts for societal change, is to work for reform rather than the Revolutionary change our founders understood to be necessary. Sam Adams and Ben Franklin helped set forth the radical demand of "No Taxation Without Representation," but when the Crown offered them Parliamentary representation, they refused it! To Adams and Franklin, representation could never be meaningful within the colonial system. What good would it do if Americans had three or four representatives who really cared about their desires, when there

A JAIL OF THE SAME PERIOD

were hundreds of others who regarded Americans as children and subjects? What was needed, they knew, was revolutionary change of their society, not a reform on the order of more representatives in the British legislature. Likewise, educational reform today is meaningless without a general reorientation of our society. If we are to live up to our Revolutionary heritage within our educational system, then our social, economic and political structure must reflect that Revolutionary past. Student and teacher organizers should be aware that many of the demands they raise can be met within the current educational system, but that such victories are not enough. *It should be understood that education can never serve and arm the people against tyranny until society itself serves and arms the people as a whole for the same purpose.* Students and teachers can never really take control of the educational process from administrators, Boards of Education and the needs of big business and demagogic politicians until the people of America have taken control of our society from the neo-Tories who run our government and economic system.

Reform in education is not enough. It is an important step toward reaffirming our heritage. But as the student movement of the 1960's showed, meaningful educational change cannot be achieved without support from Americans outside the school system. The immediate goal is to democratize the educational system; the long-range goal is to restructure society in keeping with the philosophy that founded this country. It's a big job, but not as big as taking on King George.

AND IN THE END

"The moral purpose of revolution is to instruct; not to destroy," wrote Tom Paine. Likewise, the purpose of education today is to instruct. But something has gone wrong. Today's educational system destroys: destroys the self-reliance and creativity of students; destroys what should be the natural bond between students and teachers; destroys the vision our founders had of the power of a Revolutionary education and ultimately destroys the first principles and ideals of the American Revolution.

The need for change is clear. The Bicentennial provides a theme, a set of principles, a list of demands that are common to the experience of all Americans. If we *believe* in these principles, and use them to raise our just demands, we can create a fresh vision of education and society with appeal not just among students and teachers, but beyond the campus walls.

What follows are some organizing ideas and programs for high school and college students and teachers that fit into the Bicentennial theme of reaffirming America's democratic heritage. These are only a beginning. Use your imagination to put America's radical past back to work to resurrect democracy today.

High Schools and the Bicentennial

> We are always equal to what we undertake with resolution . . . If you always lean on your master, you will never be able to proceed without him. It is a part of the American character to consider nothing as desperate; to surmount every difficulty by resolution and contrivance.
>
> —THOMAS JEFFERSON

In the 1790's, a young schoolteacher named Noah Webster looked at this country's educational system and wrote, "The laws of education are *monarchical*. [They] deprive a large proportion of the citizens of a most valuable privilege." Almost two hundred years later, our educational system is still monarchical, and it still deprives a large proportion of citizens—namely, the tens of millions of grammar and junior and senior high school students—not only of a valuable privilege, but of the fundamental rights for which the American Revolution was fought.

It is certainly an odd fact that as America prepares to celebrate its two-hundredth anniversary of independence, America's students are denied their *own* independence. In the 18th century, there was a term for people who were forced by circumstances to place themselves in bondage for a number of years in order that they might one day be free: indentured servants.

High school students today are told that the loss of *their* freedom for a few years of schooling is little compared with the long-term gain. Students are encouraged to see themselves as "children," or, if not that, certainly not responsible human beings, and are taught to place more reliance in their teachers than upon themselves. This is just what the rebels of the 1770's were told by the Crown. But they finally stopped listening to that hogwash. And that is what America's high school students are doing today.

WHERE TO BEGIN

High school activists (we use, throughout this section, "high school," but these ideas and programs can easily be adopted by junior high and grammar school activists) who want to use the principles of the American Revolution as a theme for organizing for educational change should consider founding a Peoples Bicentennial Commission on their campus. (See the advice on organizing your own PBC in the college section of this chapter, beginning on page 138.) Forming a PBC will help give you visibility on campus, and can promote unity in the formulation of student goals and tactics.

When your core group of activists is together, you should turn your attention to the specifics of your program: what your goals are, how to state your demands and how to shape a program that addresses both the general issues of student freedom and self-determination and the more specific and immediate problems of student day-to-day life—dress codes, textbooks, open campus, etc. *It is only by working on both levels at once*

A PATRIOT RALLIES THE TROOPS

that a program for meaningful change can be sustained. By tying in the specific issue of the dress code, for instance, to the overall concept of the powerlessness of students in determining their own lives, you will be able to go far beyond the concept of a student's right to wear long hair or jeans—for your fellow students will understand that even though they've won the battle of the dress code, the overall issue of democratic power still remains. A victory over the issue of the dress code is a drop in the bucket, and students will go on to fight other battles in the name of student power and rights. Working on both levels will draw connections between the oppression on campus and the oppression in society as a whole. Students who understand that they have little power to determine their own lives in school will also realize, once they've graduated, that things aren't much different on the outside.

To help make these connections, and in order to sustain a movement on campus, your PBC might consider beginning your organizing activity by issuing a Declaration of Student Independence to dramatize the oppression common to all students.

THE DECLARATION OF STUDENT INDEPENDENCE

In 1776, the Continental Congress appointed a committee of five men to draft a document stating the "common sense" demands and grievances of the patriots. That document became known as the Declaration of Independence—one of the most revolutionary statements of basic human rights in history. The purpose of the Declaration was to state the case of the rebels, in plain, everyday language, so that all could see the justice in it. It proved to be a catalyst for action, and a way of unifying people who had previously thought themselves different from one another. In other words, it gave people who had once considered themselves New Yorkers or Georgians a common identity as patriots who were being oppressed and abused by Royal tyranny. At the same time, it made them feel that their gripes and concerns were the same as those of millions of other people. By doing that, the Declaration made folks feel strong, united and capable of taking successful action to gain control of their lives.

High school activists, like the founders of this country, can make the common sense of their grievances known to fellow students and the community by issuing their own Declaration of Student Independence. The first step, of course, is to get together with the other students who make up your PBC and read the original Declaration. Talk about its language, its grievances and its general ideology. Then relate the original to your own situation. Is your school, like King George's empire, destructive of your rights as human beings? Are your grievances similar to those of 1776: Has your school's administration refused to institute any rules "wholesome and necessary for the public good," such

CONTRARY TO THE MODERN CORPORATE VIEW, JOHN HANCOCK WASN'T AN INSURANCE SALESMAN. HERE HE IS SHOWN IN A TYPICAL POSE, IN THE ACT OF COMMITTING TREASON AGAINST THE CROWN

as freedom of press and assembly for students? When students are suspended, are they deprived "of the benefits of Trial by Jury"? Has your school's administration answered your demands for democratization of your education "only by repeated injury"? After you've asked these kinds of questions, work together to draw up a document that follows the original form and tone and present it to the student body. Consider, for example, this sample Declaration:

As the 200th anniversary of the American Revolution nears, we, the students of ________________ High School, pledge ourselves to reaffirm and live the Revolutionary principles and ideals that founded this country. It is clear to us as students that our education today is run on the same basis on which King George III ran his empire—inequality, arbitrary regulations and lack of personal freedom. Therefore:

We hold these truths to be self-evident, that all people are created equal, that they are entitled to an education and that the purpose of this education is to secure for them the inalienable rights of Life, Liberty and the pursuit of Happiness; that to secure these rights, education must be designed with the full participation of students; and that when education no longer meets these requirements, students have a right, and a duty, to participate in changing the educational system, so that it *will* meet these needs and adhere to the principles that founded this country.

The history of our present education is a history of repeated injuries and abuses of our rights—all having the object of making students conform, pitting one student against another, separating the teacher from the student and channeling us into predetermined slots in society. To prove this, let Facts be listed in our favor:

As students, we are forbidden the basic rights that are fundamental to this country—among these, freedom of speech, the press, assembly and thought.

As students, we are denied any meaningful decision-making as to what our education and classes will be like.

As students, we are at the mercy of the whims of teachers and administrators, none of whom we have had any part in hiring, and of none of whom are we allowed to call for dismissal when there is good cause.

As students, we are at the mercy of arbitrary rules and regulations, none of which we have a part in forming.

As students, we are divided and segregated according to artificial categories we do not believe in. Women are separated from men when they are forced to take home economics classes and men are required to take shop. Students of non–middle-class background are tracked into non–college-preparatory courses because they score poorly on I.Q. tests that are based on the values of the middle class.

As students, we are forced to compete, rather than allowed to participate cooperatively and in the spirit of the common good. Students are told they are "cheating" and "only hurting themselves" when they help one another; students are told they are "model pupils" and "good citizens" when they participate in a cutthroat manner.

Therefore, we, the Students of ______________________ High School, endorse and present this Declaration to the school and our community, and declare that students are, and of Right ought to be, Free and Independent human beings, fully participating in and shaping their education. We pledge to one another that, having stated and endorsed these grievances, we commit ourselves, as the founders of America did, to right these wrongs, to take control of our lives and our education and, as patriots proclaimed in 1776, to use every method in our power to secure our rights.

The value of such a Declaration of Student Independence is obvious. It allows students to state their grievances against the school administration. It is serious, yet engaging enough to hold people's attention—many organizing efforts have died because organizers felt that political action had to be dull and doctrinaire to be "really political." Another advantage of such a document is that it gives nonactivist students a chance to participate without demanding a commitment greater than they are willing to give.

A Declaration of Student Independence is effective only if the students endorse it. So after printing up copies of the Declaration, the members of your group should spend a week or so gaining signatures on it. This gives you a chance to begin political education, to hear the views of students outside your group of friends and fellow activists and to begin discussing the upcoming two-hundredth birthday of the Revolution and what it can mean to students.

Present the signed Declaration to your principal to put him or her on notice that students feel the need for change in your school. Make large copies, and paste them up prominently around school as broadsides. Place them in student hangouts, stores, etc. Once 70 percent or so of the student body has endorsed the Declaration, you might try holding a public festival to celebrate your independence. (See the following section on Freedom of Speech and Assembly.) Be creative! Be theatrical!

THE BILL OF STUDENT RIGHTS

As the patriots of 1776 learned, proclaiming your independence is one thing; gaining it in any real way is quite another. Independence is never handed to people on a silver platter—it has to be fought for. After the

PROPOSED DESIGN FOR A SCHOOL, CIRCA 1880...

endorsement of the Declaration, you should consider moving to the next logical step of going beyond listing the grievances of students to the listing of demands in a Bill of Student Rights. Most likely, the Declaration will be drawn up only by the core group in your PBC, but if your signing campaign was successful, you will have come into contact with many other students who feel that they deserve the right to determine their own lives. Talk to them now about a Bill of Student Rights. Invite them to a meeting to discuss drawing up such a Bill. You might want to let it be known around campus that a general open meeting of your PBC will be held to discuss the document, and invite all who are interested. Remember, if your goal is democracy in the school, then your organization should be a model of democracy and should involve all who are interested.

A sample preamble to a Student Bill of Rights, in keeping with the language and philosophy of the Revolution, might read:

Thomas Jefferson wrote, "A bill of rights is what the people are entitled to against every government on earth, general or particular, and what no just government should refuse, or rest on inference."

Our school is run like a government—a monarchy—in which we, the students, are the subjects and the principal and other administrators are the royal tyrants. Having already issued our Declaration of Student Independence, and having received no satisfaction on our well-founded grievances, we now endorse this Bill of Student Rights to protect ourselves from the arbitrary, discriminatory and unjust practices of this school.

Demands will be plentiful. Here's just a sample of a few:

- The school shall make no rules, regulations or policies restricting the students' right to freedom of speech or of the press, right to assemble and right of free thought.
- Students shall be free from cruel and unusual punishment including corporal punishment and the punitive use of grades.
- All students have the right to participate in the full educational process, extracurricular activities and school-sponsored programs, and shall not be discriminated against on the basis of race, sex, creed, political beliefs, appearance, marital status, pregnancy, grades or other unreasonable classifications.
- Every student has the right to participate in planning his or her education and in the democratic process of establishing rules and regulations, both in the school as a whole and in the classroom.
- A student who is to be suspended or expelled must be given the right of due process and receive a trial by a jury of his or her peers.

These are just a few sample rights. There are many more, but as you list them, you should try to keep the number small, and make them general enough so that they can provide an overall theme or backdrop for your organizing. For instance, if students feel that one teacher is particularly poor—misinterpreting facts, emphasizing the wrong points or using a racist or sexist textbook—by use of the Bill of Student Rights, that one particular case can be linked up to the right of calling for democracy in the classroom. The issue then becomes not just a bad textbook or teacher, but the very process that allowed that book or teacher to be selected in the first place.

HOW TO USE THE BILL OF STUDENT RIGHTS

It is a simple maxim of politics that power is rarely given up freely. The group in power (in this case, the faculty and administration) must be made to see that the group out of power (the students) are not merely asking for a part, but are united and demand their proper role. Those in power tend to see petitions and lists of grievances as meaningless and harmless, because they do not really put pressure on them. They are often regarded as good ways for dissidents to channel their anger so that no direct action will take place. For this reason, you shouldn't be disappointed or allow yourselves to fall into confusion and disarray just because the administration disregards statements endorsed by hundreds of students. After all, that's why students are powerless in the first place!

But this is not to say that petitions such as the Declaration and Bill of Student Rights are useless. Their real success isn't gauged by whether or not their programs are immediately agreed to, but by what effect they have on the people involved. Beyond providing a backdrop for specific organizing, such petitions can have many other effects:

First, petitions put the administration on notice that students are dissatisfied both about specific issues and about the general quality of their lives in school. Your school's rulers will most likely disregard the petition, but at the back of their minds, they'll sense trouble brewing.

Second, a petition drive has an educational value. People who read the petition and discuss it learn about new issues and how different problems all tie in. It also brings about a certain commitment: the very act of signing the petition puts students on a side in the question, and becomes an act of resistance against the arbitrary authority of the school.

Third, a petition as an initial organizing tool shows that you are reasonable and that you've tried moderate methods to effect change. If the administration won't listen to your just demands, you have a right to go on to other tactics. That's the lesson of 1776.

Fourth, a petition helps build drama. When hundreds of students all sign the same piece of paper, and present it to the administration, then a certain suspense begins. It's also a visible sign of the united protest of massive numbers. Putting up a banner that reads 264 MOLLY PITCHER HIGH SCHOOL STUDENTS DEMAND OUR RIGHTS can be a powerful sign of student power.

...AND AN INTERIOR VIEW OF THE JAIL AT LOWELL, MASSACHUSETTS, FROM THE SAME PERIOD

Fifth, a petition drive puts organizers in touch with the students. It breaks down the isolation between activist and nonactivist students and can help to expand your group of co-workers.

The Declaration of Student Independence is mostly an exercise in psychic guerrilla warfare, so instead of formally presenting it to the administration, you might just want to nail it to the door of the office building, or something equally dramatic. But the Bill of Rights is another matter: it is the student body's program to end their oppression and assert their rights. After its endorsement, send a delegation to the principal to present the document, and demand some action on the matter. Have a network ready to spread the results of the meeting. If the administration *does* begin to address your demands, let it know that all of your grievances are of equal importance, as they all deal with your right to control your lives. Repeal of the dress code is simply not enough if students still can't help determine what is to be taught, how it will be taught, what books will be used, etc. Be aware that the administration may try to co-opt your protest, by setting up some kind of committee or board that will "consider" the matter. Such committees are usually a way of stalling and making the administration appear reasonable and concerned by giving you "token" input into the decision-making. If your principal offers to put you on a committee, keep in mind that battle fought by Sam Adams for "No Taxation Without Representation" and how he rejected token representation once it was offered, stating that representation under the present system could never be just.

If, as is more likely, the administration refuses your demands, claiming the decision is not its own or that student control of education is unrealistic, then you should be ready to act. Remember that the struggle is ongoing. The fact that you have mobilized 70 percent of the student body to demand their rights by petition does not mean you can rest. Victory often immobilizes activists. You should have a strategy that will allow you to quickly move from one step to another. For instance, the administration's refusal to deal with the Bill should be made widely known through leaflets, speeches, etc. Beyond that, you should force the issue of your rights by implementing the different points of the program.

BRING THE BILL OF RIGHTS HOME!

If your student body supports the Bill and the administration fails to act on it, you should try bringing the Bill of Rights to your school without official approval. For instance, if you feel your school doesn't have freedom of the press, you should begin pushing the issue. What follows are some issues high school activities can organize around, using the Bicentennial as an overall theme: freedom of the press; freedom of speech and assembly; student evaluation of the teachers; discipline procedures; tracking and honors; curricula and textbooks.

Freedom of the Press

> An evil Magistrate, entrusted with a power to punish Words, is armed with a Weapon, the most destructive and terrible. Under the pretense of pruning off the exuberant branches, he frequently destroys the tree.
>
> —JAMES ALEXANDER, 1735

Few high schools in this country guarantee a free press to their students. If there is an "official" school newspaper funded by the school system, it is usually a waste of paper. Articles center on a clean campus, sports events and human-interest stories about teachers. Where, James Madison might ask, are the stories that are to "arm us with the power that knowledge gives"? The plain answer is that any such stories are banned from the paper. The reason is simple: established school newspapers are not only funded by the school system, but also *controlled* by the system. Faculty advisers and administrators have the power to censor any articles that might lead students to rebel against the tyranny of modern education (i.e., any article that appears relevant to student life on campus). The result is journalistic pabulum.

High school activists should have control of some sort of media outlet at an early stage of their organizing. Weekly newspapers, broadsides and messages sent through the Committees of Correspondence were the ways the founding radicals spread the message of revolution in 1776. Even though we're now in the era of electronic media, a creative, together newspaper is still one of the best ways of spreading the word, stirring up interest and bringing people together.

When you decide the time is right to begin distributing information through some sort of newspaper, and

you'll probably decide this very early in your work, you'll find there are several ways to proceed. If your school has an "official" paper, you might get on its staff and attempt to combat the censorship of relevant ideas and articles from within. Or, if you could center your demands on the notion that the censored paper does not represent the needs and views of the students and, out of fairness, your group should be allowed use of the school's resources to put out a second paper. (Don't put too much faith in this tactic. Schools are obviously unconcerned about fairness.) Finally, your PBC can begin its own paper, independently financed and controlled solely by students.

The "Official" Paper

Official school newspapers are usually run like a closed corporation: often, students must take an entire semester of "Journalism class" for the "privilege" of writing for the paper. Such courses are notoriously boring. Often, the faculty adviser has the power of appointment to every position of importance on the paper—the general editor, editorial and news editors, managing editor, etc. To crack this undemocratic system, one of your first actions might be to agitate for democracy in the school paper.

Opening up the school newspaper to the entire school is what democracy is all about. Begin agitating for the end to Journalism class as a requirement to write for the paper. Write some stories on your own; chances are they'll be better than the stuff printed in the paper, even though you haven't "learned" how to write from a teacher and a textbook. If the adviser refuses to allow your stories to be printed and for you to become a full staff member, then let other students know about it, and begin a campaign for an open newspaper. You'll have a good case, as students seldom enjoy the tripe that the school paper usually prints and would enjoy something more interesting. Demand that the paper have public meetings and that the positions of importance—such as editorships—be filled by a vote at these meetings. Another goal of democratization of the school paper is that all staff members have a part in determining the editorial stand of the paper. In that way, even if administration-oriented and power-hungry people have the top positions on the paper, there will still be room for input from all of the staff.

If you crack the outer shell of the paper and join the staff, you should begin pressing for stories and features that help students in their struggle to participate in decisions affecting their education. Good stories, for instance, might center on historical struggles that parallel what's happening in your school today; a calendar of events in the school and community; drug information; legal-rights information; critiques of different textbooks used in your school.

Eventually, if you're doing your job, two things will happen. First, students will become interested in the paper and look forward to reading its articles; and second, the administration and faculty censors will begin to come down on your stories. The first time your story is censored, you might try talking it out with the censors, reasoning with them, pointing out your First Amendment rights. But, as people in power within the school hierarchy rarely relate to students as responsible

humans, they will probably tell you to pull the story, or, at least, cut the objectionable parts. You should *never* cut your story if you think its central message is hurt by the deletion. Refuse to allow the story to go in at all, rather than have it censored.

If you can sneak it by, a good tactic is to leave the space blank where your story should have been, and just print the word CENSORED in the space. If they censor that too, write a story about freedom of the press historically, and the battles that went on over it. You might do something like:

> With the nation's 200th anniversary approaching, it is important to examine our society to see how well we live up to our Revolutionary tradition. Take the issue of freedom of the press, for instance. One of the big grievances the patriots of the 18th century had against the Royal government was that any articles they wrote that strayed the slightest bit from the official administration line were censored. Not only that, but often the editor of the paper was thrown into jail, and the paper closed down. Penalties in Maryland for the offense of printing antiadministration material were typical of the harsh treatment independent-thinking journalists have been given: "Whipping, Branding, Boreing through the Tongue, Fine, Imprisonment, Banishment, or Death."
>
> In their own version of "Love It or Leave It," the Royal governments of the time branded any criticism of their administrations as nothing short of "Publishing, Uttering, and Spreading Malicious and Seditious papers . . . Tending to the Disturbance of the Peace and Subversion of the present Government."
>
> To the Tories of the day, the thinking behind such a philosophy was simple and direct: disenchantment with official policy led to criticism by the people; criticism inevitably led to rebellion in order to set things straight; rebellion to revolution; revolution to the deposing of the monarch who was ruling at the time. To the colonial rulers of the day, a free press was indeed a danger and evil to be ferreted out and destroyed.
>
> Early American journalism abounds with the stories of editors and publishers who became entrapped in this web of Catch-22 logic. In 1695, for instance, Thomas Maule published a book that was deemed so subversive to the rulers of Massachusetts that he was almost immediately arrested for "wicked Lyes and Slanders . . . upon Government, and likewise divers corrupt and pernicious Doctrines utterly subversive." Maule was thrown into prison, his books burned and his press smashed. But still he continued. He was eventually jailed six times and whipped twice for daring to exercise his right to freedom of the press.
>
> John Peter Zenger, whom we've all read about in American History class, was also a fearless journalist who insisted on printing the truth, whether the administration liked it or not.
>
> Unfortunately, the issue of a free press wasn't resolved with the Revolution. When the Federalists came to power in the 1790's, one progovernment editor stated the administration position: "He that is not for us, is against us. Whatever American opposes the administration is an anarchist, a jacobin, and a traitor . . . It is *Patriotism* to write in favour of our government—it is Sedition to write against it." On the other side of the question stood Thomas Jefferson and other radicals: "Were it left for me to decide whether we should have a

government without newspapers, or newspapers without a government, I should not hesitate a moment to prefer the latter."

Today, it seems, some people feel there is still a question as to how free the press should be. There are still some Tories and Federalists around who think that they are fit to determine what the people have a right to read in their papers. If Tom Jefferson were around, he'd know what to call this attitude among some of our present-day tyrants: un-American and unpatriotic!

With a story like that, you can be sure that students are going to understand what you're talking about!

You might also try mimeographing the article that was censored and handing it out to students, with a note at the top of the story that the principal or faculty adviser has ruled it unsuitable for publication. You might also include on the leaflet a few choice quotations from the founders about freedom of the press. After this happens a few times, students will get the idea that a free press is free only when you've got access to one. If enough students support you, you might ask them to boycott the paper, sending letters to the editor explaining that they did so because your article was censored. What would the administration think if no one picked up a single copy of the paper one week?

While the advantages of trying to take over the campus newspaper are great—you can gain control over vital resources and the necessary money to put out a paper—there are also disadvantages. For one thing, school-newspaper bureaucracies are deeply entrenched, and it might take over a year before the paper begins to represent the students. Also, there's often so much red tape you have to cut through that it just might not be worthwhile. And unless you manage to get a lot of good people on the staff and really gain control of the paper, you'll still find those tired old stories about a clean campus.

So you might consider starting your own "underground" paper. True, you won't have as many resources, and the quality won't be as good as that of the "official" paper for a while, but the paper will be under the total control of students; it can take a consistent and radical editorial stand; it can be a model of collective action and student democracy, and it will be seen as more daring than working through "the proper channels." Also, administrations are generally opposed to underground papers, and it will give you a chance to reveal them for their unpatriotic attitude in their opposition to a free press.

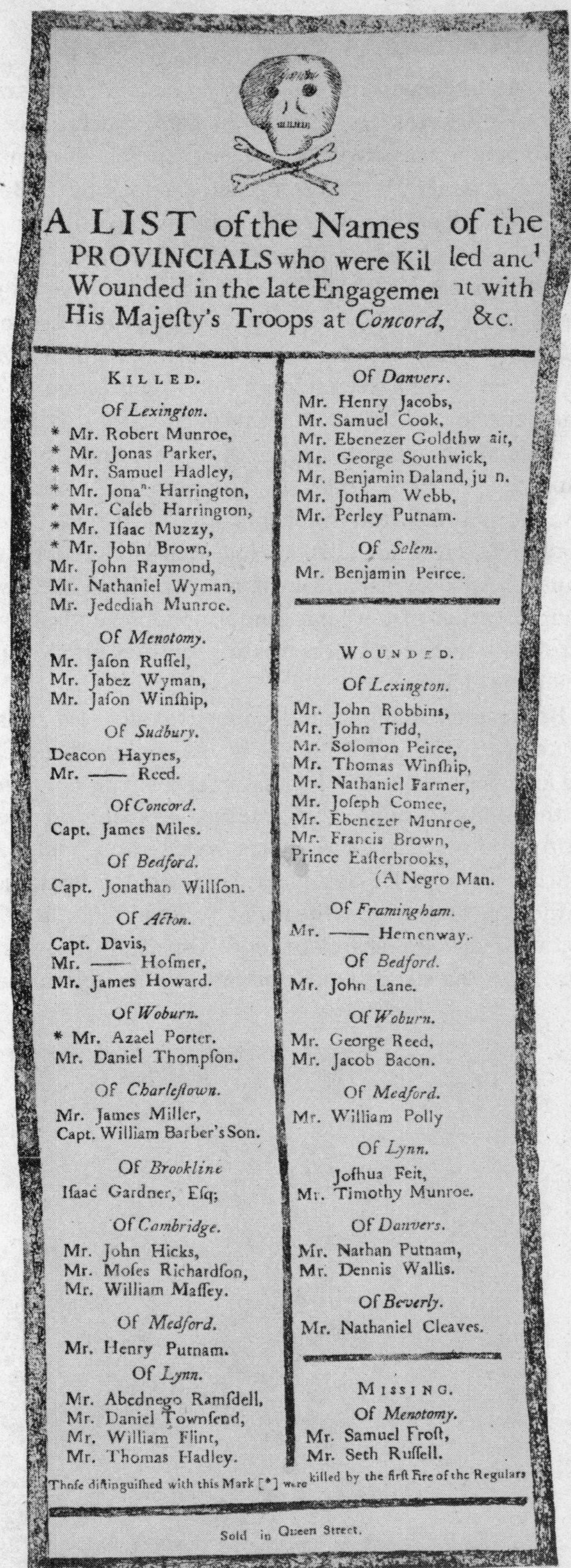

A LIST of the Names of the PROVINCIALS who were Killed and Wounded in the late Engagement with His Majeſty's Troops at *Concord*, &c.

KILLED.

Of *Lexington*.

* Mr. Robert Munroe,
* Mr. Jonas Parker,
* Mr. Samuel Hadley,
* Mr. Jona[n.] Harrington,
* Mr. Caleb Harrington,
* Mr. Iſaac Muzzy,
* Mr. John Brown,
Mr. John Raymond,
Mr. Nathaniel Wyman,
Mr. Jedediah Munroe.

Of *Menotomy*.

Mr. Jaſon Ruſſel,
Mr. Jabez Wyman,
Mr. Jaſon Winſhip,

Of *Sudbury*.

Deacon Haynes,
Mr. —— Reed.

Of *Concord*.

Capt. James Miles.

Of *Bedford*.

Capt. Jonathan Willſon.

Of *Acton*.

Capt. Davis,
Mr. —— Hoſmer,
Mr. James Howard.

Of *Woburn*.

* Mr. Azael Porter.
Mr. Daniel Thompſon.

Of *Charleſtown*.

Mr. James Miller,
Capt. William Barber's Son.

Of *Brookline*

Iſaac Gardner, Eſq;

Of *Cambridge*.

Mr. John Hicks,
Mr. Moſes Richardſon,
Mr. William Maſſey.

Of *Medford*.

Mr. Henry Putnam.

Of *Lynn*.

Mr. Abednego Ramſdell,
Mr. Daniel Townſend,
Mr. William Flint,
Mr. Thomas Hadley.

Of *Danvers*.

Mr. Henry Jacobs,
Mr. Samuel Cook,
Mr. Ebenezer Goldthwait,
Mr. George Southwick,
Mr. Benjamin Daland, jun.
Mr. Jotham Webb,
Mr. Perley Putnam.

Of *Salem*.

Mr. Benjamin Peirce.

WOUNDED.

Of *Lexington*.

Mr. John Robbins,
Mr. John Tidd,
Mr. Solomon Peirce,
Mr. Thomas Winſhip,
Mr. Nathaniel Farmer,
Mr. Joſeph Comee,
Mr. Ebenezer Munroe,
Mr. Francis Brown,
Prince Eaſterbrooks,
(A Negro Man.

Of *Framingham*.

Mr. —— Hemenway.

Of *Bedford*.

Mr. John Lane.

Of *Woburn*.

Mr. George Reed,
Mr. Jacob Bacon.

Of *Medford*.

Mr. William Polly

Of *Lynn*.

Joſhua Feit,
Mr. Timothy Munroe.

Of *Danvers*.

Mr. Nathan Putnam,
Mr. Dennis Wallis.

Of *Beverly*.

Mr. Nathaniel Cleaves.

MISSING.

Of *Menotomy*.

Mr. Samuel Froſt,
Mr. Seth Ruſſell.

Thoſe diſtinguiſhed with this Mark [*] were killed by the firſt Fire of the Regulars

Sold in Queen Street.

PATRIOTIC NEWS STORY OF 1775 LISTING THE CASUALTIES AT LEXINGTON AND CONCORD

How to Do It

An underground paper is easy to start. A typewriter, stencils and access to a Mimeo or Ditto machine are all that is really necessary. A thousand copies of a stapled five-page paper can be printed for under $20. But if you have the money, you should really try using an off-set press—a slightly more expensive process, but one that will give a real newspaper effect, complete with pictures. If no one in your group has any previous experience in putting together a paper, contact the folks in your local community underground organization, a college paper or students in another high school. For easy-to-understand information on how to print your own paper, write FPS/Youth Liberation, 2007 Wastenaw Avenue, Ann Arbor, Michigan 48104, for its 25-cent pamphlet "How to Start a High School Underground Paper." Another useful bit of material from FPS is its sample packet of ten high school underground newspapers ($1) and a booklet reprinting ten FPS articles from past issues (50 cents).

Because an underground paper is controlled by students, it can print anything it wants. Research articles, for instance, can be used to hammer away at conditions in the school—how much money is spent on men's sports compared with women's sports; how many students were expelled last year, and why; a critique of textbooks, and who writes and selects them. Radical historical articles are also good, especially those that show how the struggles of students in your school tie in with other movements out of our past and present. Each issue should include a copy of the Declaration of Student Independence and the Bill of Student Rights and articles about specific issues that relate to the general themes of these documents. You should also go beyond the school gates and search out news of other schools, and of America and the world in general. Write FPS for a list of other underground high school papers and begin exchanging copies with them and reporting on what they're doing. Student resistance to high school tyranny is happening all over the country, and by exchanging and reporting news from other schools, you can give students an idea of just how large the movement is.

If the administration decides your paper is too radical (in other words, your criticisms of the school are too popular with other students), school officials may try to suppress it. The usual method of suppression is to suspend anybody who distributes the paper, and to confiscate the copies of any students reading them on campus. There are three things you can do in this instance: distribute the paper off campus, try to go through "channels" to get the rule changed or ignore the rule and hand it out anyway. In most cases, the last choice is best. If the administration harasses you, arouse students to your defense by talking about your First Amendment freedoms. (You might consider contacting a lawyer to file suit for your rights. The advantage in going to court—if you win—is that you will have a court order on your side that your school will be forced to obey. Your case may also set an important precedent

WASHINGTON EVACUATING LONG ISLAND

EVERY AGE AND GENERATION MUST BE AS FREE TO ACT FOR ITSELF, IN ALL CASES, AS THE AGES AND GENERATION WHICH PRECEDED IT . . . MAN HAS NO PROPERTY IN MAN; NEITHER HAS ANY GENERATION A PROPERTY IN THE GENERATIONS WHICH ARE TO FOLLOW. — TOM PAINE

that will apply to other schools. The disadvantages: possible expense, and the probable dissipating of student energy and concern as the legal battle draws out.) Take the school to task for teaching about how dictatorships deny a free press while your school is doing just that. Point out that you are only practicing what the school teaches in your History course—the Bill of Rights, the Zenger case, etc.

Have your friends put together a King George exhibit, showing what kind of people have been opposed to a free press—King George III, Alexander Hamilton, Adolf Hitler—and who has supported a free press—Thomas Jefferson, John Peter Zenger and others. Make the exhibit colorful—pictures of people, quotations, a copy of the Bill of Rights—and set it up one day during lunch for everybody to see.

If your paper is really a paper of the students, then administration attempts at suppressing it will fail. Administrators and other people in power still go on the assumption that if something is suppressed, it will be controlled—when, of course, the truth is that efforts at repression of a people's movement always lead to resistance. If students are to relate to your underground newspaper as something more than the "official" paper, then they must feel that it really is *theirs*. Don't bog the paper down in useless rhetoric, militance or ideology that most people don't understand; if you do, students will see you as just a small radical clique of boring troublemakers.

Keep a balance between editorial-type stories and simple human-interest articles that are easier to read and more enjoyable to students who don't consider themselves interested in politics. Humor and satire can often be more effective in attacking a target or stating a grievance than trying to be militant and calling your principal a "pig." Try using the rhetoric of the Revolution. Call your principal a Tory if he is unresponsive to your demands, and explain in your paper what a Tory was in 1776—a loyal subject of the King who valued power and wealth above all else and had only contempt and hatred for the common people who were demanding their own independence. Now, doesn't that sound like your school administration?

Freedom of Speech and Assembly

> Every age and generation must be as free to act for itself, in all cases, as the ages and generation which preceded it . . . Man has no property in man; neither has any generation a property in the generations which are to follow.
>
> —TOM PAINE

Everyone who has gone to high school has had the boring experience of sitting through compulsory assemblies. The subject matter of these assemblies is right in keeping with the philosophy of the administrators—*My Fair Lady*–type productions by the drama department, pep rallies, a lecture by a visiting "dignitary." In other words, they're a bore that students would rarely attend if they weren't forced to.

If you want something better than these stale, hour-long sleep-ins, there are several things you can do. You can agitate for optional assemblies, petition your grievances or even suggest a boycott. Boycotts are one of the oldest forms of protest in this country. In fact, the Revolutionary movement of 1776 actually began back in the 1760's when patriots got together to boycott taxed British goods and the Tory merchants who sold them. The same tactic can be used by students of the 1970's to pressure school officials to accede to student demands.

Working to make assemblies optional is important; but even if the school administration agrees to this, students who would rather be at an assembly than in a class or study hall (even at their worst, assemblies are often better than required classes) should still be able to see something interesting. So another demand should be for student power to determine just what the assemblies will be like. After all, students make up at least 90 percent of the audience, so why shouldn't they have 90 percent of the decision as to what the assemblies will be about? Find out who controls the decision-making on this issue, and begin to work to have that decision-making democratized. If there is already a student-faculty board or committee that makes these decisions, get on it, poll students for what they'd like to see and begin proposing programs that will be of interest to students.

Why not put on assemblies that are celebrations of our Revolutionary heritage? Instead of learning history out of dry textbooks, students could have a chance to see what our past is *really* all about, and even have a chance to participate in it! And besides, you'll be able to raise issues important to all students—issues the administration might try to suppress if it weren't for the history slant.

You might, for instance, propose that the school hold assemblies on some dates out of our past, such as:

- *January 29*—Tom Paine's birthday
- *March 5*—The Boston Massacre
- *March 23*—Patrick Henry's "Give me liberty or give me death" speech
- *April 13*—Thomas Jefferson's birthday
- *April 19*—The battles of Lexington and Concord
- *September 27*—Sam Adams' birthday
- *December 16*—The Boston Tea Party

An indoor assembly, using these dates to talk about our Revolutionary principles and the coming Bicentennial, has all sorts of possibilities. Some students might want to put on a play about 1776, presenting it as more than just history by making it pretty clear that the principles people fought for in the 1770's should still be

AS GOVERNMENT TROOPS RETREAT FROM CONCORD, PATRIOTS COUNTERATTACK GUERRILLA-WARFARE STYLE

LEXINGTON CITIZENS' MILITIA STANDS UP TO THE KING'S SOLDIERS

struggled for today. To help students realize the parallels, stay away from language like "British," and "Colonies," and "independence." Instead, put it in the language of today: use administration for "British"; radicals, common people and patriots for "colonists"; human rights and self-determination for "independence." That makes it fairly obvious that conditions then weren't so different from those today. At such an assembly, you might also read excerpts from early speeches of such people as Sam Adams, Patrick Henry, Joseph Warren and John Hancock. These were some of the most famous orators of their day, and their speeches weren't designed to befuddle people, as politicians today seem intent on doing, but to stir them to action. They were the rabble-rousers of their day. Other ideas are easy to come up with; imagination is really the key.

If you don't have any success working through the "system," your PBC should consider sponsoring its own outdoor event—either during school time or on a weekend. If your administration is particularly uptight about you, they might come down on such a celebration. But if they do, you have a perfect case to accuse them of being un-American and unpatriotic. After all, what's more American than having a good old patriotic, red, white and blue celebration in honor of the Founding Fathers and Mothers of the country? On the lowest level, you might simply set up, during lunchtime, an outdoor exhibit of radical American tradition, or a King George exhibit exposing the authoritarian, antidemocratic tradition of corporations and demagogic politicians throughout our history. You could set up a soapbox—another American tradition—and open it up as a free-speech platform. You might lead off, for instance, with some sort of general discussion about the Bicentennial and how it relates to students. Allow anyone who wants to to come up and speak. Our school system pressures people into conformity and silence. Giving students a chance to speak out in public is a good way to break through the myth that "adults" are the only people with ideas worth listening to.

On a grander scale, you can put on an outdoor celebration like those that were held during our early Revolutionary days.

STUDENT EVALUATION OF TEACHERS

> It is much easier to restrain liberty from running into licenciousness than POWER from swelling into tyranny and oppression.
>
> —JOSIAH QUINCY, 1774

Imagine America in 1774. King George thought of

the people of this country as "my children" and felt free to lay down laws to them and criticize them whenever he felt they were "misbehaving." For a long time, Americans accepted this attitude, confident that when the King did something *they* didn't like, they could, in a reasonable manner, offer suggestions and criticisms to the King about *his* behavior and methods of ruling. After all, they reasoned, America was a free country, and it was in the best interest of everyone concerned to have grievances and opinions openly aired. Imagine what they thought, then, when on February 7, 1774, the King rejected a very reasonable petition from Americans requesting a change in one of his policies, dismissing their opinion as "groundless, vexatious, scandalous, and calculated only for the seditious purpose of keeping up a spirit of clamour and discontent!"

Most high schools are run on this two-hundred-year-old King George philosophy. Students are told what to do and how to do it, tested to see if they've absorbed (even if it's only for a few hours) the lessons the teacher has selected as being important to their education and then graded by the teacher's standards. Not only is this whole method of education undemocratic, it just plain doesn't make sense.

Democracy in education means that students and teachers are free to share opinions and thoughts, to let each other know how they feel about their classes, to help each other grow and learn. A good way to begin getting some democracy into the classroom is by starting a system of student evaluation of teachers.

There's one important difference between King George and teachers, however. King George was the *enemy* of the patriots. He swore to either make them his subjects, or destroy them in the process. Teachers, on the other hand, are essentially people who are interested in helping other people. The trouble is, they've gone through years of oppressive schooling themselves, are forced by the school system to maintain "control" of students and are faced with the loss of their jobs if they do anything that is too obviously in the students' interests. Of course, there are always some tyrants in every situation. But overall, if teachers are approached with understanding, with responsibility and with a genuine feeling that teachers and students are not *natural* enemies but fellow victims of an undemocratic system and thus natural allies, teachers may be quite open to input from students. They'll probably even be surprised at how much they've misjudged students.

You might try approaching your teacher on a personal level—bringing up points about the purpose of education and democracy, how conditions change too rapidly for one person alone to deal with, how students have valuable things to say about their education, how a teacher *whose sole purpose is to help students* should know what students are thinking and if they really feel they are being helped. Suggest that some sort of student committee be set up in the school to devise an evaluation form. It might include questions about the teacher's methods; selection of material; how open the teacher is to differing ideas; whether students are allowed to carry out individual projects or forced to follow the lesson plan; whether a student would take his course if he or she knew as much about it as he/she does now . . . The committee could take the results from each class, sort through them and then print them up for student and teacher consideration. After the evaluations are published, time should be set aside in the classroom to talk about the results and why students voted on a teacher as they did. That way, teachers would understand what students really thought about their courses, and students would know what to expect from a certain teacher.

The eventual goal of an evaluation system is to be able to use the material compiled to make decisions on the firing or retaining of teachers. If evidence is clear that students think a teacher is very poor, unresponsive to student needs or biased in presentation, a student delegation should be sent to talk to the teacher. Re-

Betsy Ross
sewed more
than flags!

NO AMERICANS WERE SAFE DURING THE REVOLUTION.
HERE, THE CIVILIANS OF CHARLESTOWN ARE SAVAGELY BOMBARDED BY ROYAL HENCHMEN.

member, in such a situation it does no good at all to be abusive, sarcastic or angry. The teacher should be made to feel that you are genuinely interested in your education and feel that his/her course can be improved so that it will meet students' needs. At the same time you should make it clear that you aren't requesting privileges from the teacher, but asserting your rights—rights that are naturally yours and not something a teacher can confer when it suits him or her. If the teacher refuses to hear you out, or make any changes, and follows the King George route, you should launch a student campaign to bring pressure upon the teacher. Ultimately, teachers will have to decide whether they stand with the students in their efforts for a democratic education, or with the administration in its efforts at control.

Evaluations are a two-way street. While bad teachers should be opposed, students should always support those faculty members who are really responsive to their needs. You should do this because, first, good teachers are often the ones who are fired, and so one day you may have to agitate in their favor, and second, other teachers will see that students don't dislike and oppose all teachers, just those who try to control their lives.

As students begin to assert their rights and demand their independence, a system must eventually be instituted that will allow them their rightful share in the hiring and firing process of their teachers. This, of course, is a long-range objective, and can be achieved only when students have taken control of their own lives and education. And this can happen only when the people once again take control of the country. Until that time, there will be many who will argue that students aren't concerned or sophisticated enough to exercise such power. What they don't understand, of course, is that when people *are* the system—whether it's government or a school—then the system becomes their life. And *everybody* who has a chance wants to control his or her life.

DISCIPLINARY PROCEDURES

Men who injure and oppress the people under their administration provoke them to cry out and complain; and then make that very complaint the foundation for new oppressions and prosecutions.

—ANDREW HAMILTON, 1735

On April 19, 1775, the Redcoats marched on Lexington and Concord. Their mission had two purposes: to seize a storehouse full of rebel weapons and to arrest Sam Adams and John Hancock, the two most militant patriots of the time. Once arrested, Adams and Hancock were to be shipped to England, where they would be given a "fair" trial (before Englishmen, not their American peers)—and then hanged.

Students today are in the same position as Adams and Hancock were two hundred years ago. They're not likely to be hanged, of course, but they are subject to arbitrary discipline, in which there is no effort made at ensuring the Constitutional rights of due process, representation by a lawyer or trial by one's peers.

THE TORIES' DAY OF JUDGMENT

Students who are struggling to control their lives and education must also control the enforcement of the school rules and regulations. Why, for instance, do only teachers and administrators have the right to determine who gets punished, expelled or suspended? And why is it always students, and occasionally a worthwhile teacher, who are charged with breaking rules? In insisting on their right to fair disciplinary procedures, students can move in several ways.

First, of course, a student board should be set up to hear the case of any student who is charged with breaking a rule. The final determination of punishment belongs to this board, and this board alone. This is a fundamental foundation of student power and, as such, will probably meet with administration resistance for a long time. As you work toward this goal, you should enlist the support of sympathetic teachers, perhaps run a petition campaign among students and print up articles that talk about the tradition in this country that reaffirms the rights of an accused. You should seek community support for a cause like this—especially among lawyers and legal scholars. If you've made inroads into assembly subjects, you might try to have an entire assembly devoted to student rights and the historical struggle for legal rights in this country. Or on a day like Law Day (May 1), you could set up an entire day of seminars, meetings and discussions with all kinds of people concerned with legal matters—ex-prisoners, lawyers, students, scholars, historians. If a student is unfairly suspended from one of your classes, you should bring pressure on the teacher to democratize the classroom and let everyone in the class decide whether the student should be expelled—one person, one vote.

All punishment in school is ultimately political—for every act of resistance, whether it be smoking in the rest room, or handing out an underground newspaper, constitutes a rebellion against rules students had no part in making. You should make this clear in any informational materials you prepare, and let teachers know you feel this way, too.

On a lighter level, you might print up a broadside suspending the principal or some other teacher who has grossly violated student rights. Paste up copies around school, listing the reasons why you think that person, instead of a student, should be punished. Of course, you won't be able to pull off the suspension of your princi-

Was this
nation born
in Revolution?

pal, but the idea will probably appeal to a lot of students he or she has suspended in the past!

TRACKING

> Where learning is confined to a *few* people, we always find monarchy, aristocracy and slavery.
>
> —BENJAMIN RUSH, 1786

The subtlest form of discrimination in high school, and the form most subversive of the radical democratic ideals of 1776, is tracking. Tracking, under the "liberal-reform" guise of "to each according to his or her needs," is in reality the cornerstone of Tory education in America.

The original idea behind tracking was that some students "learned" faster than others. By being in the same class, the argument ran, "slow" students were hurt by being taught faster than they could learn, and "fast" students were stifled by being held back from learning all they were capable of knowing.

Over the years, it's become pretty obvious, though, that tracking is a dismal failure in its stated goal. What tracking *does* succeed in doing is serving the needs of the corporate interests of America by beginning the training, at an early age, of people to fit into the job categories big business has decided it needs. Because of this undemocratic system, students in the low track find themselves forced into factory, secretarial and service (including housewife) roles, while students in the upper track usually go on into college, there to receive the additional training necessary to become technicians, professionals and scientists, etc.

Tracking not only begins the training process for future jobs—without the student's knowledge or approval—but does so on the basis of race, sex and economic and social background. If you don't believe it, just look around your school and ask yourself what the people in the upper and lower tracks are like.

Tracking must be stopped if we are to have a democratic education. And not just in high schools. Already, some of the more "liberal" high schools have ended the tracking system—not because they were philosophically opposed to it, but because they found it was simply not necessary. The use of tracking in elementary and junior high school had simply been more successful than anticipated! By the time students reached high school, administrators found, they were already so programmed that most of them just accepted their roles passively.

Breaking Down Tracking

Dealing the death blow to tracking should be a major long-range goal of any high school Peoples Bicentennial Commission.

One place you can begin attacking tracking is within your classroom. In History and Social Studies classes, for instance, students often learn about the ethnic groups that have played a part in shaping America. You can press the point in these classes that it certainly is strange to learn how different peoples, working together, made America unique and how different peoples are separated in your very own school.

Or you might discuss tracking in relation to social Darwinism, a 19th-century concept that was used to justify slavery and the rule of the wealthy over the workers and farmers. Social Darwinism held that the fittest people would rise to the top in the struggle for survival, and that democracy was a "radical" concept that ran against this natural process. It was even argued that it was really more humane to leave poor people where they were, rather than upset the balance of nature. Tracking seems to line up right beside this reactionary philosophy.

Using historical material like this, you might consider looking at who might have been on what side of the tracking question. In other words, historically what kind of people favored giving special education to an elite, while doing just enough for the "common people" to keep them quiet, and who was committed to a democratic system, where all had equal opportunity.

On a wider scale, you should use your school or underground newspaper to raise the issue of tracking. Your PBC, for instance, might conduct a survey of students in the different tracks of your school as well as the views of school administrators on the "benefits" of tracking. The study might include questions on family occupation, family income, family educational background, area of the community lived in; expectations about post–high school college or jobs; what kind of equipment and educational material is used in classes of the upper and lower tracks; how students in each track relate to their teachers; whether students in one track are punished or suspended more frequently than those in another; how students in each track feel about the quality, relevance and personal interest of their courses, etc. When a representative sampling of students is completed, publish the results, comparing the students' feelings with the bogus theories of the administrators.

With such a study, you will have some powerful ammunition to assault the tracking system. You might consider working with parents on the basis of the information. Most parents really don't have any idea what tracking is all about; in fact, most probably don't even know it exists.

Demand that students be allowed to take the courses they prefer. If the argument arises that students will be hurt by such a step, point out that if students helped run their courses on a democratic basis, they could collectively decide what pace they should move at, and how students could help one another to progress instead of competing to rise above the rest.

Because tracking is such a subtle, institutional form of discrimination, you might want to conduct other studies to build a well-documented case. Such studies will make clear that student dissatisfaction with classes is not "youthful rebellion" or the result of old-fashioned teaching methods, but arises because a whole system is serving not the needs of the students but those of big business interests, and the fears of government leaders who understand that democracy and cooperative education in schools could be a dangerous thing for their world. Here are three possibilities for in-depth studies:

POOR MAN

- I.Q. Tests. There is a wealth of information that exposes I.Q. tests as relevant only to the experiences of the white middle and upper classes in America. Because of this, they are inherently discriminatory against people who don't come out of this background. Yet these same tests are often an important basis for assigning students to different track levels. Find out what part I.Q. tests play in tracking in your school.
- Tracking by Sex. In high school, male students are assigned to take shop courses, while women are forced into home economics classes. Men compete on sports teams (which are generously funded), while women have little chance to develop athletic skills. In grammar schools throughout the country,

RICH MAN

there's much more playground space provided for males than for females. Research the sexist philosophy that has set up this artificial division between men and women students. How does this kind of male/female segregation corrupt the principles of the right of all people to "life, liberty and the pursuit of happiness"?

- Counselors. Talk to students about their counselors. Do some of these counselors advise certain students to "learn a trade" and then persuade others that they should try for college? Do they give college- and professionally oriented advice to men and attempt to convince female students that their ultimate fulfillment will come only from marriage, a home and children?

A counselor's job should be to provide information on all the possibilities that await people after high school —not channel them into slots on the assumption that people are *not* all created equal. Such counselors should be opposed. If they won't listen to reason, begin a campaign against them, calling for their ouster. Make up WANTED posters of them and stick them up around school. List their crimes: corrupting the minds and potential of youth; robbing students of their right to the pursuit of happiness; denying the equality of all people; serving the interests of corporations instead of people. When you see *your* counselor, find out what he or she is like. Maybe *you* should be the one giving advice!

If the counselors at your school are generally destructive of your rights, you might consider writing to Vocations for Social Change Work Force, 4911 Telegraph Ave., Oakland, Calif., for information about setting up your own counseling service. The goal in breaking down tracking is not to give everyone the "opportunity" to become a rich, well-educated professional, but to allow all students the freedom to select the education and career that will be fulfilling for them and beneficial for society. And that's what VSC is all about. A student-run counseling service could be an important aid to many students, and will allow you to better understand what the student body is feeling and thinking.

In the end, one of the most effective actions you can take against tracking is to reject it yourself by breaking out of your assigned track. If you're an honor student, refuse the honors bestowed on you, both during the school year and at graduation. Make it clear that you are refusing because, as long as your fellow students are being robbed of an education, you cannot glory in honors. In 1971, Vietnam veterans threw their war medals away at the Capitol to show their disassociation from America's foreign policy. You might try something similar with your awards and certificates. Quote Ben Rush's words that appear at the beginning of this section as a justification for your actions. Whichever track you're in, you can press to take classes that have been denied you in the past. By breaking down tracking on a personal level, students of different backgrounds can unite to form a democratic movement to reaffirm the Spirit of '76.

TEXTBOOKS AND CURRICULUM

> [The founding principles] should be the creed of our political faith, the text of civic instruction, the touchstone by which to try the services of those we trust; and should we wander from them in moments of error or of alarm, let us hasten to retrace our steps and to regain the road which alone leads to peace, liberty, safety.
>
> —THOMAS JEFFERSON, 1807

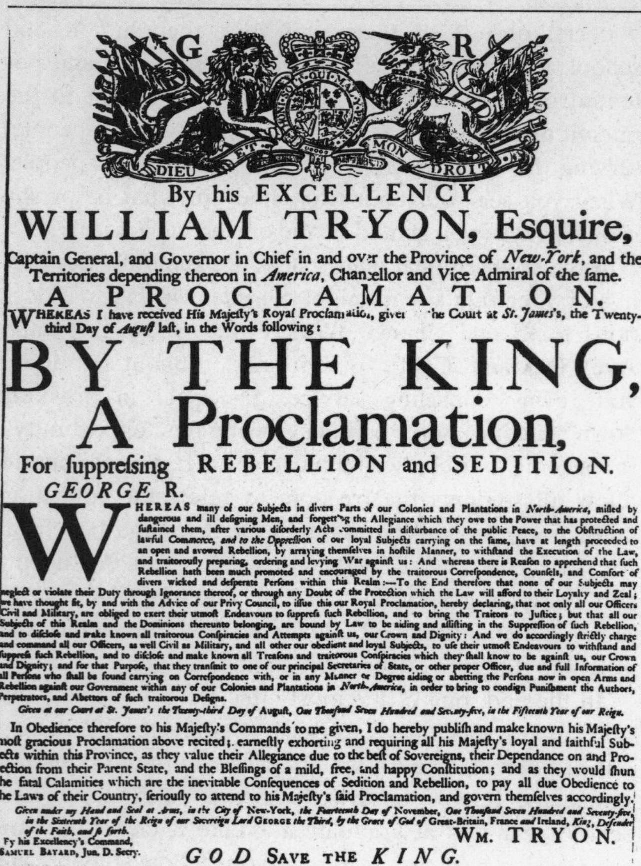

G R

DIEU ET MON DROIT

By his EXCELLENCY

WILLIAM TRYON, Esquire,

Captain General, and Governor in Chief in and over the Province of *New-York*, and the Territories depending thereon in *America*, Chancellor and Vice Admiral of the ſame.

A PROCLAMATION.

WHEREAS I have received His Majeſty's Royal Proclamation, given at the Court at *St. James's*, the Twenty-third Day of *Auguſt* laſt, in the Words following:

BY THE KING,

A Proclamation,

For ſuppreſsing REBELLION and SEDITION.

GEORGE R.

WHEREAS many of our Subjects in divers Parts of our Colonies and Plantations in *North-America*, miſled by dangerous and ill deſigning Men, and forgetting the Allegiance which they owe to the Power that has protected and ſuſtained them, after various diſorderly Acts committed in diſturbance of the public Peace, to the Obſtruction of lawful Commerce, *and to the* Oppreſſion of our loyal Subjects carrying on the ſame, have at length proceeded to an open and avowed Rebellion, by arraying themſelves in hoſtile Manner, to withſtand the Execution of the Law, and traitorouſly preparing, ordering and levying War againſt us: And whereas there is Reaſon to apprehend that ſuch Rebellion hath been much promoted and encouraged by the traitorous Correſpondence, Counſels, and Comfort of divers wicked and deſperate Perſons within this Realm:—To the End therefore that none of our Subjects may neglect or violate their Duty through Ignorance thereof, or through any Doubt of the Protection which the Law will afford to their Loyalty and Zeal; we have thought fit, by and with the Advice of our Privy Council, to iſſue this our Royal Proclamation, hereby declaring, that not only all our Officers Civil and Military, are obliged to exert their utmoſt Endeavours to ſuppreſs ſuch Rebellion, and to bring the Traitors to Juſtice; but that all our Subjects of this Realm and the Dominions thereunto belonging, are bound by Law to be aiding and aſſiſting in the Suppreſſion of ſuch Rebellion, and to diſcloſe and make known all traitorous Conſpiracies and Attempts againſt us, our Crown and Dignity: And we do accordingly ſtrictly charge and command all our Officers, as well Civil as Military, and all other our obedient and loyal Subjects, to uſe their utmoſt Endeavours to withſtand and ſuppreſs ſuch Rebellion, and to diſcloſe and make known all Treaſons and traitorous Conſpiracies which they ſhall know to be againſt us, our Crown and Dignity; and for that Purpoſe, that they tranſmit to one of our principal Secretaries of State, or other proper Officer, due and full Information of all Perſons who ſhall be found carrying on Correſpondence with, or in any Manner or Degree aiding or abetting the Perſons now in open Arms and Rebellion againſt our Government within any of our Colonies and Plantations in *North-America*, in order to bring to condign Puniſhment the Authors, Perpetrators, and Abettors of ſuch traitorous Deſigns.

Given at our Court at St. James's the Twenty-third Day of Auguſt, *One Thouſand Seven Hundred and Seventy-five, in the Fifteenth Year of our Reign.*

In Obedience therefore to his Majeſty's Commands to me given, I do hereby publiſh and make known his Majeſty's moſt gracious Proclamation above recited; earneſtly exhorting and requiring all his Majeſty's loyal and faithful Subjects within this Province, as they value their Allegiance due to the beſt of Sovereigns, their Dependance on and Protection from their Parent State, and the Bleſſings of a mild, free, and happy Conſtitution; and as they would ſhun the fatal Calamities which are the inevitable Conſequences of Sedition and Rebellion, to pay all due Obedience to the Laws of their Country, ſeriouſly to attend to his Majeſty's ſaid Proclamation, and govern themſelves accordingly.

Given under my Hand and Seal at Arms, in the City of New-York, *the Fourteenth Day of* November, *One Thouſand Seven Hundred and Seventy-five, in the Sixteenth Year of the Reign of our Sovereign Lord* GEORGE *the Third, by the Grace of God of* Great-Britain, France *and* Ireland, *King, Defender of the Faith, and ſo forth.*

WM. TRYON.

By his Excellency's Command,
SAMUEL BAYARD, Jun. D. Secry.

GOD SAVE THE *KING*.

At the core of demands for student rights are the questions what will be taught in the classroom, how it will be taught and who has the power to determine these and other important classroom issues. Unlike other matters, such as underground papers and assemblies, these are the issues that students come in touch with every day, in every class that they attend. It is wise to concentrate a lot of your energies as an organizer on the issues of Curriculum and Textbooks.

Textbooks

Textbooks, especially those on "nonscientific" subjects such as history, economics, social studies and political science, are notoriously atrocious. History chapters on the American Revolution, for instance, often follow the school of conservative thought that claims that the Revolution wasn't a "real" revolution at all! A textbook that takes positions like that is likely to be not only boring, but downright untruthful.

One Bicentennial project that relates directly to the needs of high school students is the reexamining of textbooks for the values they set forth, as well as the kinds of material they emphasize. The best way to begin is by drafting a set of questions that you can use to analyze each text. Here are some sample questions to guide a critique of your American History books:

- Does the book begin the course with the Pilgrims or with the American Revolution?

  If the book excludes the Pilgrims and Puritans, or deals with them only in stereotypes of black clothes and the First Thanksgiving, chances are that the impact of traditional Protestant theology on America is ignored. This theology was not what we now call the "Protestant" ethic. It infused into American culture the strong conviction that human beings had an obligation to worship a just God by performing good works in the community. We Americans have never totally lived up to this creed, but its impact on the culture is reflected in a variety of radical movements that fought in its name.

- Does the book argue that the American Revolution changed little in the social structure of the United States, or that it was in some measure a democratic as well as an anticolonial revolution?

  If the text holds that the American Revolution was fought merely to preserve those rights that British citizens already enjoyed and that nothing within American society had changed fundamentally, the chances are that the book will take a conservative attitude toward the principles of liberty and justice that the Revolutionaries tried to preserve.

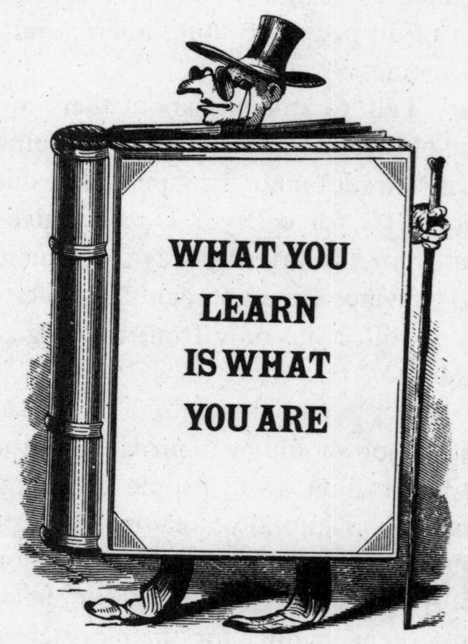
WHAT YOU
LEARN
IS WHAT
YOU ARE

A HIGH SCHOOL

- Does the book ignore the Antifederalist case against the Constitution?

  The Antifederalists were a diverse lot, but the best of them made accurate predictions about what would happen to the United States under this "most complicated" government.
- Does the textbook view Jefferson's compromise, late in life, with Hamiltonianism as a healthy adjustment to changing conditions?

  If so, it will probably later defend technological and economic progress almost uncritically. The early Jefferson fought to preserve a decentralized, agrarian society as the best means to fulfill the goals of "life, liberty and the pursuit of happiness" outlined in the Declaration of Independence. His own Administration, however, witnessed an almost uncontrolled pattern of manufactures along the Eastern Seaboard.
- How does the text treat the Jacksonian Era?

  Does it argue that Jackson was really representing not democrats but local capitalists in his veto of the National Bank? The position makes a monumental error in composition, equating conditions of a preindustrial society with those following the Civil War. It also ignores completely the moral basis upon which the Jacksonians based their objections to the Bank, as well as the political institutions which emerged in the struggle.
- Does the textbook maintain that the Civil War represented a great victory for the forces of Truth and Right?

  If so, it either ignores the economic consequences of the War or approves of them. Whatever Emancipation did for blacks—and, as is well known, it did not do much—its main result was to ensure the triumph of Northern industrial capitalism over a century.
- How does the text deal with the Populist movement?

  Many texts represent the Populists as jingoistic, racist, nationalistic and reactionary precursors of the McCarthyism of the 1950's, raising a few radical economic demands to gloss over a fundamentally dangerous political program. This view is simply a rehash of the invectives launched against Populism by its wealthy, entrenched enemies.
- Does the book contend that the Progressives were America's true radicals in the 20th century?

  If so, it will try to convince you that a modest

TEXTBOOK WRITERS ARE NOT NEUTRAL OBSERVERS OF HISTORY. MOST AUTHORS STILL PICTURE WOMEN AS PLAYING PASSIVE ROLES, MERELY SUPPORTING THEIR HUSBANDS AND FATHERS . . .

effort to eliminate concentrations of power—without democratizing large institutions—together with a social-welfare program borrowed from Bismarck's Germany is an adequate solution to the problems of industrial society.

- Does the text believe that the New Deal was the final triumph of decency in American social policy, after which there can be only modest rearrangement and improvement?

  A reading of the morning newspaper is enough to shoot holes in that theory.

- Does the text include an extensive discussion of blacks, women, ethnic groups, Indians and unions in its treatment?

You can also develop such questions for the texts used in any other class. Here are some general guideline questions for three other subjects:

- *Science:* Does your textbook deal only in the technical aspects of "pure science" and neglect the moral, ethical and political questions involved in the application of scientific knowledge? Is science seen in a vacuum of intellectual research, or in the context of serving the needs of society?
- *Social Studies:* Does your textbook set forth the "melting pot" theory of American society and neglect theories relating to the ongoing conflict between different social and economic classes? What role do women and Third World people play in the social analysis? Are the traits and living conditions of people rationalized by arguments of inherent, biological differences, set forth in relation to the socialization process?
- *Health:* Does the textbook take the physical differences between men and women and attempt to build a case from these for the emotional and psychological "strengths" of men and the "weaknesses" of women? Does your book picture women as inherently emotional, dependent and family-oriented,

...WHEN IN REALITY, WOMEN WERE EQUALLY IMPORTANT IN CREATING AND WINNING THE AMERICAN REVOLUTION. HERE NANCY HART, "THE GEORGIA GIANT," DEFENDS HER HOME AGAINST FIVE TORIES

while men are seen as aggressive, detached and the natural breadwinners? On the questions of drugs, sexuality, health, etc., does the text use government-supplied information, or attempt to consult non-government sources? Are new developments in health, food and drugs branded as fads or dangerous practices, or carefully analyzed as to their merits?

When you've developed a good understanding of which of your textbooks are particularly worthless, and for what reasons, you should begin organizing to have the books assigned to the trash bins, where they belong. Bring your specific objections to the teacher and your classmates.

You might dramatize your objections by rewriting a chapter you are currently studying. To be really effective, this kind of "Peoples Textbook" must be done with a lot of care and responsibility. Say, for instance, your history book, as is likely, doesn't have much information on the women's movement of the early 20th century. To write a Peoples Textbook on this stage of the suffrage movement, you might begin by reading a number of books describing the period. You should consult old newspaper accounts to see what the women's struggle looked like at the time. Finally, you should seek out women in your community who lived through the time and ask for their recollections. Often you'll find that the people who lived through such great events are a much more interesting and accurate source of information than all of the scholarly treatises combined.

When you've accumulated the resource material, you should distill it down into about ten pages, have it run off (by offset if possible, so that you can include pictures) and hand it out to the class when you reach that historical time period. Ask for an evaluation from the class of the way your paper and the textbook treat the subject. If you've really done a job, your fellow students, and probably the teacher, will like the Peoples Textbook version better. And if you've done the job you should,

SAM ADAMS LAYS DOWN THE LAW

you'll gain an insight into what an incredible responsibility it is to try to write truthful history—something, unfortunately, that most textbook authors don't seem to understand.

From this beginning, you might attempt to have your class organized in groups of four or five, each group taking one chapter of the book and rewriting it if necessary. Each week, a different "chapter" of the Peoples Textbook can be read and discussed in class, and compared with the official text.

Another classroom activity could be the substituting of selected readings from outside sources to replace portions of the textbook. For instance, when your History gets to the labor movement of the late 1800's and early 1900's, select portions of such labor histories as Jeremy Brecher's *Strike!*, Joyce Kornbluh's *Rebel Voices* or Ronald Radosh's *Debs* to give a fuller picture of what the early workers' struggle was like. You can easily type these selections on stencils and run off copies for the class.

One more way to get beyond the sterile and misleading textbooks is to begin an Oral/Visual Project in your class. Oral/Visual history is people's history, told by the folks in your community who lived through important events and time periods. If you're studying antiwar protests in Social Studies class, you could invite in a former antiwar organizer to speak about the massive protests of the 60's. Or you might have some senior citizens talk to your class who participated in the labor movement and fought for survival during the Depression. (For information on how to conduct an Oral/Visual history project, see the section entitled Oral/Visual Projects beginning on page 169).

As you work on these projects, remember that all of these ideas should be discussed in the classroom among both students and teachers. Many teachers realize that the texts the Board of Education provides are sterile and contain many omissions and untruths. Discussing your texts, criticizing them in a constructive way and making a decision among all those concerned—teachers and students—in a democratic way can be an important step toward revolutionizing curriculum, and eventually the entire educational process.

Curriculum

Students usually begin a new course by walking in, sitting down and being told what the teacher has decided the course is all about—everything you're supposed to study and learn, and how it will all be taught. This is called Curriculum, and by the way it is presented, it seems that Curriculum, like death and Mount Everest, is just there, and not much can be done about it.

But something *can* be done, if students win the input into curriculum decisions that is rightfully theirs.

A good way to begin working to change the curriculum in individual classes is to start on the first day in your own classes.

After the teacher has laid out his or her version of the course, make some additions and comments on the proposed semester. You might, for instance, ask that the first week of classes be devoted to just discussing what material is to be covered, with the idea in mind that if the class decides that some parts of the curriculum need amending, such suggestions will be followed through on. A week-long discussion like this can provide a chance for students and teachers to work together on a concept of the course, and allow students to work cooperatively instead of competitively.

Your Peoples Bicentennial Commission might sponsor some sort of curriculum questionnaire (or, if the conditions are right, pressure the Student Council into running such an evaluation) to begin a dialogue between students and teachers about their education. To ensure that the questionnaire gets answered, ask just a few general questions that will give you a good idea of what people are thinking:

- What classes are you taking (or teaching)?
- How do you rate these courses individually on: Being a significant contribution to your education? Having relevance to dealing with the world and its problems? Developing an understanding of what society should be like?
- What classes that aren't offered at this school would you like to take or teach?

You can use the results of this questionnaire to persuade the school to schedule a "free" week—a time when all kinds of classes are taught, by whoever wants to teach them. The fact that you don't have a teacher with a thorough knowledge of American blues or the history of peace movements in America doesn't mean that you can't have a course in either subject. Students can do the bulk of the teaching, and teachers can learn. That's what democratic education is all about.

Hundreds of constructive activities can be offered during a "free" week. One possibility is child-care classes. Another is community work: as examples, restoring a vacant building for use as a community center or food co-op; working with local switchboards or local drug clinics. The entire school can be restructured on a democratic basis. Students can attend any courses they want. Tests will be unnecessary. As John Adams wrote: "Let us dare to read, think, speak and write. Let every order and degree among the people rouse their attention and animate their resolution. In a word, let every sluice of Knowledge be opened and set aflowing."

A free week also serves to show students the possibilities of what a democratic education can be—something they've probably never seen. Use the free week to gain student support for similar programs. After all, if it can be done for a week, why not all the time?

A more specific questionnaire can be developed to

THE WONDERFUL PIG OF KNOWLEDGE

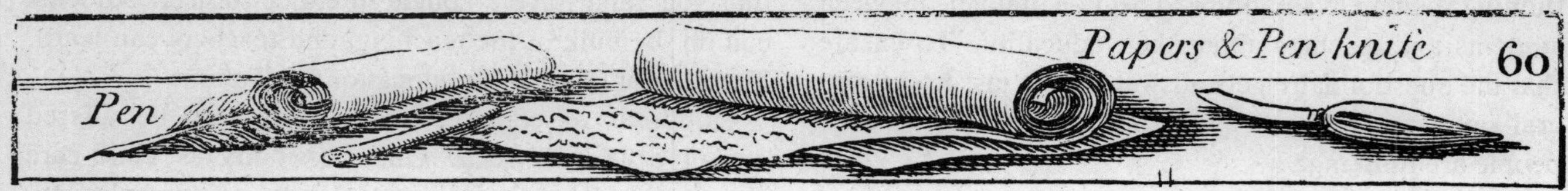

accompany a teacher-evaluation form. Toward the end of each semester, students should fill out the form for each of their courses, evaluating the work done in the course in a specific way. The results of the evaluation can be printed up and made available to students before the start of the next semester, to help them in deciding which courses are worth taking.

The questionnaire not only should ask questions about the value of the course, how fair tests were, the teacher's ability to lecture, etc., but should be mainly concerned with issues of democracy: what kind of input students had into decision-making; how open the teacher was to student demands; if the teacher did all of the teaching, or whether students also served as teacher; how open the teacher was to learning from students; how much of the class involved competition between students and how much was based on cooperative learning.

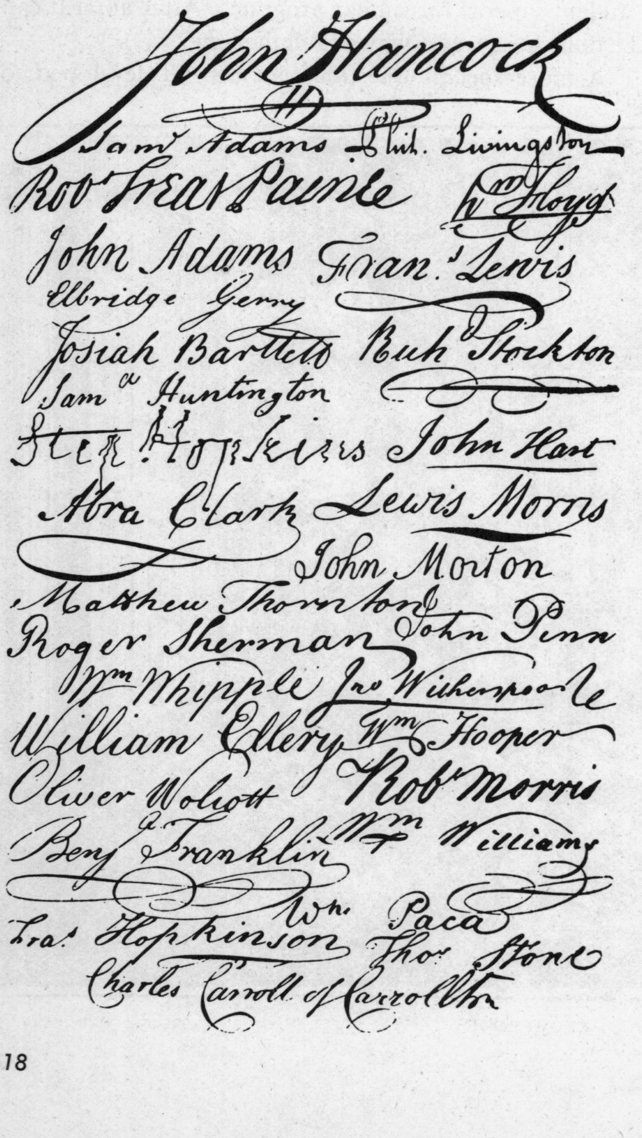

Curriculum change is a matter vital to democratic education. It's also a good place to break down student dependency on teachers and other artificial teacher/student divisions. Because curriculum reform takes place in the classroom, students and teachers must work together to achieve any meaningful results. As you demand the control over your courses' content that is rightfully yours, keep this in mind. Alienating the teacher from your just demands from the outset will do little in bringing about change. Curriculum reform is just a transitional demand on the road toward democratic education. In fact, the administrators in your school may be quite pleased that you've decided to channel your energies "constructively" instead of agitating around more "radical" issues.

What these people don't understand, of course, is that working around curriculum change also gives you an opportunity to raise other issues fundamental to a Revolutionary education. You can, for instance, bring up student dissatisfaction not just with a particular class, but with a system that makes *any* classes mandatory. Freedom of selection is a democratic demand that can be raised here. Or you can agitate for seminars taught by students, with the teacher serving only as an adviser to recommend reference material. Grades, exams and homework are other issues arising from a questioning of the curriculum status quo.

CONCLUSION

Because we so often find politicians, business tycoons and deceptive school textbooks mouthing praises of "democracy," many of us have forgotten just how revolutionary a concept democracy is. To those who understand what democracy is all about, it's clear we have a long way to go before we can truly call our education, or our society, democratic. Democracy in education, and for our society, is our demand.

This section on High School Students and the Bicentennial is just a brief introduction to the issues and problems students face. And it touches on just some of the possibilities for organizing within a framework of our democratic heritage.

We have tried to outline a philosophy and an analysis of our past and present. That philosophy and analysis can be used on many more issues of importance to high school students than the few we've listed. Other issues must and can be addressed during the Bicentennial years: the "confidential" records the school keeps on you, but refuses to allow you to see; compulsory school attendance; access to school resources (buildings, audio-visual equipment) for organizing; dress codes; open campuses; mandatory physical education.

The lessons of the American Revolution all point to a single fact: a revolutionary democratic movement is successful only when it has wide appeal. In schools, this should mean appeal to both students and teachers. Some teachers, it's certainly true, are tyrants who have taken their jobs simply because they enjoy being in control of hundreds of lives from nine to three. But most teachers are people who really want to serve other people. Teachers are not the problem; the educational system, which forces them into their roles, is the problem.

Good teachers should be fully supported (if they're good, chances are they'll soon be in trouble with the administration) and work to reform others who are not meeting your needs. Let them know you are aware of the pressures they face, their own socialization, how their jobs are important to them and their families. But also be firm, and make them understand that standing tall and refusing to move won't be tolerated for long by students.

The largest group a campus Peoples Bicentennial Commission can reach, of course, is the student body. Reach people where they are, not where you'd like them to be. In 1765, people considered themselves loyal subjects of the King who had a right to correct the King's errors. In 1776, Americans felt that the King should have *no* power over their lives and that it was no longer a case of the King's occasional error in judgment, but a Royal plot designed to deprive Americans of their natural rights. How did the general attitude change so drastically? It was the work of ten years of ongoing organizing by patriot activists. Ten years of hard work. Such patience is something we often forget in our instant-everything world.

TOM PAINE, AN ENGLISH CORSET MAKER, TURNED AMERICAN REVOLUTIONARY

In the end, the patriots of 1776 should teach us not only patience, but that revolutionizing individual institutions in society without a societal revolution is meaningless. After all, we go to high school for just three or four years. We live in American society for sixty or seventy. We can begin laying the basis for a Revolutionary education, but we can not genuinely change it until we have revolutionized society.

As we work toward this goal, we should keep in mind the first principles of the American revolution:

- All people are created equal.
- All people are entitled to Life, Liberty and the pursuit of Happiness.

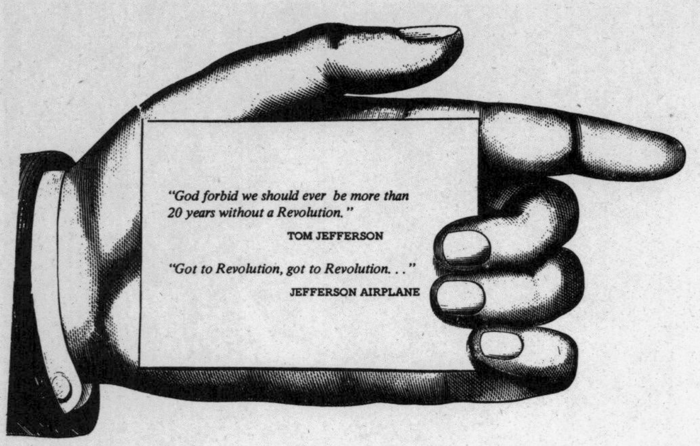

"God forbid we should ever be more than 20 years without a Revolution."
TOM JEFFERSON
"Got to Revolution, got to Revolution..."
JEFFERSON AIRPLANE

- The people have the right, and the duty, to alter or abolish unresponsive institutions.
- The Earth Belongs to the Living.
- The people have the right to freedom of speech and of the press, and the right to assemble and to petition the government for a redress of grievances.

To live by these principles is our task. To change America to conform with these principles is our duty. They are our birthright.

Teachers and the Bicentennial

High school students can demand their basic human rights. College and university students can battle against the pacification policies of their schools. But neither effort can succeed without the support of faculty members. Students may have the overwhelming numbers in schools, but teachers have the positions of power and influence, though they don't really run the show either. The two groups working together can be a powerful force for educational change.

Democracy demands cooperative effort and equality, yet our educational system places the teacher above the student and makes enemies of the very people who have the most at stake in our schools.

Students must be aware that problems of our schools are not the creation of teachers, but the effect of the selfish needs of our corporate/government aristocracy. In general, teachers are not the *enemy*; they too are the victims.

On their part, teachers must understand that students are human beings and should be treated as such. The purpose of education is not to keep these human beings in check during their school years, nor is it to mold them into conformity. Even the federal government has decided that people who are eighteen years old are at least as sensible and mature as are the rest of older Americans and should exercise all of the rights of full citizens —including making the decisions as to who our elected representatives are to be. Yet in high school and college, students are rarely treated as full-fledged members of society.

During the Bicentennial years, students will inevitably demand the fulfillment of the Revolutionary promise of education, and faculty members who are really concerned about democracy must respond positively. The role of a teacher is to provide knowledge and new experiences that will allow students to question values, beliefs and concepts. Only by questioning can people become active participants in the democratic process. Shouldn't teachers subject their own beliefs and teaching methods to the same sort of questioning process?

TEACHER VS. STUDENT

- Education, as conceived by our founders, was a revolutionary weapon used to arm the populace against tyranny, the arbitrary abuse of power and encroach-

THE FOUNDING FATHERS RECEIVE A TREASONOUS DOCUMENT —THE DECLARATION OF INDEPENDENCE

ment on the inalienable rights of the people. As a teacher, do you feel you must sometimes resort to playing the tyrant's role? Is such a role necessary, or can the classroom situation be somehow altered so that an atmosphere conducive to learning can prevail while allowing you to avoid the role of villain?

- How democratic is the physical setup of the classroom? Is your desk or lectern situated in front of the room, slightly elevated above the students? If so, is this kind of setting used simply because it is most suitable to lectures, or because it has a deeper psychological purpose? If it is simply best suited to lecturing, is a learning process based primarily on lecturing democratic? Do you feel comfortable placed at the front of the class, or do you sense a tension and separateness from the students?
- Must students raise their hands to speak? Must you? Does this mean that what you have to say is inherently more worthwhile or correct than the thoughts of students? Do you address students by their first names and require they call you Mr. or Ms.? If you don't require it, but they still call you Mr. or Ms., what does this mean?
- Does a discussion ever arise in class over just what students and teachers have in common in the educational experience? Do the students realize the pressures and regulations under which you are forced to work? Why is it teachers are supposed to listen to the personal and collective problems and complaints of students, but students are never to know the teacher except as instructor?
- Are there subtle, unnecessary distinctions made between teacher and student in your school? Do teachers have their own cafeteria? In the high school, are students forbidden to smoke, while teachers are permitted a nicotine break? Do teachers have a private lounge, closed to students? Is it fair for one segment of the school population to have privileges denied another? If not, do you lend support to students who are agitating for equal rules for all?

PATRIOTS MAKE THINGS HOT FOR THE BRITISH AS THE KING'S TROOPS RETREAT FROM LEXINGTON

COOPERATION VS. COMPETITION

- Do you encourage group projects and work, or primarily the competitive efforts of individuals? Is it necessarily the case, as we've been led to believe, that competition makes students rise to their highest level of achievement? If it does, is this necessarily best for the student or society?
- When students work together against your wishes on homework or exams, do you tell them they're "cheating" and "only hurting themselves"? Is it better to fail on your own and learn from the experience, or succeed with the help of others?
- What do grades do for students? How do classmates relate to the student who always gets A's? What do students who always fail think about themselves? Are students who receive poor grades motivated to improve, or do they just write themselves off as being "dumb"?
- If your class were run democratically, with a free-flowing discussion and you playing the role essentially of a resource person instead of leader, how would you react?
- What *do* tests test? Do students integrate the knowledge into their world view, or just cram in answers, and forget them as soon as possible?

LESSON PLANS VS. CREATIVITY

- When discussion arises over some interesting point in the classroom, do you let it flow, or try to curb it to stay within the range of the lesson plan? Do you feel you've fallen behind when you don't accomplish as much in a day as you had planned?
- How do students feel knowing you have a master plan of what is to be taught? Do they still feel they have a meaningful part in their education, or do they resign themselves to quietly taking notes?
- If you opened the lesson plan to general discussion and amendment, how would you react if students decided to substitute something of interest to them for an entire section you feel is more important to the class?
- Do you draw up a lesson plan for yourself, for the students or on demand of the administration? Which way do you think it should be?
- Do you teach the same course, year after year, using essentially the same notes? Does the subject remain static in reality, or just in your lecture?
- What would you think of drawing up two lesson plans —one to satisfy the administration and one to actually teach? Would this be dishonest, or responsive to the needs of the students?

TEXTBOOKS AND CURRICULUM

- What is your honest opinion of the texts you use? Are they just "the best we can hope for" or something you really stand by? If you were a student, would you be eager to read them?
- If students aren't doing the assigned reading, is it because they're just lazy, or because the texts aren't interesting? Do you demand that students do the reading whether they want to or not? If students dislike the texts, do you encourage them to try to write something better? If students *did* write a sample "Peoples Textbook" chapter, would you accept it, or view it as a rebellion against your authority?
- When you present the curriculum, do you make a conscious effort to examine it for its political content? *Is* curriculum, on any subject, political? Or is it possible to be "objective"? If you teach history and ignore the role of women and working people, is this a political decision? What do you think women and workers would say?

The Bicentennial is upon us. Americans who are truly interested in the Promise of Democracy must reexamine our institutions in the light of the Revolutionary ideals of 1776. Teachers can go beyond the general questioning of their role in the school system and look at the entire educational process for its contribution to democracy. Virtually every course taught in high school and college can be evaluated in this light. What follows is an essay describing the ideals of the Revolution, and how they can be applied in courses ranging from Debate and Speech to Geography.

CURRICULUM SUGGESTIONS

What Are We Celebrating on July 4, 1976?

The document signed in Philadelphia on July 4, 1776, is the cornerstone of our liberties. Women and men who have fought tyranny and inequality in America have repeatedly returned to this basic statement of the democratic ideal.

Here's what Abraham Lincoln said about the Declaration:

> [The Founding Fathers and Mothers] meant to set up a standard maxim for free society which should be familiar to all, constantly labored for, and, even though never perfectly attained, constantly spreading and deepening its influence and augmenting the happiness and value of life to all people of all colors everywhere . . . Its authors meant it . . . as, thank God, it is now proving itself—a new stumbling block to all those who in after times might seek to turn a free people back into the hateful paths of despotism.

ACTIVITIES:

- Introduce the Declaration of Independence at an opening ceremony during the school programs and assemblies. Ask the students to compare it with the Pledge of Allegiance.
- In class discussions, ask students to grade our society according to how closely it approximates the "standard maxim" of the Declaration.
- Ask the class, individually or collectively, to construct models of a society that would adhere strictly to the principles of the Declaration.

Q. R. and S. come here & confefs.

General Educational Theory

The Founding Fathers and Mothers were Renaissance people, at home in varied disciplines and arts. Franklin was called the "American Leonardo." David Rittenhouse, Franklin's successor, was leader of the Pennsylvania intellectuals, an advocate of the democratic movement and a renowned astronomer. Washington was a surveyor. Tom Paine was a brilliant engineer, who designed the longest single-span iron bridge of his time. He also designed an early version of Bunsen's burner and introduced a stream of inventive propositions such as the draining of marshes in order to combat yellow fever. Ben Rush, a signer of the Declaration of Independence and the most celebrated physician of his day, delved into techniques of psychoanalysis a century before Freud. Tom Jefferson was a respected naturalist, inventor and architect.

The Founding Fathers and Mothers assumed that people ought to be complete, balanced human beings, able to function in a number of areas. They did not believe that American citizens of the future should be cramped, limited people, stuffed into pigeonholes and molded according to bureaucratic dictates.

QUESTIONS:

- What is your school doing to produce the kind of citizens the Founding Fathers and Mothers admired?
- Has the school ever made a statement of its philosophy, of what kind of individual it seeks to produce and how it tries to accomplish its purpose?
- If so, how do the school's announced goals and practices compare with the Founding Fathers' and Mothers' educational theory as expressed in their careers?

THE AMERICAN FLAG—
AN ENDURING REVOLUTIONARY SYMBOL

ACTIVITIES:

- Ask alumni to discuss whether the school prepared them for lives the Founding Fathers and Mothers would have thought happy and fulfilling.
- Ask current students how their educational experience at school compares with that of the Founding Fathers and Mothers.
- As a project, have students plan alternative schools, and discuss their varying models.
- Have students survey the student population of their own school to determine the quality of education they are experiencing.

Art

Student artists may find inspiration in the Revolutionary themes discussed in this section. A class may want to develop a Bicentennial art show for the community, depicting the Revolution of 1776 through the eyes of contemporary Americans, or create a series of posters on American Revolutionary themes.

RESOURCES:

The Peoples Bicentennial Commission offers a multimedia team—using slides, music, readings, etc.—to dramatize the American experience. Illustrations, including some of those in this section, are available in slide form, accompanied by a written narrative.

Debate, Speech

College students in the 1700's debated mainly natural-rights questions. In order to understand the thought of Revolutionary America, debate or speech classes might take up such questions of rights and liberties. Here are some questions debated by Harvard students during the Revolutionary era:

- Is civil government originally founded on the consent of the people?
- Is the voice of the people the voice of God?
- Is an absolute and arbitrary monarchy contrary to reason?
- Is civil government more favorable to human liberty than a liberty free of any legal restriction?
- Are the people the sole judges of their rights and liberties?

Also, classes can invent their own questions on the theme of natural rights, or debate statements by the founders of the nation. Or the class might debate the question: If the philosophical arguments of the early founders are taken as valid, should we then have a revolution? How would the Declaration of Independence be written today?

Drama and Media

Yankee Doodle was once a well-known symbol; he was the country bumpkin of the Colonies, a fool, a figure of fun. When Americans rebelled against the King, they accepted the label "Yankee Doodle" and made it a term of pride instead of derision.

Yankee Doodle is only one of the folk figures whose memory has dimmed with the years. Other legendary and semilegendary people, such as Will Democrat, Uncle Sam, Pecos Bill, and Johnny Appleseed, can be rich sources of dramatic material. Such figures are part of the American Dream, and each is in itself a statement of that dream.

The American Revolutionary Road Company has distilled a statement of the American Dream into a powerful play in the tradition of the Italian commedia dell' arte. The play, *Americomedia,* focuses on the career of Yankee Doodle and the struggle of Ms. Liberty.

The Peoples Bicentennial multimedia project uses a variety of media techniques, including live music, to present the American Dream.

Drama and media classes can depict the American Dream through the eyes of a legendary character, as the Road Company is doing; through scenes and words of the democratic tradition, as the multimedia project is doing, or by re-creating events or life stories out of the American past.

Economics

> No hereditary emoluments, privileges or honors ought to be granted or conferred in this State . . . Perpetuities and monopolies are contrary to the genius of a free State and ought not to be allowed.
>
> —NORTH CAROLINA DECLARATION OF RIGHTS, 1776

Painting.

Tim Vizard | Tom Fearfull

It is at all times necessary, and more particularly so during the progress of a revolution and until right ideas confirm themselves by habit, that we frequently refresh our patriotism by reference to first principles.

Thomas Paine

The Jeffersonian theory that "the Earth belongs to the Living" was both the philosophical and the economic summation of the Revolutionary ideal. The ending of the feudal inheritance code was seen as the logical extension of the Spirit of '76 into economics. If (wo)-man was born free and equal, then why should society artificially award a few with unearned wealth? Insofar as possible, the economy should be arranged to put everyone at birth on an equal footing. Talent and industry rather than the names of one's parents should be the vehicles of success.

In reaction to the destruction of the aristocratic inheritance laws, the wealthy part of the citizenry devised a new legal form for controlling the riches of the republic: the corporation. Radical democrats saw the corporation as a new guise for the ancient feudal code, and they fought it bitterly. The Workingmen's Party of New York resolved in 1829:

> Hereditary transmission of wealth on the one hand, and of poverty on the other, has brought down to the present generation all of the evils of the feudal system, and that, in our opinion, is the prime source of all our calamities.

Corporation charters were ruled by the Supreme Court to be perpetual, which is to say that legislatures, having created them, could never uncreate them. Like the great estates of pre-Revolutionary days, they were above ordinary law. The Equal Rights Party's Declaration of Rights (1836) denounced this new arrangement:

> We declare our hostility to the dangerous and unconstitutional creation of vested rights by legislation. All acts of incorporation passed by one legislature can be rightfully altered or repealed by its successors.

The working-class Equal Rights Party based its argument upon the position of Jefferson, who had written in 1816: "I hope we shall crush in its birth the aristocracy of our monied corporations, which dare already to challenge our government to a trial of strength, and bid defiance to the laws of our country."

Working people, demonstrating against the "creation of vested rights by legislation," carried banners proclaiming THE EARTH BELONGS TO THE LIVING. The Equal Rights Party statement in 1837 complained:

> . . . that the working classes of modern times are kept in debasement and poverty. Aristocrats have discovered that charters are safer weapons than swords, and that cant, falsehood and hypocrisy serve all the purposes of a Highwayman's pistol, while they leave their victims alive and fit for future exactions . . . Here as elsewhere, Man is the slave of Money. Law rules the poor and Money rules the Law.

Ralph Waldo Emerson, very much in the mainstream of American thought, sneered at inherited wealth in his "Essay on Self Reliance":

> A cultivated man becomes ashamed of his property out of a new respect for his nature. Especially he hates what he has, if he sees that it is accidental—come to him by inheritance, or gift, or crime; then he feels that it

is not worth having; it does not belong to him, has no root in him, and merely lies there because no revolution or robber takes it away.

Expressing the deep American tradition that privilege should not be passed from generation to generation, successive waves of reform movements attacked the glaring inequity of inherited corporate wealth and power. The inheritance tax was invented as a method of impeding the transmission of unearned wealth. Theodore Roosevelt's Progressive (Bull Moose) Party of 1912 declared:

We believe in a graduated inheritance tax as a national means of equalizing the holders of property.

Senator George Norris of Nebraska thought the great corporate holdings were simply the aristocratic system in disguise. Since that system was illegal, and had been since the Revolution, it should not be tolerated.

The U.S. Commission on Industrial Relations Report of 1915 pointed out that inheritance of great wealth is not an American doctrine and that it came from the English code, the avowed purpose of which was the support of a privileged nobility.

While vast inherited fortunes, representing zero in social service to the credit of their possessors, automatically treble and multiply in volume, two-thirds of those who toil from eight to twelve hours a day receive less than enough to support themselves in decency and comfort.

AFTER HEARING THE NEWS OF THE DECLARATION OF INDEPENDENCE, NEW YORK PATRIOTS PULLED DOWN GILT-COVERED LEADEN STATUE OF KING GEORGE. THE GOLD COVERING WAS USED TO HELP FINANCE THE REVOLUTIONARY EFFORT; THE LEAD WAS MELTED INTO BULLETS FOR USE AGAINST THE KING'S TROOPS

During the Depression of the 1930's, pressure for action against inherited wealth grew. President Roosevelt, responding to public opinion, told the Congress in 1935:

The transmission from generation to generation of vast fortunes by will, inheritance or gift is not consistent with the focus and sentiments of the American people.

English

WORDS AND TERMS TO DISCUSS:

- aristocracy
- monarchy
- republicanism
- inalienable rights
- natural rights
- tory
- patriot
- despotism
- tyranny
- arbitrary power
- liberty
- freedom
- common sense
- revolution
- the rights of man
- self-evident truths

DISCUSSION:

What part did literature and the writer play in the American Revolution? Read Thomas Paine's *Common Sense,* Thomas Jefferson's Declaration of Independence. Examine the life of the poet Philip Freneau.

TO CELEBRATE JULY 4TH, BOSTON'S PATRIOTS REMOVE KING'S COAT OF ARMS AND BURN IT IN THE STREET

Sociology

Sociology is a relatively new discipline in America, but it is closely aligned with democratic principles. To make an open and critical analysis of contemporary society requires complete freedom to investigate all aspects of social experience. But sociology does not stop with investigation—its role is to identify social problems and injustices and attempt to correct them. It is an activist's discipline. Sociologists must be willing to take risks in their efforts to identify and alleviate the many problems confronting our society today.

In the classroom, it is necessary for teachers to make students aware of this unique role sociology plays, and to offer students the opportunity to be critics of society and social activists. The most basic classical sociological concepts can be made relevant to students when discussed in terms of the founding principles of this country and how these principles are acted out today. Stratification, bureaucracy, social change, race relations, ecology are some of the issues that the early patriots confronted. A historical perspective can only increase our understanding of contemporary society.

PROJECTS:

1. Do a comparative study of how the Founding Fathers viewed one or more of these social issues (or any of the numerous others not mentioned) and how contemporary sociologists analyze the same issues. How have historical changes over the last two hundred years affected our criticisms? Which problems have been alleviated and which have grown worse?

2. Suggest that students investigate the Sociology Department at your school to analyze how completely the teachers are living up to their role as critics of society. If any teachers disapprove of this sort of project, ask them why they are sociologists.

French

The destinies of America and France were closely intertwined in the 18th century. The Marquis de Lafayette and the Baron de Kalb were among the beloved heroes of the war against King George. De Kalb was killed in battle, covering a retreat; his last words were "I die the death I always prayed for—the death of a soldier fighting for the Rights of Man."

Lafayette participated in the French Revolution and later, as an old man, visited the United States to receive one of the most splendid welcomes in American history. He was made an honorary American citizen.

The French king sent troops to aid the Yankee rebels, and it was those troops who finally defeated the British. But the spirit of revolution the king aided in the New World soon spread to the Old World and toppled King Louis from his throne.

A REVOLUTIONARY SOLDIER

Working people in America and France admired and supported each other's Revolutions. One of the great figures of the French movement was Jean Paul Marat, publisher of a radical paper called *L'Ami du Peuple* (The Friend of the People). Marat himself, idolized by the poor people of France, was called the Friend of the People. He was frequently pursued by the authorities because of his attacks on corruption, and once was forced to hide in the Paris sewers.

Marat was also revered by working people in America. When Thomas Jefferson became the leader of the democratic movement, he too was honored with the title "The Friend of the People." When the great populist William Jennings Bryan won the Democratic Presidential nomination in 1896, someone among a small group watching the ticker-tape report at a conservative newspaper is said to have shouted, "Marat, Marat has won!!"

ACTIVITY:

Learn the songs of the French Revolution, including "Ça Ira." They were also the songs of the democratic movement in America. By singing these songs, classes will learn both French and American history as they learn the French language.

Geography

In 1787, Noah Webster asked himself and his readers, "In what does real power consist? The answer," he continued, "is short and plain—in property."

Not only Webster, but James Madison and others based their ideas about the political structure of the new nation on the principle that power and property were synonomous. Property meant wealth: it included land, money, paper securities, factories, ships and slaves.

Those of the Founding Fathers who wanted America to be a new kind of society in which the great majority could be happy felt that the only way was to ensure that property was as widely distributed as possible. Wealth had to be dispersed among as many citizens as possible: otherwise there could not be a "republic" in the sense in which the radical Fathers and Mothers used the word. A society composed of small farmers and artisans meant a wide distribution of property and therefore of political power. The people could then guard their rights and liberties.

If we wish to determine how close we are to the ideal "republic" that the Founding Fathers and Mothers envisioned, we must know something about the distribution of property. While land ownership is only one aspect of property, we may learn a good deal about a society from it.

Geography

ACTIVITY:

Draw a map of your community and investigate the types of ownership to be found in it. Color each species of property differently:

1. Houses owned by the people who live in them
2. Houses and buildings owned by landlords (Find out who the *big* landlords are and trace their holdings.)
3. Corporation property (Who owns the corporations?)
4. Federal property (Which part of the federal government? What for?)
5. State property
6. City or county property
7. Owned by public-utility companies

When the map is completed, find the oldest available maps of your area, or of other areas. Compare the two geographic entities. If, as James Madison and Noah Webster insisted, "power follows property," your map represents the real "constitution" of your community.

History

> Every child should be acquainted with his own country. He should read books that furnish him with ideas that will be useful to him in life and practice. As soon as he opens his lips, he should rehearse the history of his own country. He should lisp the praises of liberty and of those illustrious heroes and statesmen who have wrought a revolution in his favor.
>
> —NOAH WEBSTER

Law

THE DUTY OF GRAND JURORS

> We who are returned by the several towns in this county to serve as grand jurors at the superior court . . . being actuated by a zealous regard for peace and good order, and a sincere desire to promote justice, righteousness and good government, as essential to the happiness of the community, would now gladly proceed to the discharge of the important duty required . . . could we persuade ourselves that doing this would *add* to our own reputation or to promote the welfare of our country . . . [but] we believe in our consciences that our acting in concert with a court so constituted and under such cir-

cumstances would be betraying the just and sacred rights of our native land—which were not the gift of kings but were purchased solely with the toil, the blood and treasure of our worthy and revered ancestors, and which we look upon ourselves under the most sacred obligations to maintain and to transmit whole and entire to our posterity;

Therefore, we unanimously decline serving as grand jurors to this court.

—STATEMENT SIGNED BY TWENTY-TWO BOSTONIANS, INCLUDING PAUL REVERE, AUGUST 30, 1774

In 1787, Thomas Jefferson wrote to James Madison to tell him of an exciting idea that had come to him. He had combed the writings of all the great thinkers and discovered that no one had said it before: The Earth belongs to the Living, and the dead have neither rights nor powers over it.

From this simple axiom, he proposed a Revolutionary principle: laws should expire when half the generation alive at their enactment were dead. After a few actuarial estimates, he settled on the period of twenty years.

The idea was dismissed, as Jefferson predicted it would be, "as the dream of a philosopher."

PROJECTS AND QUESTIONS:

- Examine federal, state and local laws. How many were passed by a dead generation? What is the effect of these laws?
- Estimate the costs of enforcing ancient laws. Conduct a survey, asking citizens how they feel about their contributions to enforcement of these laws. If they were asked to donate money for that purpose, would they do so?
- Construct a model of a system that allows laws to expire, or requires them to be repassed, after twenty years. Include review and evaluation procedures so that the system functions smoothly.

Music

Several years ago, the musical group The Fifth Dimension put the Declaration of Independence to music. Student musicians may find more good lyrics in the words and deeds of the Founding Fathers and Mothers. (Those who would like to submit their songs for possi-

THE DECLARATION OF INDEPENDENCE IS CELEBRATED BY SOLDIERS AT NEWPORT, RHODE ISLAND

ble broadcast on some six hundred radio stations in the United States may submit sheet music or tapes to the Bicentennial Network, in care of the Peoples Bicentennial Commission.) Such musical compositions can also be used for school and community events. Half times at sports events might be turned into celebrations of the Revolutionary heritage and the Revolutionary dream with the help of music students.

More Music

The movement for human rights that began in America was felt in Germany, where Ludwig van Beethoven composed a Revolutionary symphony to celebrate the new spirit; the *Eroica* Symphony broke with older musical tradition and began a new era of music. Schiller composed an Ode to Freedom but had to change Freedom (*Freiheit*) to Joy (*Freude*) in order to get it past the authorities. Beethoven later turned Schiller's Ode to Joy into powerful symphonic music (the fourth movement of Beethoven's *Ninth*).

Play the *Eroica* for your class. Ask the students to compare the movements; many admirers of Beethoven have heard in them a profound statement of radical change.

There are several short, popular versions of the Ode to Joy. They will help students understand the spirit of the massive 18th-century Revolutionary movement which began with the Declaration of Independence.

Philosophy

The founders of modern democracy believed in the theory of natural (i.e., inherent and inalienable) rights. Many critics have considered this concept naive. When Vice President Agnew first saw the inscription above the entrance to the Justice Department which begins JUSTICE IS FOUNDED IN THE RIGHTS BESTOWED BY NATURE UPON MAN, he took issue with this ancient theory and presented an alternative view:

> I do not believe the first sentence is true. It is only when society acknowledges it as a right and backs it by the power of the state and the respect of a majority of its *responsible* citizens that the right exists.

Two centuries ago, debates raged over the origin of human rights. Thomas Paine dismissed the arguments:

> Why not trace the rights of man to the creation of man? I will answer the question. Because there have been upstart governments thrusting themselves between and presumptuously working to *unmake* man.

ACTIVITIES AND QUESTIONS:

At the 1952 convention of the American Philosophical Society, whose early leaders included Ben Franklin

(the founder), Thomas Jefferson and David Rittenhouse, a scholar posed the following questions, which will help to open discussion of the natural-rights theory:

- When people discourse on human rights, what light does such discussion throw upon the discussants? This, I submit, is a significant question even if there are no human rights. Even outside the field of ethics, we often find more information about the speaker than about the object of his discourse . . .

- What ethical implications follow logically from the assertion or denial of any given human rights?
- What sort of evidence can establish a human right?
- Are there any human rights, and if so, what are they?
- The founders made a distinction between natural, inalienable rights and civil rights. The former were absolute, the latter intended to secure the former. Is such a distinction reasonable?
- Consider various rights. Is there an order to these rights?
- Can rights be divided in classes? Arranged hierarchically?
- What about privileges? What is the relationship between privilege and right?

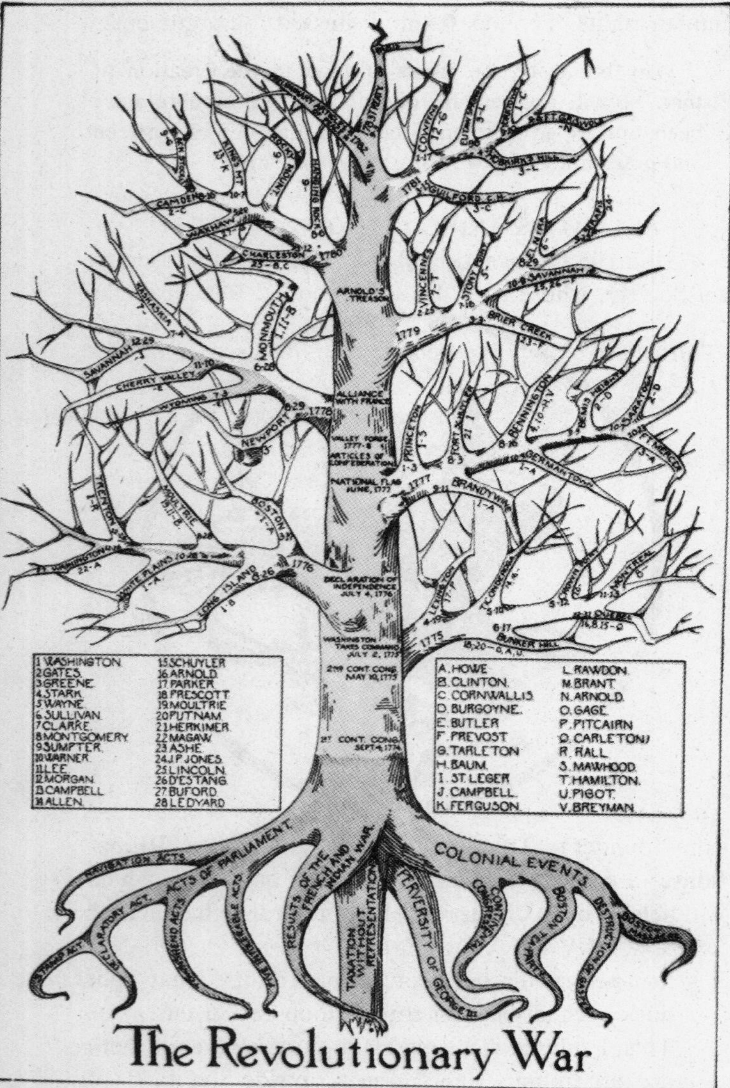

The Revolutionary War

Political Science

Q: *What is man in a state of nature, without society?*
A: A weak, helpless, feeble, unprotected animal . . . Hence the necessity and utility of a state of society.

Q: *What is society?*
A: Society is a natural or voluntary combination of individuals together to comfort, assist, strengthen and support each other. Natural society is that into which we are born, as into families, which families belong to communities, etc. But voluntary society is that into which persons enter by their own choice, as into the state of marriage.

Q: *What are the natural and inalienable rights of man?*
A: Life, liberty and the pursuit of happiness, and several others which ought always to be reserved in the hands of the people and ought not to be delegated.

Q: *What then shall we think of those who would wish to keep youth, and the common people in general, from the knowledge of their rights?*
A: The same as we justly think of those blind guides of former ages, who kept the common people from reading the Scriptures.

Q: *What is the great secret of government?*
A: Not to govern too much.

—ELHANAN WINCHESTER
"A Plain Political Catechism," 1796

These questions and answers from an 18th-century civics textbook represent part of the basic political theory the American democrats believed in.

The founders of modern democracy had little patience with abstract theories of government. Tom Paine scoffed at the idea of dividing political thought into a few theoretical "systems," saying that a thousand systems could be conceived of as well as two or three.

During the agitation that led to the overthrow of monarchical government, street orators and radical preachers reiterated the word Happiness again and again. When Happiness replaced the standard gentleman's word Property in the Declaration of Independence, it had become second nature to Americans. Jefferson insisted that happiness is the only legitimate end of government.

PROJECT: STUDY AN INSTITUTION IN LIGHT OF

1. The purpose of government as understood by the founders.

WE CALL IT MIDTOWN MANHATTAN NOW, BUT IN THE 1770'S WASHINGTON AND HIS MEN KNEW IT AS THE SITE OF THE BATTLE OF HARLEM HEIGHTS

2. The announced goals of the institution.
3. The actual operation of the institution.

Compare the three. Are they identical? If not, where and why do they diverge?

QUESTIONS TO ASK PUBLIC SERVANTS:

- How do they see themselves functioning as "instruments of human happiness"?
- In their decision-making, how do they move from the purpose of their work (happiness) to the practical matters of their work?

QUESTIONS TO DISCUSS:

- Are there any institutions that do not serve the goals of government?
- If so, why not?
- What is the responsibility of the citizen toward these institutions?
- What does such an institutional failing say about the political process through which the institution was created and is sustained?
- What is needed to repair the flaw in the process?

ROTC

In 1768, Sam Adams wrote, "It is a very improbable supposition, that any people can long remain free, with a strong military power in the heart of their country; unless that military power is under the direction of the people, and even then it is dangerous."

Distrust of the military was a common feeling in the Thirteen Colonies—especially in Boston, where the King's troops were stationed against the wishes of the people. To avoid the dangers of an army, like the British Army, run by a few professionals and unpopular among the citizens, patriots organized Colonial militias. Unlike the soldiers of the British Army, the men who joined the militia did so because they believed it was the best way to protect their rights and freedom. In the militia, the officers were elected by their men, most of whom were their friends and neighbors. If an officer gave unpopular or unfair orders, his men could vote him out of office. Further, all received the same pay, and if an officer was given more than his men, he divided the difference equally among his troops. In the 1770's this equality among officers and enlisted men was called "levelling," because it made everyone's status, rights and privileges the same.

When the militia went into battle, one general remarked, they "carry the spirit of freedom into the field, and think for themselves." Baron von Steuben noted the contrast between American and European troops. In Europe, he recalled, an officer said to a private, "Do this; and he doeth it." In America, one had to say, "This is the reason why you ought to do that; and then he does it." It was because of such a spirit that Lyman Beecher remarked in the 1840's, "The militia was our only safeguard . . . it was the people, spread over the land, armed and organized for defense."

ACTIVITIES AND QUESTIONS FOR DISCUSSION:

1. Restructure your class or unit according to the principles of 1776.
2. Examine the military today. Is it organized in the same way that the Colonial army was?
3. Could America today develop a democratic military service? What might happen if soldiers elected their officers?
4. Is it important for soldiers to believe in the principles for which they are fighting—as they did in the Revolution? As a class project, study how the military service today explains the principles of the nation to its soldiers.

BEN RUSH—DOCTOR, FOUNDER OF AMERICA'S FIRST ANTI-SLAVERY SOCIETY, SIGNER OF THE DECLARATION OF INDEPENDENCE

Science

The scientific background of the founding radicals is mirrored in their attitude toward science. Jefferson wrote:

> I am for encouraging the progress of science in all its branches, and not for raising a hue and cry against the sacred name of philosophy, for awing the human mind by stories of raw head and bloody bones to a distrust of its own vision, and to repose implicity on that of others—to go backwards instead of forwards for improvement, to believe that government, morality and every other science were in the highest perfection in ages of the darkest ignorance.

But Jefferson also said:

> If science produces no better fruits than tyranny, murder, rapine and destitution of national morality, I would rather wish our country to be ignorant.

ACTIVITIES:

Explain your own view of the purpose of science to your classes and find out those of your students. Invite scientists to discuss the role of science in the community, in America and in the world.

> Is reason to be forever amused with the physical sciences, in which she indulged merely to divert her from solid speculations on the rights of man and wrongs of his oppressors? It is impossible. The day of deliverance will come, although I will not live to see it.
>
> —THOMAS JEFFERSON

DISCUSSION:

Has science made the "solid speculations on the rights of man" Jefferson demanded? Should it?

If the choice is between "tyranny, murder and rapine" on the one hand and ignorance of science on the other, which is preferable?

Evaluate the role of science in America according to the principles of Thomas Jefferson. What would he think about the role of science today?

Journalism—The Fourth of July

In the years after the defeat of the British, conservative gentlemen of wealth and power detested the Fourth of July. They proposed that Washington's Birthday and Columbus Day be celebrated so that the "glorious Fourth," as the working people called it, would not get so much attention. Federalist leader Joseph Dennie referred to the Fourth as the "unlucky day," and Fisher Ames, one of the leading Federalist writers, opposed its celebration. Alexander Hamilton, the intellectual leader and principal figure of the wealthy Federalist coalition, insisted that the American Revolution was a special kind of revolution—"grave, decorous, orderly, and dignified"—as opposed to the "rabble-controlled" French Revolution.

But the democratic-republican societies of small farmers and working people considered their Revolution and the Revolution in France one and the same. On the Fourth of July, the democrats put on their Liberty Caps, danced around the Liberty Pole and sang Revolutionary songs.

There were toasts drunk to the Revolution in America and in the Old World. The working people of Rutland, Vermont, drank to the toast "May the plebeians of the eastern states awake!" The Democratic Societies of New York and Philadelphia observed the Fourth of July by visiting prisoners who could not pay their debts or fines and donated money to help them gain their freedom.

ACTIVITY:

Find old Fourth of July speeches and examine them. How have they changed over the years? Do they seem closer to the spirit of the democratic societies or to that of Alexander Hamilton and the Federalists? Ask your students to discuss them, and compare them with recent ones—i.e., Nixon's 1971 July Fourth speech.

ACTIVITY:

Find old Fourth of July editorials. Have they changed? If so, is there any apparent relationship between the tone of the editorials and the events of their times? For instance, did editorials during the Palmer raids of the 1920's and the McCarthy era of the 1950's follow similar lines? Have students discuss them.

Invite journalists and publishers to discuss changes in the messages conveyed on the Fourth of July. How did their own publications or stations see the Declaration of Independence from year to year?

ACTIVITY:

Plan a Fourth of July celebration with your students.

The Liberty Tree

The Liberty Tree was a universally recognized symbol of the Revolution of 1776. It signified traditional freedoms won by the ancestors of the Colonists in bitter struggles, which, to be kept, had to be jealously guarded and nourished. It was a living, growing thing, not a concrete accomplishment. It had to grow and mature, or it would wither and die. The fate of the Liberty Tree depended upon the will of Americans to be free of despotism.

The Tree was decorated on special occasions, such as the repeal of the Stamp Act in 1765. A veteran recalled that occasion:

> Such a day has not been seen in Boston before or since. The bells of Doctor Byle's Church began the tune at one in the morning. The chime in Christ Church made response. The steeples were hung with flags. Liberty Tree was adorned all day with banners and illuminated in the evening, till the boughs could hold no more. Music was heard in the streets before daybreak. Subscriptions were raised to release those who were in jail for debt from confinement. The country people came in by thousands. The whole town was splendidly illuminated. The Common was covered with multitudes. Rockets, beehives and serpents blazed in every quarter. And to crown all, a magnificent pyramid was erected which shone with the blaze of about 300 lamps.

The Liberty Cap

Another Revolutionary symbol of the 18th century was the Liberty Cap, a pointed red garment of coarse wool. It was depicted on the reverse side of the seal Jefferson offered as the national symbol, and was worn by radicals in the American Revolution. Later it traveled to France and became widely recognized as the symbol of the French Revolution. During the 1790's, working people wore it to show sympathy with the French, and decorated it with the Tricolor cockade. Joel Barlow, a democratic poet, traced the tradition of the Liberty Cap to ancient Rome, where it had been worn by freed slaves.

The Liberty Pole

If a town in 1776 had a Liberty Pole in its square or common, it was a sign that the residents had gone over

PATRIOTS ERECT LIBERTY POLE, TO THE HORROR OF WEALTHY TORIES (LEFT FOREGROUND)

to the Revolution and that Tories were unwelcome—and unsafe. Putting up a Liberty Pole was a deeply felt symbol of Liberation.

ACTIVITY:

Ask students to plant a Liberty Tree or erect their own Liberty Pole. Make it a place for students to gather and discuss their own and the community's rights and liberties.

Colleges and the Bicentennial

COLLEGE OVERVIEW

> [Education must] not be left to the caprice, or negligence of parents, to chance, or confined to the children of wealthy citizens; it is shame, a scandal to civilized society, that part only of the citizens should be sent to colleges and universities to learn to cheat the rest of their liberties.
>
> —ROBERT CORAM, 1791

While young people between six and sixteen years are compelled by law to attend primary and secondary school, matters are different with higher education. College in America is not a right, it is a privilege—a privilege available to those with high I.Q.'s, high grades, the right social background and, of course, the money to afford tuition, books, board and room.

Because universities are available to the more privileged in America, there are two basic aspects to the condition of college students:

1. College students are not being trained merely to fit neatly into society, as mandatory education trains younger students. They are being trained to move into positions of power, wealth and influence in the corporate/government sphere. Assuming roles of "responsibility" educators call it; learning "to cheat the rest of their liberties" Coram branded it in 1791. (The university also holds positions of "responsibility" in society—it accepts defense contracts, bestows honorary degrees on corporate leaders and often disrupts the local community with unilateral decisions as to how it uses its land.)

2. Because college is not available to all, because it costs money beyond the school taxes all pay and because each college and university, to enhance its prestige, is competing for first-class students and their money, colleges cannot be as blatantly oppressive of the basic human freedoms of students as can high schools. After all, high school students have no choice—they have to take what the administration dishes out or risk punishment. College students, on the other hand, are quite free to drop out or transfer to other schools.

These two points determine the philosophy of administrators. In many colleges it is quite liberal—dope smoking and premarital sex in dorm rooms are overlooked; cafeterias carry health foods; students can take "incompletes" in courses and turn in their work as much as a year late and still receive credit. If the philosophy and strategy of high school administrators is built around outright repression of students, the cornerstone of a college administrator's philosophy is pacification.

Where Matters Stand Today

There is little "action" on campuses today. What activity there is usually revolves around the softball diamond, the beer hall and the library.

Some call the mood "apathy." But from where does apathy, after a decade of student protest, arise? It's a complex question. For one thing, the national economy is in such bad shape that college students are seriously worried about their futures, as they were not in the 60's. Liberal reforms in colleges, which satisfied many stu-

dent demands without getting to the heart of the issues of democracy and power, pacified many people. And then there was the war: overt military activity is no longer waged by the United States in Indochina, and the draft has been abolished. But much of the reason for the present conditions on campuses lies in the failures of the student movement of the 1960's.

In the 1960's, hundreds of thousands of students participated in demonstrations, teach-ins, strikes, riots and take-overs of buildings. In the 1970's, those hundreds of thousands have seemingly left the movement. What happened?

- *Rhetoric*. Much of the rhetoric used in the last ten years by organizers was inappropriate to the reality of the situation on campuses. In attempts to be "militant" and "revolutionary," rhetoric was often misused. Many who desired social change turned away from politics because they could not penetrate the rhetoric to hear the message. In short, many students who might have sympathized with the just goals of the student movement were justifiably frightened off by a "more militant than thou" attitude on the part of some organizers.
- *Organizing*. As activists organized during the 1960's, they found themselves more and more setting forth a foreign culture and struggle—the Vietnamese—as a model for the actions of Americans. The problem that arose from this, as became evident in the early 70's, was, first, that people began to fall away rapidly from the movement as the end of overt warfare clouded the issues involved in Indochina. Secondly, it became increasingly evident that people are not successfully involved on a long-term basis around only the oppression that is imposed on another people. While working to support the struggles for freedom and independence of others, Americans must also have a clear understanding of how those struggles relate to their own demands and battles waged in this country. Our attempts at educating people around this concept were only secondary to the issue of peace. As peace seemingly came, protest ground to a halt.
- *Roots*. Coupled with the organizing done around the war in Indochina was a denial of our own radical democratic roots. Time and again, organizers decried America as representing the worst of everything. Forgotten was the revolutionary strain that has run throughout our history: a strain that we can aim to reaffirm in our lives today; a strain that is common to all of our lives, as the cultures of other countries are not.
- *Apocalypse*. During the 60's, the visions and goals of the movement were generally set forth in apocalyptic terms. Each demonstration was the one that would finally end the war. Each action was the "last" one that would be tried, because either it would win this time, or else it would prove that nothing at all could work. When the visions of ultimate victory couldn't be fulfilled, many people lost confidence in their ability to bring about change. Overwhelmed by the visions, organizers forgot that small victories were nonetheless true victories, even though they did not produce the ultimate goal.

FORTIFYING BREED'S HILL IN THE NIGHT, JUNE 16, 1775

- *Patience.* America is a society of instants. Add water to powder, and you have instant milk. Put a TV dinner in the oven for a half hour, and you have an instant meal. Social change has been viewed in the same way. Forgotten was the truth that revolution is a long-term process. Ten years of organizing in America seemed to many like an ultimate commitment of one's time and effort, but in historical terms of working for change, it is but a moment. People forgot patience: patience to understand that many years of work may be necessary—coupled with an understanding that the moment for great change may come at any time, and should always be anticipated.
- *Infighting.* The 60's showed that any group that claims to have the *only* correct formula for change and analysis of the problems of society is doomed to failure. Political infighting reached such a plateau that many people finally concluded that *all* political groups were equally absurd and manipulative. How many people just gave up in the face of meeting after meeting of ranting and raving and dumping on other groups?

Combating Apathy

"Apathy," the dictionary explains, is "calmness, immobility, lethargy, unconcern." But it is not unchangeable. "Nothing is unchangeable," wrote Thomas Jefferson, "but the inherent and inalienable rights" of humankind.

To reaffirm our Revolutionary heritage, we must rekindle the energy and commitment Americans have displayed in the past. In fighting unconcern, we would do well to keep in mind the dictionary-defined antonyms of apathy—"agitation, disturbance, excitement, turbulence." This is the first job of any campus Bicentennial movement—to begin setting a climate of excitement; to establish a presence of visible agitation; to replace calmness with constructive turbulence in the best American tradition.

There are a number of procedures that activists can follow to begin their organizing efforts. Too often, we forget the obvious and become overinvolved in our concentration on dealing with bureaucracies like student government, the board of regents and the office of the college president. The best way to start is by working on those programs and goals that are most easily reached. Once you've established a base, you can then proceed to tackle the major issues central to your university and its role in society.

The first step you should take is the setting up of your own Peoples Bicentennial Commission. Establishing a PBC on your campus will help your efforts in a number of ways. Primarily, of course, a PBC will be an organization that can give some structure to your work. Meeting as a group, members of a Peoples Bicentennial Commission will be able to discuss the philosophy of America's radical democratic movements, past and present, as well as important political questions and strategy. It will also be something visible that students who become interested in organizing can join. Something concrete, like an established campus Peoples Bicentennial Commission with committed and visible members, brings an important air of reality to your organizing efforts. After all, students are bombarded with theories in their classes, so why should they be interested in another theory taking up their spare time?

Building a campus Bicentennial Commission also gives a sense of movement, energy and growth. Many other campuses around the country are establishing PBC's. While all around us analysts are claiming that the movement for social justice is dead in this country, it is important to give people a feeling that this is far from the case; that in fact, students in every state, in every city, are organizing and working toward the same goals. Imagine how powerful an entire network of campus Peoples Bicentennial Commissions could make students feel by 1976!

Forming your own Commission will also give you visibility in another crucial sense. As millions of Americans are made aware of the big-business/White House propaganda campaign, the Bicentennial as a major political and social focal point of the 70's will become apparent. As students understand the corrupt and manipulative nature of the "official" plans, they will turn toward something that is constructive and in keeping with the true message of 1776. A Peoples Bicentennial Commission provides this meaningful alternative.

INDEPENDENCE HALL, PHILADELPHIA, ON THE EVE OF JULY 4TH, 1776

UTILIZING THE MEDIA

In the years leading up to the Revolution, people like Sam Adams and Tom Paine worked at spreading the concept of democracy. Most people of the time thought that divine rule by the King was the natural order of the world. Talk of democracy was so revolutionary that folks who spoke against the established order were often punished by banishment, whippings, tongue borings and even death.

But the "propagandists," as they were called, persisted in popularizing the subversive theory. As a result of Adams' work, for instance, the ministers of New England's churches preached the Revolutionary message from the pulpit. Newspapers sprang up, like *The Massachusetts Spy,* which bore the epigraph (and the political outlook to back it up): "Do thou Great Liberty inspire our Souls—And make our Lives in Thy Possession happy—Or, our Deaths glorious in Thy just Defence." At universities, like Harvard and Yale, students debated topics of democracy:

- Is civil government originally founded on the consent of the people?
- Is an absolute and arbitrary monarchy contrary to reason?
- Is civil government more favorable to human liberty than a liberty free from any legal restriction?

In short, the Revolutionaries of 1776 raised their message in every public forum available. Every institution was subjected to the constant challenge of the radical agitators of the period.

We would do well to learn from the efforts of the Sam Adamses and Tom Paines of the Revolution. After all, they were successful. A campus Peoples Bicentennial Commission should begin the constant challenging of the university by using the public forums of today—campus radio, newspaper, yearbook, video. Successful organizers, as the patriots proved, don't have to go hunting for crises. What's of prime importance is simply the continual spreading of the Revolutionary message of democracy.

When people come to understand the message, they will be able to recognize the institutions and people who stray from the democratic tradition. And like the Americans of 1776, the people will act.

Campus Radio

Radio is a major source of entertainment for college students. A PBC member might, for instance, work with the student news program. Instead of a rehash of the ABC/CBS/NBC commercial news, you could present news using the language and imagery of the Revolution. When ITT commits its newest payoff to a government official or agency, you could report it as a Tory social note, while someone who has done something particularly beneficial for the people could be given the Patriots Award. You might even try distilling several news stories of the day into a magazine news format that avoids heavy rhetoric and analysis, but ties in the undemocratic plans of government and business.

Or you might want to work on a political rock show that plays music with a progressive message, instead of the sexist commercial rock we so often hear. Make it clear on your show that being young doesn't mean you're necessarily any better than a fifty-five-year-old corporate executive. Expose so-called artists who charge outrageous prices for concerts and never use their talents to benefit anybody but themselves and their own hip jet-set habits.

You can also use the campus radio to get out programs on the Bicentennial and America's past. You might, for instance, work with some friends to come up with a series of radio dramas from the American legacy. In the 1930's and 40's, radio drama shows were the most important form of entertainment for tens of millions of Americans. Most of us have grown up without ever hearing a radio drama—complete with sound effects, music and dramatic and humorous dialogue.

Radio dramas could concentrate on events or themes from the American Revolution and other periods of American history that deal with economic, political or moral considerations that are still relevant to Americans today. Immediately after airing the presentations, the local radio station could have a guest panel discuss the historical and contemporary relevance of the event or theme under examination, and/or invite listener call-ins on the subject. Discussion topics and questions should accompany each program.

Campus Newspaper

Another campus institution that can certainly use some "excitement and turbulence" is the school newspaper. In college, school papers are usually pretty free to print what they want, yet most of the articles are less interesting than the average copy of *Reader's Digest*.

Spicing up your school paper should be fairly easy. One of the most neglected, yet creative and enjoyable, journalistic devices is the satirical/editorial column. This style of writing can get across important political messages without the use of boring rhetoric, or super-serious analysis that most students find about as enthralling as their textbooks.

There's also always plenty of room for good old-fashioned reporting—especially some in-depth investigative journalism about different aspects of your university and community. Nothing interests readers like a well-documented and previously unknown scandal. Don't be intimidated if you have never tried any sleuthing like this before; the two newsmen for *The Washington Post* who broke the Watergate scandal, and subsequently won the Pulitzer Prize for their investigative journalism, were just two young reporters assigned to the City Desk who covered only local Washington, D.C., issues. The Watergate was their first try at looking into political espionage!

One campus issue you should research and report on is your school's tie-in with "official" Bicentennial plans. In the schemes of the White House and big business, America's colleges and universities are to have a big part in the festivities. It's just possible that your school

has been given a large sum of money to initiate some kind of Tory spectacular in 1976. Look into it.

Student Activities Board

The Student Activities Board is a little-noticed but highly influential campus group. Not only is it in charge of bringing entertainment and speakers to campus, but it has access to plenty of university money to do it. This is probably *the* most important campus organization to have some influence on. By taking part in the Board's decision-making, you can, of course, get speakers on campus who have vital political messages that you would like students to hear. You can ensure that entertainers who are really responsive to their audience, and who use their visibility as artists to speak and sing out for justice and freedom, are brought onto campus. In many states, local political theater groups are touring with plays about the radical heritage of their areas. By being on the Activities Board, you can promote these groups —they will get much-needed, and deserved, money to continue their work, and your PBC will be helped in getting out the message of the country's Revolutionary heritage.

On a larger scale, you can push the SAB to sponsor an entire week of events each semester. With the two-hundredth birthday of the country coming up, for instance, an entire "Bicentennial" week could be set up in 1974, '75, and '76. (Many campuses, in fact, are already considering this.) Speakers on radical democratic history, the women's movement, labor and Third World struggles in this country could be invited. Seminars might be conducted involving both well-known authorities and people from the community who have lived through and experienced important events at first hand—the suffrage movement, civil rights, the labor movement, antiwar demonstrations, the Depression, the McCarthy witch-hunts. Folk, bluegrass and jazz musicians could play little-heard native American music, and street theater, old-time celebrations and fairs could be held on the campus main lawn.

Yearbook

The yearbook is an element of campus life that activists usually ignore. It's not as important and immediate as some of the other university institutions, but it does represent something that stays with graduates most of their lives, and it's from the yearbook that ex-students remember what their college years were like. When students who went to college during the late 60's and early 70's look through their yearbooks, they'll probably find scenes of Vietnam, campus protest and police riots. One yearbook of the period, for instance, scattered a

THE STAMP ACT PROTEST

picture of a napalmed Vietnamese baby throughout the formal portraits of the members of the graduating class. There's not much doubt that students from that university will remember more than dating and classes when they look through their senior yearbook.

With the Bicentennial upon us, you might try giving the yearbook the general theme of the upcoming two-hundredth anniversary by using line cuts (like the ones in this book), old photographs from your campus' past, quotations from the Founding Fathers and Mothers that might serve to guide the graduating class, etc. A yearbook with that kind of tone will not only remind graduates what their college years were all about, but also point out to returning students that an event of importance—to take part in, not watch from the sidelines—is occurring during this period.

Video

If your school has a video center, you should consider working with the people there. Videotape has all kinds of possibilities. It can be used to conduct interviews with students that can be compiled to show what students on your campus think about the college and society. Events and speakers can be taped for future use. You can present a videotape in place of the usual term paper for courses like Sociology, Political Science and History. Or you might want to go further by adapting a radio drama to a form suitable for videotape. Such a program could be used as a teaching aid in classrooms, lent out to community organizations or shown in conjunction with other films your PBC might sponsor on campus.

Film Festivals

Beyond working with established media organizations and departments on campus, there are a number of other activities a campus PBC could launch to establish an initial presence. Campus film festivals, for instance, are always popular at colleges. There are a number of good films available from political cinema organizations. You might also consider renting commercial films—some of the older ones are quite inexpensive. Showing an old John Wayne or Ronald Reagan Western might stimulate a discussion about the misrepresentation of America's past. People in your art department are sure to have catalogs listing commercial and underground films that are available.

If you have good relations with a number of professors on campus (as you must, if you hope to succeed), you might arrange with them to put on a Peoples Film Festival. College professors are usually given a film budget which allows them to order three or four films a semester or quarter to be shown in their classes. You could work with several of them to set up a schedule for ordering the films in such a way that for two or three weekends in a row, the professors would obtain a film or two each at the same time. On Friday, the pro-

IN 1767 FRANKLIN DESIGNED THIS CARTOON AND SENT IT TO FRIENDS. IT PROPHESIES THE SAD PLIGHT OF BRITANNIA STRIPPED OF HER COLONIES

fessors could show the film in their classes, and since the films usually don't have to be returned until the next Monday, your PBC could show them free on the weekends. If you work it right, you should end up with six or eight free films for three weekends in a row. (It might be best to show the films near, but off, campus—in a sympathetic church, for instance. In that way, community people who might not feel comfortable about going to a college campus could come and take in the movies and the message.)

Orientation

Though the academic year is usually just nine months long, you should make sure that the PBC members stay in close contact during the summer break. There will, of course, always be work to do if your school has summer session, but it's also important to be prepared for the start of each fall semester. It's at that time, each year, that hundreds, perhaps thousands, of freshmen get their first exposure to your college. If you're prepared when school starts, you can offer these new students an orientation and tour of the campus. (Even if your school already has an orientation session, chances are that it will add little to a student's knowledge of what your campus is really all about. If there is already an orientation program, either work to reform it or, if that's too much trouble, as it probably will be, just set up a counterorientation.)

A student-orientation program allows for all kinds of educational work. PBC members can take groups of twenty or twenty-five students around campus on a tour. Point out different buildings and what their functions are—military research, ROTC, devising "urban redevelopment" programs—and explain what bearing those functions have on the kind of education you get at your school. You can make note of historic sites on campus, from the time of the founding of the school to the last time the National Guard occupied the front lawn. If there are other student-movement organizations on campus, you should explain what these groups are and what they're trying to do. You can also use the orientation program to discuss how the founders viewed education (as outlined in the introduction to this guide) and how your college lives up to or strays from those first principles.

Pamphlets

Beginning with orientation and running throughout the school year, a PBC could issue Common Sense pamphlets about the university. Such subjects could

THEIR PORT CLOSED BY THE KING AFTER THE TEA PARTY, BOSTONIANS CAN RECEIVE PROVISIONS ONLY FROM PATRIOTS OF NEIGHBORING COLONIES

be dealt with as who sits on the Board of Regents; what kinds of research take place on campus; what rights are denied students; who some of the most "influential" alumni are and what role they play in the corporate/government system. Look back into the historical records of the Alumni Association for profiles of famous Tories and patriots that the school has produced over the years. A series of such Common Sense pamphlets would go a long way toward raising important issues about the university that the administration would probably rather not have brought up.

Slide Shows

Slide shows are excellent organizing tools that are rarely used on campuses. During orientation, for instance, if tours aren't possible, a few people taking a slide show around to different dorm floors for a solid week could reach a great number of students with a creative program that could parallel an actual, physical tour. Slide shows are also a great way to raise issues new to many freshmen, as well as interest students in working with the PBC. All that's really needed for a good slide show is some borrowed slide equipment, fifteen or twenty minutes' worth of slides and a script that will give the idea that there's more to a university and its past and present than books, wealthy alumni and football.

Literature Tables

Finally, and so obvious a resource that it is often overlooked, are the good old-fashioned literature tables. When the weather's nice, just get a table and a few chairs, make a sign or fly a DON'T TREAD ON ME flag and staff a table full of material about the Peoples Bicentennial Commission and information about the community and university.

HIS IMPERIAL MAJESTY, KING GEORGE III OF ENGLAND

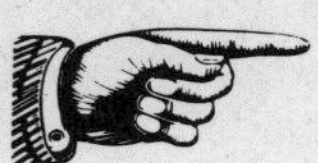

AWARENESS PAYS DIVIDENDS

If you work on all, or at least a fair number, of these possibilities, you're sure to evolve into a people's expert on the university. Many of the processes of a university are run like a closed corporation or the top-secret projects of the government. As a people's expert on your campus, you'll have an understanding of how your university works and where it is vulnerable to exposure and attack. And just as with big business and the government, the administration of your university is anxious to maintain its secrets.

Your school's charter is probably similar to that of the City University of New York. The University's mission, the Draft Statement of Purpose of CUNY says, is "to view its primary responsibility as that of imbuing devotion to justice and freedom and to the search for truth and its dissemination among its students, faculty, and community." Universities that make similar claims are obviously not eager to be exposed for forbidding their custodial and cafeteria staffs the right to unionize; denying young, progressive professors tenure because of their political beliefs; drawing up secret development plans that call for devastating land and homes in the areas neighboring the university or holding defense contracts. College presidents and other bureaucrats know they'd have a hard time explaining these efforts in the light of their stated purpose of expanding "justice, freedom and the search for truth." A people's expert should be able to blow the whistle on these antidemocratic administrators. In a democracy, there are no secrets from the people.

When you've laid the groundwork by creating an initial awareness among students of the Revolutionary premise of America, there are a number of substantial issues any Peoples Bicentennial Commission can tackle. You'll undoubtedly find dozens of important problems to deal with. Consider the following three areas: Diversifying the Campus, Curriculum and The University and Society.

Any college Peoples Bicentennial Commission that addresses itself to these three areas will have made great progress toward establishing the radical democratic society that the college must one day serve.

GOVERNMENT TAX COLLECTOR HUNG IN EFFIGY BY REBELLIOUS PATRIOTS

THE PRICE OF LIBERTY

DIVERSIFYING THE CAMPUS

> Even under the best forms [of government], those entrusted with power have, in time, and by slow operations, perverted it into tyranny; and it is believed that the most effectual means of preventing this would be to illuminate, as far as practicable, the minds of the people at large . . . without regard to wealth, birth or other accidental condition or circumstance.
>
> —THOMAS JEFFERSON, 1779

In ancient Greece, the philosopher Plato developed his model society—one that would be ruled by an elite class of scholar nobles. Trusting the benevolent intentions of these scholarly despots, Plato felt he had constructed the best of all possible worlds.

America's universities are the heirs of the Platonic legacy. To be sure, every institution of higher learning in this country maintains token quotas and minority-admissions policies, and scholarships *are* provided for many of those who can't afford to pay. But on the whole, our country's colleges are ivy-covered training grounds for the corporate and government scholar despots of tomorrow.

Jefferson and the other founding radicals were on guard against just this sort of undemocratic philosophy. Politically, they rejected the Platonic school of thought and took as their heroes the Romans Brutus and Cassius, who struck down the tyrant Caesar. What was needed, they knew, was not an academy to train students, but an educational system in which all segments of the population could learn, mingle and develop their talents to best oppose tyranny.

Reaffirming our heritage in education demands the restructuring of universities along democratic lines.

A democratic university must be based on diversity —not just because an adherence to the founding principles of this country requires that *all* people have *real,* not symbolic opportunity, but because we must learn to come to grips with diversity in society itself. A democratic university must involve "citizens" as well as "scholars" in teaching and learning. A democratic university must break down the artificial barriers between intellectual research and community life and action. The ultimate goal of democratic education is not to "close the gap" between those who go to school and those who cannot. The ultimate goal is to create a system in which such distinctions will be meaningless; in which students will also be citizens, and citizens will also be students.

REACHING INTO THE COMMUNITY

Poor Richard's Community Almanac

College education has been built up throughout our history as an awesome institution, surrounded by a powerful mythology. It is the center of knowledge with which only a segment of America comes into contact. It is home to millions of young people, with their distinct life-styles, politics and social values and the unusual freedom to assume very little real responsibility. It is a status symbol of success that stamps one as wealthy, talented and intelligent. And it is the road to well-paying jobs, big homes and positions of power.

It's no wonder that college students are often disliked simply for being college students! If we're to break down the barriers surrounding our colleges and universities and make them institutions responsive to the needs of society at large, students are the ones who must initiate the needed action.

College students have three common characteristics: they usually frequent only the college area of town, and thus learn little about the surrounding city; they have developed research skills and they have leisure time that most Americans don't possess.

A good way to start diversifying the campus is to combine these three conditions into one project. An interesting and needed beginning is to compile a listing of the people's institutions in your community (or, if you live in a sparsely populated area, the people's institutions of the whole state) and print the results in an inexpensive catalog—nonprofit stores, community-service organizations, activist groups, coffeehouses, churches, parks, food co-ops.

There are already some resource-compiling projects in several areas of the country. In Boston, the local Vocations for Social Change publishes the *Peoples Yellow Pages*; Philadelphia has the *Whole City Catalog*; San Francisco, the *Red Pages*; North Carolina, *Carologue*.

Once you begin, you'll probably find that you'll have a hard time limiting yourself and your catalog. At the outset, to avoid being swamped, your PBC should set some guidelines:

- Will the catalog be designed to serve mainly the needs of the student/youth community, or will it be something useful to all citizens in your area?
- Should only nonprofit organizations—stores, food co-ops, etc.—be listed, or should businesses that make a small profit, while still serving the needs of the people, also be recommended?
- Will you list some political and social-activist organizations and leave out others? What criteria will be set up to decide?

PRINCE WILLIAM HENRY, born 21 August. 1765.

PRINCESS AUGUSTA SOPHIA, born 8 Nov.r 1768.

GEORGE the III^d KING of GREAT BRITAIN, &c.

CHARLOTTE QUEEN of GREAT BRITAIN, &c.

When you've resolved these and related issues, you should draw up a questionnaire to be sent to people, groups and businesses you feel might be included in the listing. Keep the questionnaire short, asking for just enough information to get an insight into what they're all about:

- What services do you provide? Who uses your services?
- Do your services or products cost money? If so, how do you determine the prices? Are you willing to barter?
- Are you willing to teach others your skills?
- What hours are you open or available?
- Is your organization structured along corporate or democratic lines?

Along with the general questions, ask for a brief, specific description of the business, service or organization.

When you receive replies, work them into an easily readable, concise form and divide them into logical categories (be sure to also include an alphabetical index at the back), such as community services, education, social action, health, legal help, communications, recreation.

An almanac of such resources in your area could be more than a simple listing of institutions. Use the catalog as a way of spreading the message of the Revolutionary ideals of 1776 with graphics, quotations and historical sketches from the founding era. In an introduction, you might briefly explain America's democratic philosophy, and how this kind of public-service project fits into that world view. While the local government and Chamber of Commerce are probably planning a new visitors' center or a military parade to commemorate the two-hundredth birthday of the Revolution, your PBC will be making a *real* contribution to the people of your school and community.

Aid to Community Organizations

A campus PBC can also use its research abilities in a more substantial way: providing aid to community groups concerned with social action.

Many universities already have work/study and independent-study programs. Others that do not offer these full-time options now provide a January term in which students can undertake field work in a city of their choice. There are even Universities Without Walls—community-based academic institutions which cater especially to those who must or wish to work while they pursue a college degree.

But there are often problems with these programs. Work/study often simply involves performing community jobs that do not necessarily have any relevance to work involving social change. Students who undertake independent studies often find they deal more with books and theory than with actual community work for want of knowing just how they can best help.

A Peoples Bicentennial Commission should serve to channel this energy in constructive ways, instead of allowing it to dissipate through frustration and uncertainty.

Every community organization needs information, but few community groups have either the time or the resources to do the kind of research they need. A campus PBC working with local community groups can provide them with valuable research services, and in the process break down university/community barriers.

If your PBC has worked on getting together a community almanac, you'll have a good idea of what organizations exist in your area, and what their needs are. But if you don't have a clear picture of what's happening in your city, you should talk with the people at your local underground paper, switchboard or movement center. After just a little looking around, you're sure to come in contact with a number of social-action groups—tenants' unions, welfare rights, senior citizens, civil rights, consumer action, legal aid, environmental protection, etc. Approach any of these groups volunteering your help, and chances are pretty good you'll be put to work right away.

To publicize your efforts, get a story in the campus newspaper about what you are doing and why, what the tradition of education has been and how community action helps fulfill that tradition.

You might also discuss with sympathetic professors the possibility of their conducting courses on community problems that would combine classroom sessions led by different community organizers—each stressing a different aspect of community work—and field work in the city. The professor's role in such a class, unless he or she has had actual organizing experience, would be minimal—perhaps just recommending a syllabus, providing some theoretical reference material to go along with the day-to-day organizing experience or preparing statistical handouts and other technical information.

Such a course should be presented as more than a one-semester or one-quarter affair. It should be seen by students as an introduction to problems that will take years—perhaps a lifetime—of commitment. Too often in the past, similar courses have simply been means toward soothing the guilt of liberal students instead of motivating them to ongoing struggle.

Support for Community Struggles

Research alone is not enough. Part of the myth of academic life in America is "scientific detachment" and "objectivity." Social Sciences tend to look at social problems simply as intellectual issues that can be thoroughly studied only on a theoretical level. While some of these insights may be valuable, they certainly have little to do with addressing this society's problems.

If students are to avoid this trap that many professors

THE NEW YORK STOCK EXCHANGE, CIRCA 1869

BY THE LATE 1880'S, THE CLOSE PHYSICAL RELATIONSHIP OF THE UNIVERSITY CAMPUS TO THE COMMUNITY PRESAGED THE CONFLICTS BETWEEN "TOWN" AND "GOWN" OF THIS CENTURY. THIS IS YALE UNIVERSITY, CIRCA 1885.

have fallen into, not only must they help community organizations with research, and whatever else these groups feel is necessary, but they must also *identify* with the struggles for justice waged by the community.

If, for instance, the Farm Workers are calling for a boycott of lettuce, a PBC should contact the local UFW office, get its material and hand it out on campus. You should research to find out where your university stands on the issue. Is your cafeteria serving nonunion lettuce? If it is, you should petition against the abuses, and consider a boycott.

STATE NORMAL SCHOOL

Any organization striving for social justice can be helped in the same way with leaflets, boycotts and other shows of support. You can also give support to community groups by:

- Collecting money. Contributions are especially needed, and relatively easy to get, during crisis situations that the straight media are playing up—Wounded Knee, the Pentagon Papers trial, the Farm Workers.
- Arranging to have speakers on campus. Local organizers might appear just before individual classes or, if you think there's enough interest, for a speech in the school auditorium. You might even try assembling a panel of community people to discuss current issues in the city's life.
- Sponsoring an entire Community Day on campus. You could invite all of the different community groups to set up literature tables and displays about their organizations. A PBC's contribution to such an affair could be an erection of a display showing, through photographs, quotations, drawings, etc., the Revolutionary tradition in our history, and how these community groups fit right into it. You can also set up a King George III Display, exposing your local government and big business for their corruption and undemocratic policies.
- Throughout a Community Day, community activists could give short speeches, musical groups could perform and at night, a film festival of national and international struggles might take place.

In the end, the best support you can give people in your community is the continuous use of the campus as a forum for propagating the ideals of democracy. If we are ever to get away from simply responding to new encroachments on our lives and rights by the government/corporate aristocrats, we must all take the ideals of equality, life, liberty and happiness as our own.

CURRICULUM

During the Bicentennial years, as we begin reexamining our schools and other institutions in American society, we should concentrate much of our effort on critically looking at just what is taught in those schools. Curriculum, after all, is the heart of any college.

Colleges are often, and justifiably, criticized not so much for what they teach as for what they don't teach. In the 60's, for instance, blacks pointed out the lack of black history and forced many schools to institute Black Studies departments. Women raised the same demands for knowledge about their history and lives, and today many colleges have Women's Studies courses.

The demands for new classes on relevant social issues will continue to grow. Universities must maintain courses that serve the needs of the people—Community Studies, Labor Studies, American Cultural Studies.

But in the natural demand for additional courses and departments on important social issues, we often forget to subject the courses we now have to reexamination.

True, many—perhaps most—colleges today have "course evaluation" booklets that are designed to give students an idea of just what they're getting themselves into during the upcoming semester. But what do these critiques tell us? How well, or poorly, the professor lectures; whether exams or papers are required; how hard the grading system is.

What we rarely ask ourselves are the substantive questions of just what a particular professor's, and thus the course's, biases are. Courses, as part of the university process, should also fulfill the Revolutionary promise of promoting knowledge to serve as a weapon for democracy. To see where your courses stack up, you might look at them in the light of some of the following questions:

1. Are the Social Science departments dominated by theorists or behaviorists? If they are dominated by theorists, the chances are that justice will be among the important issues under consideration. Behavioral departments, however, will reject such discussion of traditional theory as irrelevant. They will, rather, discuss how to examine the attitudes of existing voting blocs, ethnic blocs and economic classes, and ignore ethical and moral considerations.

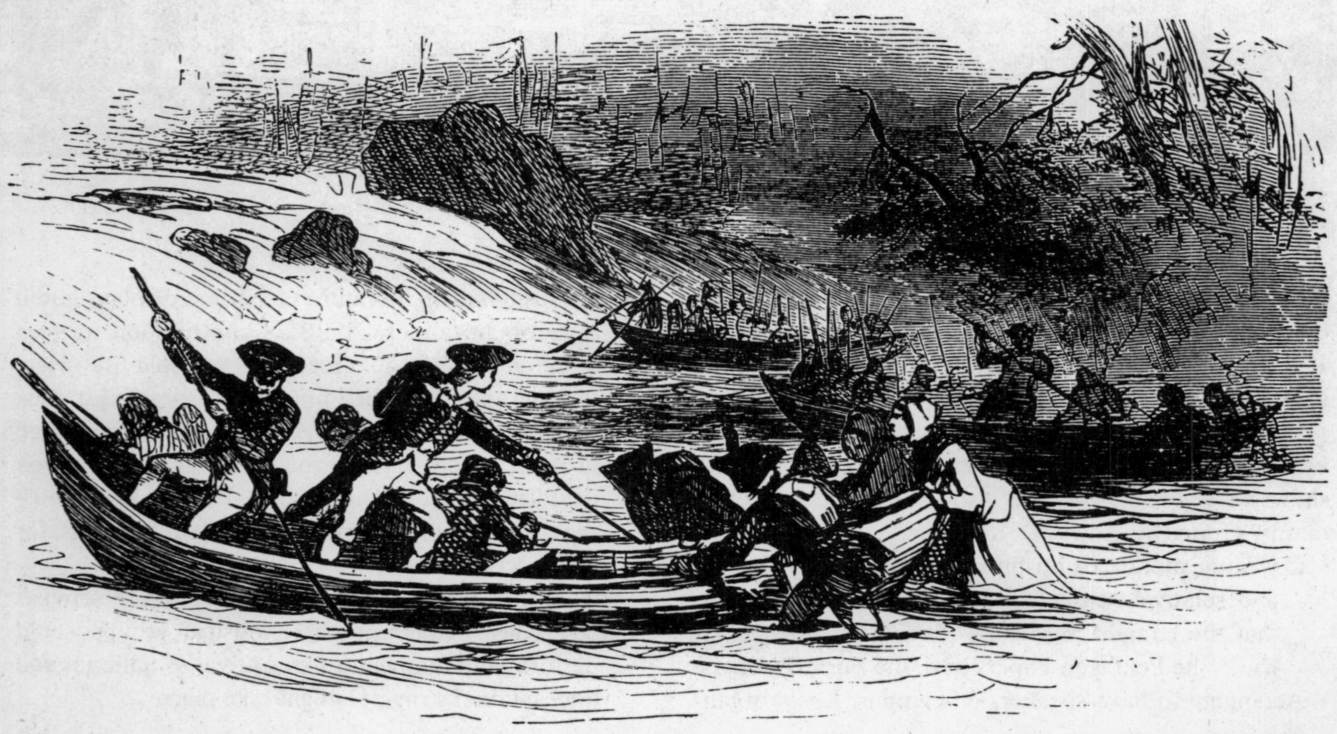

2. Do the Natural and Physical Science departments force students to examine the ethics of technology as well as the techniques? For whom should a scientist conduct research? What is his or her broader responsibility to the community? Should a scientist refuse to undertake research for something that may be destructive to human life? These are powerful moral issues that every university ought to raise with technicians. Does yours?

YES, WASHINGTON AND HIS MEN DID CROSS THE DELAWARE ON CHRISTMAS EVE, 1776.

3. Do your Humanities programs emphasize art for art's sake, stress art for society's sake or try to strike a balance between them? Do they ignore this issue altogether?

4. Do courses in Philosophy explore issues of traditional philosophy, or merely issues raised by analytical positivists?

5. Do Social Science courses demand that students retain "scientific objectivity" by concentrating on the "pure" knowledge of the classroom rather than giving emphasis to field experience? What would your Sociology professor think of Ben Franklin's maxim "Learning comes by doing"?

Here's the crux of it: Does the university take ideals and ideas seriously as ends in themselves? Is it willing to let unanswerable questions be raised, or has it surrendered completely to the materialist and positivist doctrines of the late 19th and 20th centuries? If the latter, the ideals of democracy are in serious trouble at your school.

These are a few of the general questions that you can raise with your departments. The process shouldn't end with general questions, however. For a more detailed example of how to question the democratic ideals, or lack of them, in an American History class, see the High School section on Textbooks and Curriculum.

THE STRUCTURE AND POLITICS OF THE UNIVERSITY

The crucial questions for any institution concerned about democracy in America—and for America as a whole—are who makes the decisions, and what is the motivation behind those decisions.

Battles for student and faculty power have been an important feature of the educational landscape over the past ten years, as have efforts to raise questions of war and peace, institutional racism and sexism and the economic role of America in the world. Universities have changed substantially as a result of these pressures—more, in fact, than most other institutions in society.

Yet much work remains to be done. The Bicentennial years provide us with a philosophy and theme for dealing head on with the questions of decisions and motivations in this country's colleges and universities. After all, the central issues in a democracy are power and purpose. And that's just what the events of two hundred years ago were all about. Who was going to have power—the King or the people? And how was that power to be used—to support a corporate aristocratic tyranny, or to ensure a democratic life for all, based on the principles of equality, life, liberty and happiness? These are the very issues confronting us today.

The National Student Association has drawn up a list of questions that may be helpful in thinking about the decision-making at your school (we've made some additions and deletions where we thought necessary):

1. Advising. Are students helping one another as much as they might to use the university in their own interest?
2. Orientation. Are new students finding out at the beginning how it really is?
3. Buildings. Who plans them? Who has to learn in them?
4. Community government. Who decides? What are students allowed to decide about the governance of their place of learning?

Guard against
pretended
patriotism!

5. Student workers. At $1.60 an hour? Ever hear of unions?
6. Institutional research. Who does it? What questions does it ask about your college? What answers does it publish?
7. Public relations. What image is your college projecting? It's an image, in part, of you—is it honest?
8. Student press. Does it reach the community that depends on the university? Does it deal with a learning community or with rah-rah?
9. Catalog. Who writes it? Is it in clear English or jargon? Does it describe the students' role and fate honestly?
10. Personnel and hiring. Are students consulted? If they are, is it just a token effort? If they're not, who decides?
11. Administrators. Do they teach courses? On how the college works? Do they tell the truth?
12. Parallel structures. Are there any student-run educational programs that offer alternatives to the ordinary modes?
13. Socially enfranchising living situations. Like student-run dorms, co-ops, learning living situations, etc. Can students start such things? Do they?
14. Rent strikes in the dorms. Look, if there are any rats . . .
15. Cooperative housing in the community. The college is part of the world. Why live in seclusion, unless you are preparing for a life of privilege?
16. Negative fees for students. That's right—a sliding scale of tuition by family income, allowing support for people who need money to have a chance at college. Not "scholarships."
17. Student governments As irrelevant and ugly a set of organizational forms as men have ever generated in the name of "freedom." Why aren't there student unions? Direct democracies? Parallel administrations of the university? You couldn't do worse than most imitation-U.S.A. student governments if you *planned* a caricature of representative organization.
18. Athletics. Is it possible that institutions of higher learning might be ready to grow beyond circuses? To study them, fine—but to generate them?
19. Privacy. Are students intruded upon? How can the practice be halted?
20. Rules for student conduct. In our experience, almost invariably hypocritical and contradictory. What does a two-faced system of authority teach?
21. Why don't students sit on decision-making bodies of their universities, or work as staff, for academic credit? Is there nothing to be learned there?

INDEPENDENCE HALL, PHILADELPHIA

22. Faculty are all too often stifled worse than students. Why are they so jealous of those prerogatives they do have? Why not share the wealth of authority? Tenure—pitting one against another?
23. Democracy. Present in name more than in substance at most universities. How can administrators be trained to do as they preach to students?
24. Self-starting students. Why aren't they recognized as an educational resource and paid to help in teaching and starting new programs?

IT MAY LOOK LIKE A CASTLE, BUT IT'S REALLY A HOUSE OF LEARNING

25. Summer sessions. Why aren't they used to give students a chance to experiment with different styles of learning? The opportunities are always there for this one.

The case for student power is clear; it remains in perfect accord with the spirit of the first American Revolution. Student power is a movement for democracy and egalitarianism more than it is for abstract rights. Like the Revolutionaries of 1776, students seek real, not token, representation in the governments that control them. Parliament tried to persuade Sam Adams and Patrick Henry that they should be satisfied that their views were espoused in the House of Commons, even though they themselves were not the ones espousing them. The Sons of Liberty were not convinced; nor should students be. You should always make a clear distinction between the administration's granting a change in the rules and the administration's giving up authority over an area of the rules. The one is a new privilege; the other, a power. Students demand power.

Student power is an attempt to create community between the students of a university, just as the American Revolution led to serious efforts to build a stable and fair society in its aftermath. And student power seeks to create an educational system that pays deference to the democratic standard of legitimacy—as opposed to the rules of a corporation by which universities today justify their policies. The general goals of student power are:

1. Students should run their own institutions—student-government organizations, campus press, social rules, dormitory life—anything that students and only students must obey.
2. Students and faculty should share responsibility for curriculum development.
3. Students and faculty should make the decisions affecting the entire university. Administrative personnel should come out of their ranks, chosen by students and faculty.

In short, whoever must obey a rule should make it. It's that simple. It's the Spirit of '76.

THE UNIVERSITY AND SOCIETY

The university does more than train students. It is intimately involved with decisions and policies affecting the surrounding community and society as a whole. You should reexamine these programs of your school in the light of the first principles of the country. Is your school promoting equality, life, liberty and happiness among the noncampus population, or has it become, as the Declaration of Independence branded King George and the Royal government, "destructive of these ends"?

First, a PBC should examine the university's impact on land development and housing in the surrounding community. Is it fulfilling its responsibility to improve a city, or is it a force for urban removal, bulldozer style? Universities throughout Boston, for example, exacerbate the local housing crisis by failing to construct low-income dwellings for the poor or adequate housing for their own students. Yet the student bodies remain silent in response. Similarly, Temple University's expansion programs have been a major grievance of the black community in Philadelphia, but the majority of Temple students and faculty have done little to fight them. The University of Chicago has won nationwide notoriety for its crimes against residents of the South Side and Woodlawn, but again, even activist students on campus have done little to object to these activities. These situations make a mockery of academia's claim to deal with people in an "enlightened" manner, and reformers should put an end to them.

Second, students should insist that university investments be held accountable to just standards. Why should Harvard University have supported the Mississippi Power and Light Company? Why should any university invest money in companies that thwart agencies that are supposed to regulate them, or that refuse to pay taxes to the federal government at rates that ordinary citizens have to pay, or that discriminate against women and minority groups?

Third, activists should take a close look at government and foundation grants that the university receives. Whose interest do they really serve? Does a grant to develop chemical and biological weapons serve the interests of poor people throughout the world, or of the dictatorial regimes that oppress them? Will a grant to study the effects of automation benefit working people,

UNTIL THE END OF THE CIVIL WAR, NO PRESIDENT EVER THOUGHT IT NECESSARY TO PUT A FENCE AROUND THE WHITE HOUSE

THE BATTLE OF BUNKER HILL

or the corporations that want to displace them? Will a grant to examine the attitudes of women about marriage and the family aid the cause of the women's movement, or will it be used to rationalize the old "a woman's place is in the home" argument? Can any of these research projects be said to be "value-free," serving the interests of all groups within society equally? The answer is obviously "no," and the university reformers must say so.

Fourth, students and faculty must examine university policies concerning academic enterprises that the institution owns, as well as university attitudes toward nonacademic employees. Activists at New York University, for example, have published a provocative manual, *New York University, Inc.*, describing the range of activities in which this so-called "educational" establishment had become involved. Even many professors were astonished to learn that the University owned shares in a leading spaghetti company, and its real estate holdings engulfed New York City. Elsewhere, the serenity of Yale University was ruptured a few years ago by a strike of nonacademic employees for minimum wages that brought working people and student activists together in the streets against the Board of Governors. University communities that tolerate such abridgments of equity in their midst might as well remove the word "democracy" from their catalogs. They lack even a basic understanding of what it requires.

Finally, and critically, students and faculty can examine where the university sends its graduates—where it encourages them to go. Does the placement service possess information about social-action organizations as well as established institutions? Does career counseling challenge the student to examine the moral, as well as financial and technical, aspects of a job? Does the university promote an elitist system by boasting of the number of millionaires, corporation executives and upper-income professionals among its alumni, while ignoring those who have made substantial contributions to the cause of economic and social reform? Who receives honorary degrees at Commencement—the presidents of corporations and banks, or distinguished public citizens who criticize corporations and banks? These areas may seem trivial, but they establish the priorities of the institution, the climate that it fosters. A PBC should look into them.

CONCLUSION

Democracy is the birthright of every American. Not a privilege or a gift, but a right patriots won 200 years ago, and one that Americans have fought to preserve every year since.

Too often democratic principles are reduced to innocuous platitudes. As we've all learned, it's easy to talk democracy; it's something else again to live it.

Two hundred years ago, our forefathers and -mothers saw our schools as the "training grounds of democracy." But today our educational institutions pay only lip service to the principles of a democratic life. Empty words have never been enough to maintain our "inalienable rights." Only by full participation and equal influence in our institutions—be they economic, political or educational—can we, in Ben Rush's words, reopen yet "another act in the great drama of the American Revolution."

We will have the democratic schools and institutions our birthright demands only when we recall the ideals of the patriots of 1776 who overthrew their tyrannical masters. Recall them . . . and act on them.

> The high things that are said in favor of rulers and of their dignitaries, and upon the side of power, will not be able to stop people's mouths when they feel themselves oppressed . . .
>
> —ANDREW HAMILTON, 1735

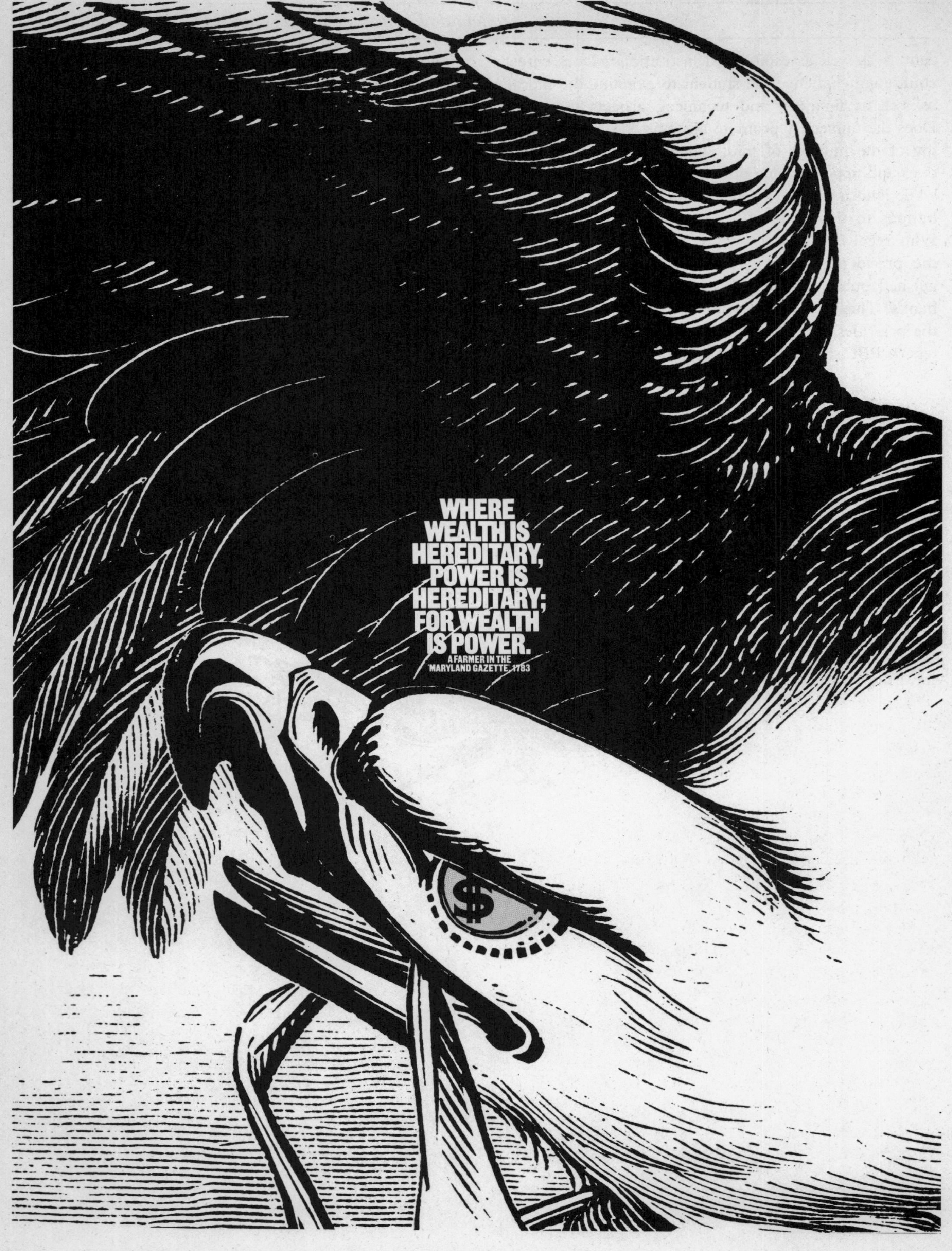
WHERE
WEALTH IS
HEREDITARY,
POWER IS
HEREDITARY;
FOR WEALTH
IS POWER.
A FARMER IN THE
"MARYLAND GAZETTE," 1783

VI

Organizing a Peoples Bicentennial Commission in Your Community

In every state of the Union, and in hundreds of communities throughout the country, "official" Bicentennial Commissions have been established to run our nation's two-hundredth birthday.

Your local or state government may be planning an official "celebration" of America's Bicentennial. If so, through your Peoples Bicentennial Commission you have the opportunity to dramatize your challenge to its legitimacy and to draw attention to your perspective and programs. Obviously, the plans of the "official" Bicentennial groups vary greatly from place to place. However, it's quite likely that the local politicians and businessmen have some plans in this regard. You'll want to research just what City Hall or the County Courthouse is up to. One thing's for sure; whatever it is, it will usually be designed to maximize business opportunities and minimize any concern with historical accuracy or social action.

Beyond countering "official" programs, your PBC can reach into the common experiences and concerns of taxpayers, workers, church people and students. It can become a valuable resource of information and research for local issue-oriented groups. Finally, with millions of Americans being deluged with "official" White House/Chamber of Commerce Bicentennial messages, a PBC has the responsibility to utilize the media and public forums to the fullest extent possible, presenting the patriots' message to the citizens of your community.

As you begin your organizing efforts, keep in mind that a PBC should be dedicated to involving the greatest number of people possible. That was the key to the Spirit of '76 (and the successful Revolution it fostered), and that's still the key today.

CORE-GROUP MEETINGS

When you are sufficiently familiar with the PBC approach, you should set up a preliminary, informal meeting to which you'll invite friends and acquaintances who might form a core group or nucleus of dedicated activists.

During this preliminary meeting, initiate detailed discussion so that those who are interested in working with you can fully understand the PBC political outlook, organizing approach and objectives. Debate and criticism of the central ideas are healthy and should be actively, and positively, engaged in. As the nucleus of activists will be your initial link to the community, they must be able to handle most of the questions interested people will naturally ask. Make sure you have an adequate amount of PBC material at this meeting to clearly explain the important ideas and help in clarifying questions. (The Peoples Bicentennial Commission in Washington, D.C., can supply you with this kind of information.)

In a week, begin a series of meetings with the core group to go over the written material for criticisms and

IF SPECIAL ATTENTION IS NOT PAID TO THE LADIES, WE ARE DETERMINED TO FOMENT REBELLION. —ABIGAIL ADAMS

suggestions. You should also begin discussion around the American Revolution seen as a social movement. Hold sessions that center on historical interpretations of the Revolution and its ideals. (At this time, you might consider group readings of J. Franklin Jameson's *The American Revolution Considered as a Social Movement,* Bernard Bailyn's *Ideological Origins of the American Revolution* and John C. Miller's *Origins of the American Revolution.* Make sure you also consult original source material—Tom Paine's *Common Sense* and *The American Crisis,* the Declaration of Independence, etc. (For a more detailed reading selection, refer to the PBC Study Guide to the American Revolution, available from Washington, D.C.)

During these core-group meetings, the issue of money should be raised. Think about your short- and long-range financial needs, and possible funding sources. (Assign someone the task of opening a checking account in the name of Peoples Bicentennial Commission so that sympathetic persons can easily make donations.) At this early stage, you'll all probably have to put up a little of your own money for immediate expenses. This initial amount will allow you to meet your first printing bills—expenses that will be necessary for the next step in the formation of your community's Peoples Bicentennial Commission.

THE FIRST COMMUNITY MEETING

When your nucleus of people feels that it is ready, you should call a meeting for the general public. Because the PBC approach attempts to expand social activism beyond the traditional audience of the student movement, you'll want to announce the meeting as widely as possible. Often, local radio stations will make free announcements for any public group that asks. Also, daily and weekly newspapers will generally run small articles announcing community events. Don't overlook church, college and underground community weeklies, either. An attractive flyer announcing your public PBC meeting can be produced at a very low cost. Someone in your group, no doubt, will have had experience doing layout. All you need is a good typewriter, some "press type" (available in various type faces for emphasis, headlines, etc.), some catchy graphics (lift some from this book), bright-colored paper and neat layout. We recommend offset printing, not Mimeograph. It may cost a little more, but you're bound to get more positive reactions to your printed material.

Put up your leaflets *everywhere*: libraries, public schools, churches, union halls, coffee shops, bookstores, community centers, barbershops, beauty salons, Laundromats. Don't make the common mistake of excluding certain types and classes of people by the "tone" of your material. People have been inundated by rhetoric. They'll find simple, straightforward language refreshing.

Your nucleus of organizers will want to prepare carefully for these general meetings. Be sure to discuss within the group the fact that people who differ by reason of age, sex, education, religion and occupation will have different concerns and priorities. Parents will tend to be more concerned about educational standards or drug-pushers, while childless small property owners may be more worried about local property taxes, urban renewal or highway-construction plans. Older people will care more about inflation, pension levels or medical care, and so on. Encourage each member of your group to talk about his or her main concerns. In this way it will be obvious that even in the core group there are varying degrees of concern about different issues.

If nucleus members have personal hostilities toward particular types of people, these should be talked about openly. Otherwise, members may publicly agree with your approach of trying to reach diverse kinds of people while at the same time unconsciously sabotaging such efforts because of their hostility.

HINTS ABOUT GENERAL-MEETING PROCEDURES

It's usually a good idea to hold the general public meetings on a week-night, beginning about seven o'clock. This will allow everyone time to get home from work, but will provide enough time for a full meeting that doesn't drag into the early hours of the morning.

An agenda should be prepared and distributed in advance of each meeting. The agenda should merely list important subjects to be covered during the meeting—program proposals, strategy, announcements, finances—and individuals should be able to offer amendments or additions to it at the start of the meeting.

An important point on the agenda for the first or second general meeting should be the creation of a democratic structure for conducting the work of the group between assemblies of the whole body. If your group is large, a simple procedure is to request nominations for the "steering committee" from the floor. While the steering committee will be empowered to make decisions on behalf of the entire group, it should, of course, be normal practice for the general body to approve or disapprove major proposals. Be sure that you encourage the nomination and election of a representative cross section of the various people who are participating.

Make sure that anyone who supports the PBC approach and is genuinely interested in the work is allowed a full voice in all major decisions. Be sensitive to the fact that because you'll have different types of people involved, some will be able to work on a daily basis, while others will be able to contribute only a few hours a week.

I hope we shall crush in its birth the aristocracy of our moneyed corporations, which dare already to challenge our government to a trial of strength and bid defiance to the laws of our country.

Thomas Jefferson

VII

Special PBC Projects

Numerous projects have been suggested throughout this book: research into the local power structure; tax organizing; labor, church and political-club programs. All are important, even vital, to your organizing efforts. And all involve hard work—work that is often unglamorous, and slow in returning satisfaction and concrete results.

To break up the long hours of hard-core community organizing, your Peoples Bicentennial Commission should also look for projects that are essentially fun, enhance your visibility within the community and in the news media, and have something for everybody to participate in. Three possibilities that fit readily into the Bicentennial theme are Oral/Visual Projects, Peoples Patriotic Celebrations and Tour Guides to your community.

ORAL/VISUAL PROJECTS

Thomas Jefferson was accused of having put no new thoughts into the Declaration of Independence; this he readily acknowledged, saying that his purpose was not to invent new wisdom but to "speak the American mind." He believed that the principles for which the Revolution was fought were the general beliefs of most Americans.

Have we lost those principles along the way in the two centuries of American nationhood? Or is there still a living American Revolutionary tradition? An Oral/Visual Project can result in a collage of "the American mind" in the 1970's, expressed directly and indirectly by the people who are the guardians of our ideals: bus drivers, parents and children, clerks, newspaper reporters—all of us. The study of the Revolution is incomplete without a study of the living Revolutionary tradition as it affects, moves and transforms America.

The overall questions to explore in your project are:

- What do the people of your community know about the ideals of the American Revolution?
- What do they think of those ideals?
- What influence have these ideals had on contemporary Americans?
- Do the institutions that affect the community operate in accordance with those ideals?
- Is the struggle between the "two American dreams" —between the authoritarian tradition and the democratic heritage—still going on?

To get at these general issues, here are a number of questions designed to reveal the feelings of people in your community:

- The Russians have the Communist Manifesto; the Chinese have the Quotations of Chairman Mao.

BETSY ROSS DID MORE THAN SEW

Do Americans have a political document to lean on for guidance?

- When the Founding Fathers signed the Declaration of Independence, they pledged their lives and their fortunes. Many of them lost everything; their possessions were confiscated and they became hunted fugitives. Do you think modern politicians are that dedicated to the people they represent? Do they measure up to the standards set by the Founding Fathers and Mothers?
- The Declaration says that people have inherent, inalienable rights—that we acquire these rights automatically, that we have these rights at birth and they are not given to us by governments. Do you think that is old-fashioned?
- The Declaration speaks of rights that include Life, Liberty, and the pursuit of Happiness. And it says the government is formed only to secure these rights. How well do you think the government is fulfilling this purpose? Is it securing your right to Liberty? To Life? To the pursuit of Happiness?
- The Declaration says that whenever any form of government turns against our rights and tries to destroy them, it is our duty to change or abolish that form of government. Do you agree with that?
- What kind of people do you suppose would write and sign a document like this?
- What did you learn, as a child, about the American Revolution of 1776? What ideas or principles did you pick up as you learned about it? Do you feel we can still use those ideas? How seriously do you take them? How seriously do you think our leaders take them?
- Do you ever think of 1776 and the things America stood for then and compare that with America as it is now?
- The Colonists complained that they had no voice in the making of decisions. Do you feel that you have

a voice in local decisions? In state decisions? In national decisions?

- Many of the Founding Fathers and Mothers believed that practically the entire population was qualified to make the most important decisions—war and peace, economic questions and so forth. Do you feel that you are able to make or contribute to such decisions, or do you feel that you need someone to make decisions for you?
- The soldiers at Valley Forge had little food, only a few rags to wear and no shoes in the middle of winter; there was no money. Why do you think they went through that? Is there anything you would do that for?
- Thomas Jefferson and others believed America should be a country of small farmers; they hoped that every family would have a small farm, enough for a decent living, and that there would be neither extreme wealth nor extreme poverty. Do you think that was a good idea?
- Of course, we can't all have small farms anymore. But do you think the basic idea is still sound? In an industrial society, could we still use those principles?

ROBERT MORRIS

BEN FRANKLIN

- The Revolutionaries of 1776 angrily denounced George III. What comes to your mind when you hear that name, George III?
- When the Founding Fathers and Mothers called for revolution, they made a list of accusations against King George—matters they considered sufficient cause for open rebellion against the government. Here is one of the accusations: "He has refused his assent to Laws [i.e., he vetoed the laws enacted by the Colonial legislatures], the most wholesome and necessary for the public good." Do you think they were right to be furious about this?
- How about this one: "He has erected a multitude of New Offices, and sent hither swarms of Officers to harass our people and eat out their substance." A lot of people today also complain that swarms of officeholders—bureaucrats, we call them now—are harassing the people and eating out their substance. How do you feel about that?
- Here's another one: "He has affected to render the Military independent of and superior to the Civil Power." The Founding Fathers and Mothers tried to organize the government so that the military

would serve and not rule the people. George Washington, even though he had commanded a victorious army and was a great hero, came before the Congress after the last battle and humbly removed his hat to tell the representatives he was resigning his commission. He took it for granted that the military was not even close to being equal to civilian authority. What kind of danger do you think the Founding Fathers and Mothers saw in a big military establishment? Do you think we have followed their advice about making the military our servant rather than our master? Can you envision a time when the military would become "independent of and superior to the Civil Power," as it is described in the Declaration?

- Here is another complaint from the Declaration: "He [the King] has combined with others to subject us to a jurisdiction foreign to our constitution, and unacknowledged by our laws." When the government ignores the laws, what is the duty of the citizen? Were the Americans justified in rebelling against the government after repeated pleas were ignored?
- All these abuses were considered typical of kings, so the American Revolutionaries tried to ensure that we would never again have a king to do these things to us. Did they succeed in forever putting an end to these abuses and injustices? If not, how would they explain it to themselves if they could see modern America? How would they react to hearing people complain about so many of the things they fought to stop? Would they think King George III was back in charge?

- The Constitution guarantees freedom of the press. How important is that right to you? How important is freedom of religion?
- The Constitution also guarantees the right to speak freely on all topics. How important is that right to you? How do you use it? The Constitution guarantees the right to assemble and demonstrate over grievances. How important is that right to you? Have you ever used it?
- Ben Franklin said that those who are willing to give up a little liberty in order to get a little security deserve neither liberty nor security, and that eventually they will lose both. Yet polls show that most Americans are ready to give up their Constitutional liberties. Are you willing to surrender some of your rights?
- What do you think about students' learning American ideals?

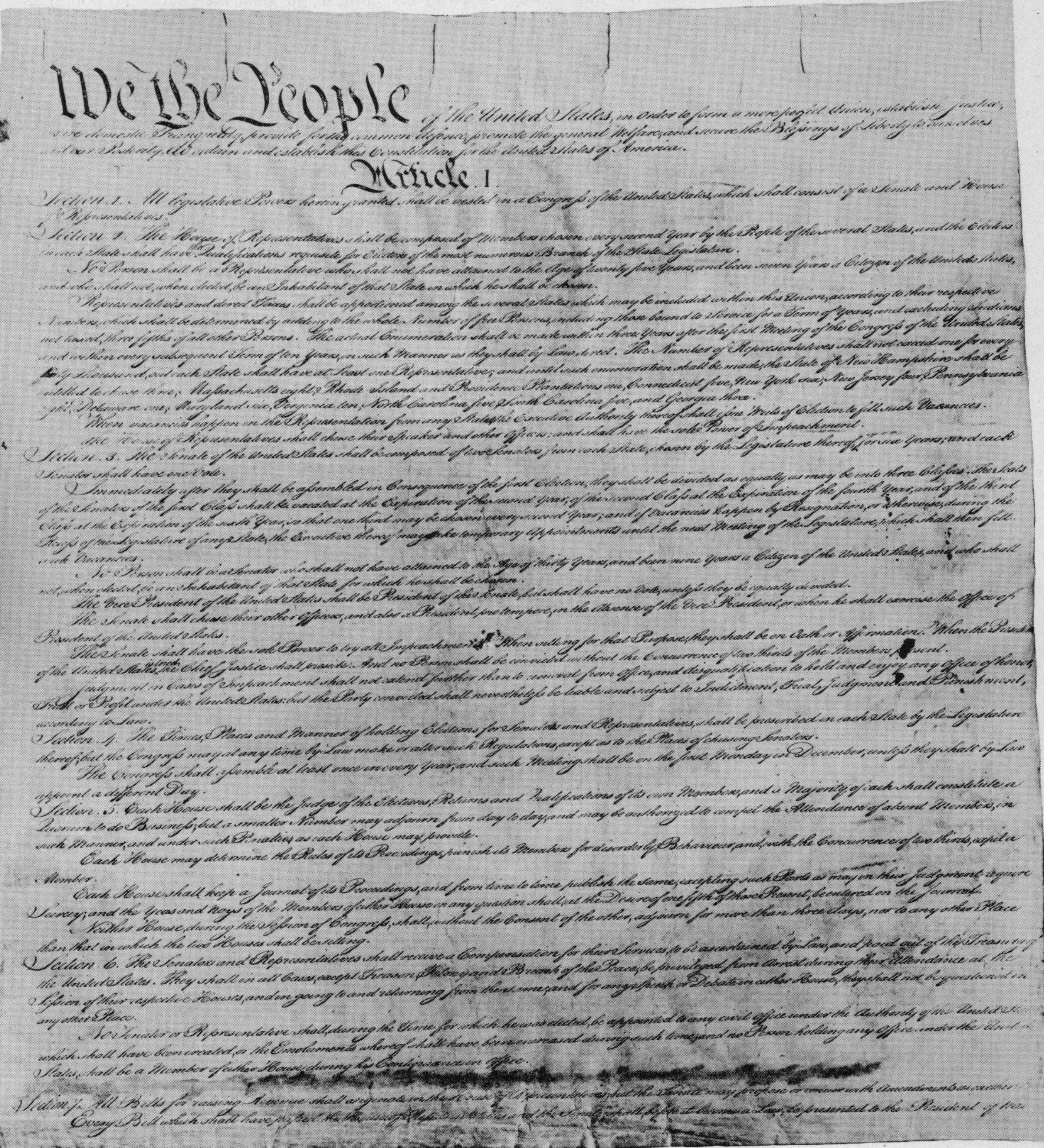

We the People of the United States, in Order to form a more perfect Union, establish Justice, insure domestic Tranquility, provide for the common defence, promote the general Welfare, and secure the Blessings of Liberty to ourselves and our Posterity, do ordain and establish this Constitution for the United States of America.

Article. I

Section. 1. All legislative Powers herein granted shall be vested in a Congress of the United States, which shall consist of a Senate and House of Representatives.

Section. 2. The House of Representatives shall be composed of Members chosen every second Year by the People of the several States, and the Electors in each State shall have the Qualifications requisite for Electors of the most numerous Branch of the State Legislature.

No Person shall be a Representative who shall not have attained to the Age of twenty five Years, and been seven Years a Citizen of the United States, and who shall not, when elected, be an Inhabitant of that State in which he shall be chosen.

Representatives and direct Taxes shall be apportioned among the several States which may be included within this Union, according to their respective Numbers, which shall be determined by adding to the whole Number of free Persons, including those bound to Service for a Term of Years, and excluding Indians not taxed, three fifths of all other Persons. The actual Enumeration shall be made within three Years after the first Meeting of the Congress of the United States, and within every subsequent Term of ten Years, in such Manner as they shall by Law direct. The Number of Representatives shall not exceed one for every thirty Thousand, but each State shall have at Least one Representative; and until such enumeration shall be made, the State of New Hampshire shall be entitled to chuse three, Massachusetts eight, Rhode-Island and Providence Plantations one, Connecticut five, New-York six, New Jersey four, Pennsylvania eight, Delaware one, Maryland six, Virginia ten, North Carolina five, South Carolina five, and Georgia three.

When vacancies happen in the Representation from any State, the Executive Authority thereof shall issue Writs of Election to fill such Vacancies.

The House of Representatives shall chuse their Speaker and other Officers; and shall have the sole Power of Impeachment.

Section. 3. The Senate of the United States shall be composed of two Senators from each State, chosen by the Legislature thereof, for six Years; and each Senator shall have one Vote.

Immediately after they shall be assembled in Consequence of the first Election, they shall be divided as equally as may be into three Classes. The Seats of the Senators of the first Class shall be vacated at the Expiration of the second Year, of the second Class at the Expiration of the fourth Year, and of the third Class at the Expiration of the sixth Year, so that one third may be chosen every second Year; and if Vacancies happen by Resignation, or otherwise, during the Recess of the Legislature of any State, the Executive thereof may make temporary Appointments until the next Meeting of the Legislature, which shall then fill such Vacancies.

No Person shall be a Senator who shall not have attained to the Age of thirty Years, and been nine Years a Citizen of the United States, and who shall not, when elected, be an Inhabitant of that State for which he shall be chosen.

The Vice President of the United States shall be President of the Senate, but shall have no Vote, unless they be equally divided.

The Senate shall chuse their other Officers, and also a President pro tempore, in the Absence of the Vice President, or when he shall exercise the Office of President of the United States.

The Senate shall have the sole Power to try all Impeachments. When sitting for that Purpose, they shall be on Oath or Affirmation. When the President of the United States is tried, the Chief Justice shall preside: And no Person shall be convicted without the Concurrence of two thirds of the Members present.

Judgment in Cases of Impeachment shall not extend further than to removal from Office, and disqualification to hold and enjoy any Office of honor, Trust or Profit under the United States: but the Party convicted shall nevertheless be liable and subject to Indictment, Trial, Judgment and Punishment, according to Law.

Section. 4. The Times, Places and Manner of holding Elections for Senators and Representatives, shall be prescribed in each State by the Legislature thereof; but the Congress may at any time by Law make or alter such Regulations, except as to the Places of chusing Senators.

The Congress shall assemble at least once in every Year, and such Meeting shall be on the first Monday in December, unless they shall by Law appoint a different Day.

Section. 5. Each House shall be the Judge of the Elections, Returns and Qualifications of its own Members, and a Majority of each shall constitute a Quorum to do Business; but a smaller Number may adjourn from day to day, and may be authorized to compel the Attendance of absent Members, in such Manner, and under such Penalties as each House may provide.

Each House may determine the Rules of its Proceedings, punish its Members for disorderly Behaviour, and, with the Concurrence of two thirds, expel a Member.

Each House shall keep a Journal of its Proceedings, and from time to time publish the same, excepting such Parts as may in their Judgment require Secrecy; and the Yeas and Nays of the Members of either House on any question shall, at the Desire of one fifth of those Present, be entered on the Journal.

Neither House, during the Session of Congress, shall, without the Consent of the other, adjourn for more than three days, nor to any other Place than that in which the two Houses shall be sitting.

Section. 6. The Senators and Representatives shall receive a Compensation for their Services, to be ascertained by Law, and paid out of the Treasury of the United States. They shall in all Cases, except Treason, Felony and Breach of the Peace, be privileged from Arrest during their Attendance at the Session of their respective Houses, and in going to and returning from the same; and for any Speech or Debate in either House, they shall not be questioned in any other Place.

No Senator or Representative shall, during the Time for which he was elected, be appointed to any civil Office under the Authority of the United States, which shall have been created, or the Emoluments whereof shall have been encreased during such time; and no Person holding any Office under the United States, shall be a Member of either House during his Continuance in Office.

Section. 7. All Bills for raising Revenue shall originate in the House of Representatives; but the Senate may propose or concur with Amendments as on other Bills.

Every Bill which shall have passed the House of Representatives and the Senate, shall, before it become a Law, be presented to the President of the

THE CONSTITUTION OF THE UNITED STATES OF AMERICA

• America will soon be celebrating the two-hundredth anniversary of the signing of the Declaration of Independence. What kind of celebration do you think would be appropriate?

Conducting the Interviews

The first step in doing an Oral/Visual Project is for the interviewers to become aware of their own attitudes about the principles of the American Revolution. Future interviewers, after some initial reading (refer to the PBC Study Guide to the American Revolution), should begin by interviewing one another. The next step is to decide what other people each one wants to begin interviewing, and why.

Most of the time, the researchers can gather information casually, by going door to door in the neighborhood and by dropping in on local merchants. Appointments should be set up where necessary. One might begin the interviews by explaining that the President has proclaimed the Bicentennial Era (1971–1976) as a time for recalling and reviving the Spirit of '76. It should be explained that the group is involved in research to determine what the community thinks the Revolution stands for, and whether or not the community operates on the principles expressed by the founders of the country. Employ the questions listed above, when appropriate.

Researchers may encounter interviewees with authoritarian biases, cynical attitudes toward American ideals or plain unconcern about those ideals. Don't be deterred from engaging in debate over the principles of 1776. Discussions of this kind may result in mutual learning.

THE STORY OF THE REVOLUTION WAS PASSED FROM ONE GENERATION TO ANOTHER BY WORD OF MOUTH

The research group should meet every week or two to discuss the work. It does not require experts to teach effective interviewing techniques—discussion among group members and an exchange of friendly suggestions will improve each member's skill. And as the work goes on, researchers will find themselves more interested in some types of interviewees than others, and more curious about certain types of questions and issues than others. This is when the project begins to take real shape.

Oral History

One intriguing aspect of an Oral/Visual Project is the community history it can produce, as told by the women and men who lived it. To begin an Oral History Project, go to those who participated in events and record their description of their experiences. Workers or union organizers usually haven't had the time or inclination to keep journals; nevertheless, many of them were involved in important parts of a community's past, and their recollection of events may be more accurate, in some instances, than the account of a scholar or historian. Certainly, the participants know better how it felt to be in the event than a scholar knows, and often the participant knows details that make history come alive. Oral History is making history from the bottom up—a process whereby we all become historians and come to understand the importance of each individual to the development of society, and vice versa.

In terms of fostering idealism in communities, moreover, Oral History has an important role to play. In areas of the country where intense labor struggles took place, for example, the rank-and-file participants can bring to light the battles that they fought for justice, equality and dignity in their youth. Almost inevitably, researchers will run across residents who remember a time when life was less hectic in the community, when a "community sense" was part of everyday life. The feeling of mutual responsibility and concern, missing from so many communities today, remains part of an American heritage that survives in the memories of many of our citizens. As Peoples Bicentennial Commissions search for alternative models of community life, the community's past itself can become a good place to start.

A history of the family might interest some researchers. Family size and composition have changed over the years; you might ask what effects those changes have had. You might also ask what changes there have been in how children are raised: what goals parents have for their children, and how they have changed; what children are taught about competition/cooperation, authority/equality; what children are taught about making choices and decisions.

A history of immigration is another possibility. Every community has residents who are first- or second-generation Americans, and residents who remember what their great-grandparents told them about coming to the United States. Why did they come? Was economic op-

ETHAN ALLEN CAPTURES FORT TICONDEROGA IN THE NAME OF "THE GREAT JEHOVAH AND THE CONTINENTAL CONGRESS"

portunity the only motive? How does America live up to their expectations? Do people in the country they left respect Americans? What did they know about America's history and the American Revolution before they came? How do the ideals of America's Revolution compare with the ideals of their former country?

Use the Right Tools for the Job

The tape recorder is the obvious medium, but using other media can make the final product of your Oral/ Visual Project richer, more varied and more informative—as well as more fun. Pictures can be taken; old photographs, scrapbooks and newspapers can be examined and copied to gain an understanding of how values and attitudes have—or have not—changed in the community. Equipment for making films, radio spots and newspapers is often available from schools, churches and community organizations. One researcher may want to take pictures; another may prefer taking notes in interviews to taping them; still others may want to research old documents from the local community, rather than do personal interviews. Some researchers might use information that others have gathered to produce their own readings or short dramatic pieces on tape around the themes of the American Revolution.

Each researcher should present the collected material to the group and discuss what (s)he found interesting, surprising or disappointing. Selections should be made from the materials, and then they should be edited and assembled for presentations. The material should be reviewed in light of the original questions:

- What do Americans know about the ideals of the American Revolution?
- What do Americans think of the ideals of the American Revolution?
- What influences do the ideals have on contemporary Americans, directly and indirectly?
- Do the members of the community and institutions affecting the community live up to the ideals?
- Do they try to live up to them? In what ways?

Exchanging Experiences

> We must all hang together, or assuredly we shall all hang separately.
>
> —BENJAMIN FRANKLIN, 1776

In 1776, communications between colonies, even between neighboring towns, was a difficult proposition. But people like Sam Adams understood that only by the exchange of information between communities could the sense of isolation and powerlessness in the face of Royal tyranny be broken down. Without an understanding of their neighbors, people are trapped in their own areas. In this situation, one cannot be expected to have a realistic conception of one's own community and its relationship to others; when one is thus isolated, it is impossible to forge a clear view of the strengths or shortcomings of one's community, its unique qualities, its peculiar problems and its special privileges or lack of privileges. Sam Adams set up the Committees of Correspondence to destroy this ethnocentrism. The Committees worked well—people in Massachusetts and Virginia, who had previously felt they had little in common, were able to band together for the common good.

Today, effective Oral/Visual Projects can serve to

CONCORD—THE FIRST BLOW FOR LIBERTY

break down these same feelings of isolation and powerlessness that many Americans feel. After you have widened your knowledge of your neighborhood, the next step is to exchange information with other neighborhoods, districts, parishes or towns. A natural outgrowth of research in your own community is contact with groups and individuals pursuing similar goals in Oral/Visual Projects in other areas.

Oral/Visual Projects Can Be the Voice of the People

After the questions have been asked, the interviews finished, the Oral/Visual material compiled, it is important to keep in mind one simple truth: that the hopes, dreams and thoughts of the people of this country have long gone unheard, and that it is our responsibility to use completed Oral/Visual Projects to let the people of America tell their story. If there *is* a silent majority, it is only because Americans have long been denied the chance to publicly speak their minds.

AN AUTHOR WHO WRITES OF HIS OWN TIMES, OR OF TIMES NEAR HIS OWN, PRESENTS IN HIS OWN IDEAS AND MANNER THE BEST PICTURE OF THE MOMENT OF WHICH HE WRITES.
—THOMAS JEFFERSON, 1786

The key to an effective Oral/Visual Project is the distribution of the material you've collected—in other words, getting the message out. This is where imagination comes into the story. Let your mind run free, and you'll probably come up with dozens of schemes. Here are just a few:

- Use your Oral/Visual material to build a "living museum." Combine excerpts from interviews, old letters, items that reflect the history of your area, old newspapers, photographs of yesterday and today, music, etc. Make your display colorful, mount it on large boards and make sure it's mobile. Take it through your community to churches, schools, libraries, town meeting halls. When the weather is nice, hold a display on your local town green, or in a park. Tie in the exhibit with Peoples Patriotic Celebrations (see the next section).
- Get together some friends and put on a play based on the material. Probably few people in your town have a very clear idea of local history beyond their own experience. Use the combined recollections of the folks you've interviewed to tell the story.
- If you have the equipment, try making a videotape of some of your interviews. Show the tape at schools, labor halls, churches, community gatherings, PTA sessions, meetings of fraternal organizations.

- A Boston group of high school students doing an Oral/Visual Project targeted a local television station with news of its work, and was rewarded with a highly effective five-minute film clip on the six-o'clock news. The report not only showed the project in action (students interviewing old labor organizers), but also included post-interview comments by both students and the senior citizens describing how "generation gap" barriers and other myths were broken down. Approach your own television stations with the story; local news programs love such "human interest" items.
- Inform your city newspaper about the project. Most dailies devote an entire section of the paper to local community news. Oral/Visual Projects, with excerpts from interviews and personal comments by the participants, are naturals here.
- Talk to the people at your local community, church, college and underground papers. Often, journals of these kinds are short on writers and stories and would be eager to have you do a regular column featuring a different interview each week.
- Don't forget radio. Most areas have at least one radio station that can help you out. Try to set up a show on which you actually interview people on the air. Or arrange to "feed" a station short tapes combining excerpts from interviews, music, sounds of the city and news items that reflect the unresponsiveness of politicians and businessmen to the desires of the people you have interviewed.

THE WASHINGTON COUNTY SEMINARY AND COLLEGIATE INSTITUTE, FORT EDWARD, NEW YORK, CIRCA 1854

Keep in mind that your presentations can be an important first step in opening up dialogue in the community around the meaning of our founding principles and their applicability today. Xerox, American Airlines, Ford Motor and dozens of other multimillion-dollar corporations have already begun *their* Bicentennial television series designed to show us all what America has been and is today. But the corporate vision of America is the King George story retold. Only the

"Were it left for me to decide whether we should have a government without newspapers, or newspapers without a government, I should not hesitate a moment to prefer the latter."

Thomas Jefferson

200 years ago, a Revolution was fought to secure the rights of a free press. The Peoples Bicentennial Commission supports those patriots who have fallen victim to the Administration's assault on the First Amendment: Earl Caldwell, William Farr, Peter Bridge, Les Whitten, Joseph Pennington, Dee Norton, Sam Sperry, Ronald Ostrow, Jack Nelson, Joseph Weiler, David Lightman, Gene Cunningham, Stuart Wilk, Dean Jensen, Sherrie Bursey, Brenda Joyce Presley. For further information, contact The Peoples Bicentennial Commission, Room 1025, 1346 Connecticut Avenue, N.W., Washington, D.C. 20036.

people of America understand America. Only the *people* can tell the whole story.

PEOPLES PATRIOTIC CELEBRATIONS

In 1776, when word of the signing of the Declaration of Independence reached New York City, thousands of patriots assembled in Wall Street to celebrate the glorious event and to pull down the gilded leaden statue of King George astride his horse.

In the Bicentennial years, Americans once again have a chance to participate in patriotic celebrations. Big-business moguls have already planned hundreds of them for us—all on the scale of "World's Fair" extravaganzas, and all requiring exorbitant entrance fees for the "privilege" of celebrating *our* Revolution!

To combat these crass, commercial ventures, your PBC should consider staging Peoples Patriotic Celebrations. The Fourth of July may be a Bob Hope Special now, but once it was a truly revolutionary holiday. (So revolutionary, in fact, that reactionaries thought up Columbus Day as a conservative answer to the Glorious Fourth.)

Envision what a *true* Peoples Patriotic Celebration might be: an event to generate energy and enliven your community; a chance for people who rarely associate to come together to celebrate a common heritage; a colorful and theatrical presentation of the Revolutionary principles of 1776.

Dates to Celebrate

- *January 29*—Tom Paine's birthday
- *March 5*—The Boston Massacre
- *March 23*—Patrick Henry's "Give me liberty or give me death" speech
- *April 13*—Thomas Jefferson's birthday
- *April 19*—The battles of Lexington and Concord
- *July 4*—The Declaration of Independence
- *September 27*—Sam Adams' birthday
- *December 16*—The Boston Tea Party

Beyond these dates, of course, there may be several that are particularly applicable to your town—days when something of historical importance happened in your community. Be sure to include these in your plans.

As you begin thinking about your people's festivities, keep in mind some of the patriotic celebrations out of our past:

- *May 19, 1774*—One thousand residents of Farmington, Connecticut, met on the village green to erect

a forty-five-foot Liberty Pole, burn a copy of the Boston Port Bill (an act that punished the people of Boston for the Tea Party) and proclaim, "We are the sons of freedom and will forever resist all efforts to bind us with the chains of slavery."
- *June 2, 1774*—Demonstrations began throughout the

THE KING'S ARMY EVACUATES BOSTON

Colonies in response to the Port Bill. Stores closed in Philadelphia, and flags flew at half-mast. In New York City, effigies of Tory Governor Hutchinson and Lord North were publicly burned.

- *November 1, 1765*—In New York City, thousands assembled to resist the passage of the Stamp Act. All of the church bells of the city rang; cannon were fired; flags flew at half-mast; eulogies were pronounced for the dead spirit of Liberty and effigies of those responsible for the tax were tarred and feathered and then hung from scaffolds.
- *November 2, 1773*—A crowd gathered under the Boston Liberty Tree and proceeded to the store of merchants who were importing taxed tea. The store was stormed by hundreds of patriots.

These early demonstrations, and props, should provide ideas for you in staging your own patriotic celebrations. Obviously, different things will be appropriate to each community, but the important thing is that the celebration be, like the demonstrations of the 1760's and 1770's, more than superficial hoopla and fireworks. It should utilize patriotic symbols, and graphically set forth the Spirit of '76. The more imaginative you are, the better your celebration will be.

An Old-Fashioned Patriots' Celebration

- Make it colorful. Fly "Don't Tread on Me" and Thirteen Star flags; use lots of red, white and blue bunting.
- Use Revolutionary symbols. In the 1770's, the three most prominent symbols at rallies were Liberty Caps, Liberty Poles and Liberty Trees. Designate a tree on your town green or in your park as the Liberty Tree, and fly a red flag from its top—as did our Founding Fathers and Mothers. In the years

just before the Revolution, patriots erected tall Liberty Poles to show that their community stood with the patriotic cause. During your celebration, commit your town to the patriotic cause—erect a Liberty Pole and attach a Liberty Cap to the top. (A Liberty Cap was made of coarse red cloth and was worn by ex-slaves of Rome to proclaim their freedom.) After your Liberty Pole is set up, follow the lead of the radicals of the 1790's: link hands, recite passages from the Declaration of Independence and hold a joyous dance around the Pole.

- Wear patriotic costumes, and recite stirring speeches from the early Fourth of July celebrations and the orations held in Boston to commemorate the Boston Massacre.
- Play early American music.
- Tar and feather effigies of present-day Tories.

GENERAL CHARLES LEE

- Hand out copies of the Declaration of Independence.
- Make public presentations of community gratitude to local patriots. City officials are always awarding keys to the city to slumlords, visiting politicians and heads of corporations. Make your awards to community members who best exemplify our Revolutionary ideals in their daily lives and work.
- Erect a "King George" exhibit exposing local Tories, as well as displaying blow-ups of Revolutionary scenes and figures and short quotes from the founders.

Remember, the patriots of 1776 would be scandalized by the Walt Disney fireworks spectaculars of today. Your Peoples Patriotic Celebration should provide an alternative to this pablum by offering an opportunity for your community to express its patriotism in meaningful ways. Some of the above ideas might be too far-out at first for your community's celebrations. Effigies, for instance, might be ill received. Don't exclude potential participants by unnecessary militance and rhetoric. Show you are sincere in your feelings about the Spirit of '76.

Make your celebration as American as apple pie, and as revolutionary as Tom Paine and Abigail Adams!

A PEOPLES TOUR GUIDE TO YOUR COMMUNITY

In 1876, America celebrated its Centennial—the one-hundredth anniversary of independence. There were 40 million citizens in 1876, and by contemporary reports, at least one out of five, or 8 million people, attended the official Centennial festivities in Philadelphia.

In 1976, there will be over 225 million Americans, most of them sharing at least two traits: the desire and ability to travel, and an interest in the Bicentennial and this country's historical sites.

dition. Oral/Visual Projects and patriotic celebrations begin that process. Formulating tour guides and actually conducting tours of your community can carry that process a step further.

How do visitors examine your community? Do they simply sight-see—taking in the tourist spots listed in a *Mobil Tour Guide*? Do they have their pictures taken in front of historic buildings? Do they buy up souvenirs—plastic Liberty Bells in Philadelphia, miniature Statues of Liberty in New York, postcards of the Lincoln Memorial in Washington, D.C.? Obviously, visitors who view your community in such a fashion gain only a superficial understanding of the heritage that has shaped your life and your area.

TOPPLING A SYMBOL OF ROYAL AUTHORITY

Look at your community. When Bicentennial travelers visit your area, what will they come to know about your town? For that matter, what do your neighbors and fellow citizens know about their community—its history and its heritage?

The Bicentennial, a time to reidentify with our Revolutionary past in a philosophical, social, political and spiritual sense, can also be a time to reexamine the nature of your community through its Revolutionary tra-

Your Peoples Bicentennial Commission can help give visitors a meaningful view of your community by

1) researching local history, 2) presenting the product of that research in pamphlet form, 3) setting up a mechanism for distributing the pamphlet to incoming tourists and 4) conducting your own tours of the community for visitors and residents alike.

PATRIOTS BESIEGE MANSION FULL OF TORIES

Research into Local History

Most communities have their share of monuments, historic markers, old houses and birthplaces of historic figures. First, familiarize yourself with these, going beyond the stories set forth in Chamber of Commerce brochures, bronze plaques and Tourist Bureau leaflets. Learn the *whole* story. Then tackle the historic moments and places out of your community's past that are generally glossed over. (Usually, you'll find that "official" markers and plaques are concerned with battles and famous men.) When your research is completed, select events, places and stories that will give visitors a sense of the ongoing struggles of your ancestors for their inalienable rights. You might, for instance, list events and historic sites of the Revolutionary Era, abolition movement, the crusade for women's suffrage and rights, different labor struggles, perhaps last year's battle for quality housing or the scene of a student demonstration of the 1960's.

The Pamphlet and the Questions

Your pamphlet should be graphically appealing (a picture to go along with each historic reference) and

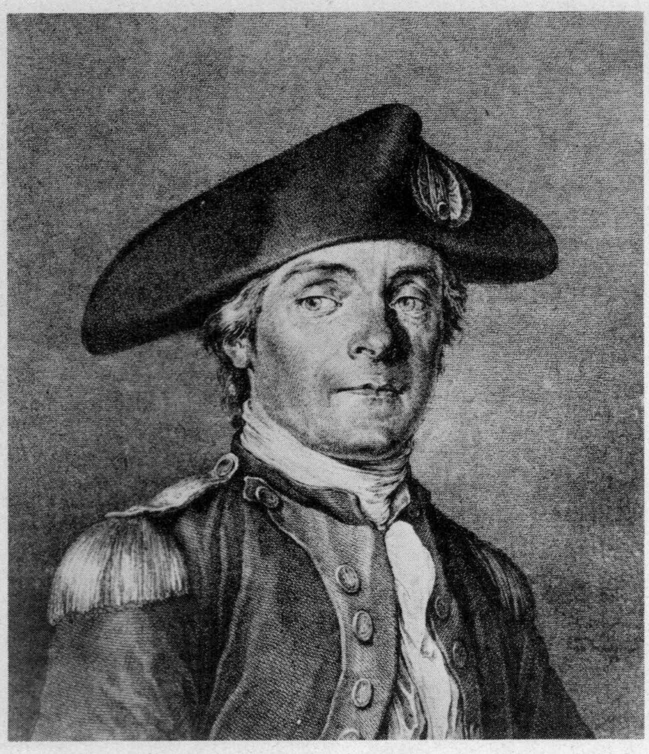

JOHN PAUL JONES—REVOLUTIONARY NAVAL HERO

should contain a simple map marking the spots to be visited and present a rundown on your Peoples Bicentennial Commission and why you have put out the pamphlet. It should include a brief, nonrhetorical text describing your community's overall history and how it relates to the Revolutionary philosophy upon which this country was founded.

Most important, you should formulate a series of questions visitors can ask themselves to give added meaning to the experience of learning about your heritage. The questions should be designed to elicit a more thoughtful response from tourists than the usual "My, isn't that interesting? Let's take a picture of it for our album." Some sample questions might be:

- "As you stand before this house, picture what life must have been like for the people who lived here in 1776. The Revolution was upon them. They were afraid, yet determined to see it through. How do you think your family would react in their situation? Were the patriots of 1776 any braver than we are today, or were they just common people, like ourselves, with a clear vision and purpose?"
- "On November 14, 1912, this factory was the scene of a bloody clash between striking workers and federal troops. Three laborers died here that day. Was their sacrifice worth making? Had they been able to foresee how their protest would end, do you think they still would have demanded their rights? Would you? Is there anything today worth dying for, as these three workers died in 1912?"
- "Now that you've learned something about our community's past, how do you think our history has been instrumental in shaping our lives and values today? Are we living up to the heritage of our ancestors, or have we failed to heed their message?"
- "In your daily routine, are *you* shaping generations to come? If yes, are you ever aware of your role in creating history? Do you think that someday your great-great-grandchildren will look back at this era and include you in *their* guide to your community?"

Distributing Your Tour Guides

Keep the cost of your pamphlet low—free if possible; otherwise, not more than a quarter. Local bookstores and tourist-oriented spots will probably carry it for you. On nice days, set up a table outside the most frequently visited tourist site and hawk the guides there. Make sure you regularly hit the community bus and train stations and the airport, if you have one. You should also launch a campaign with the community Tourist Bureau; chances are it will have been designated an "official" Bicentennial center. At first, try to sell the bureau on

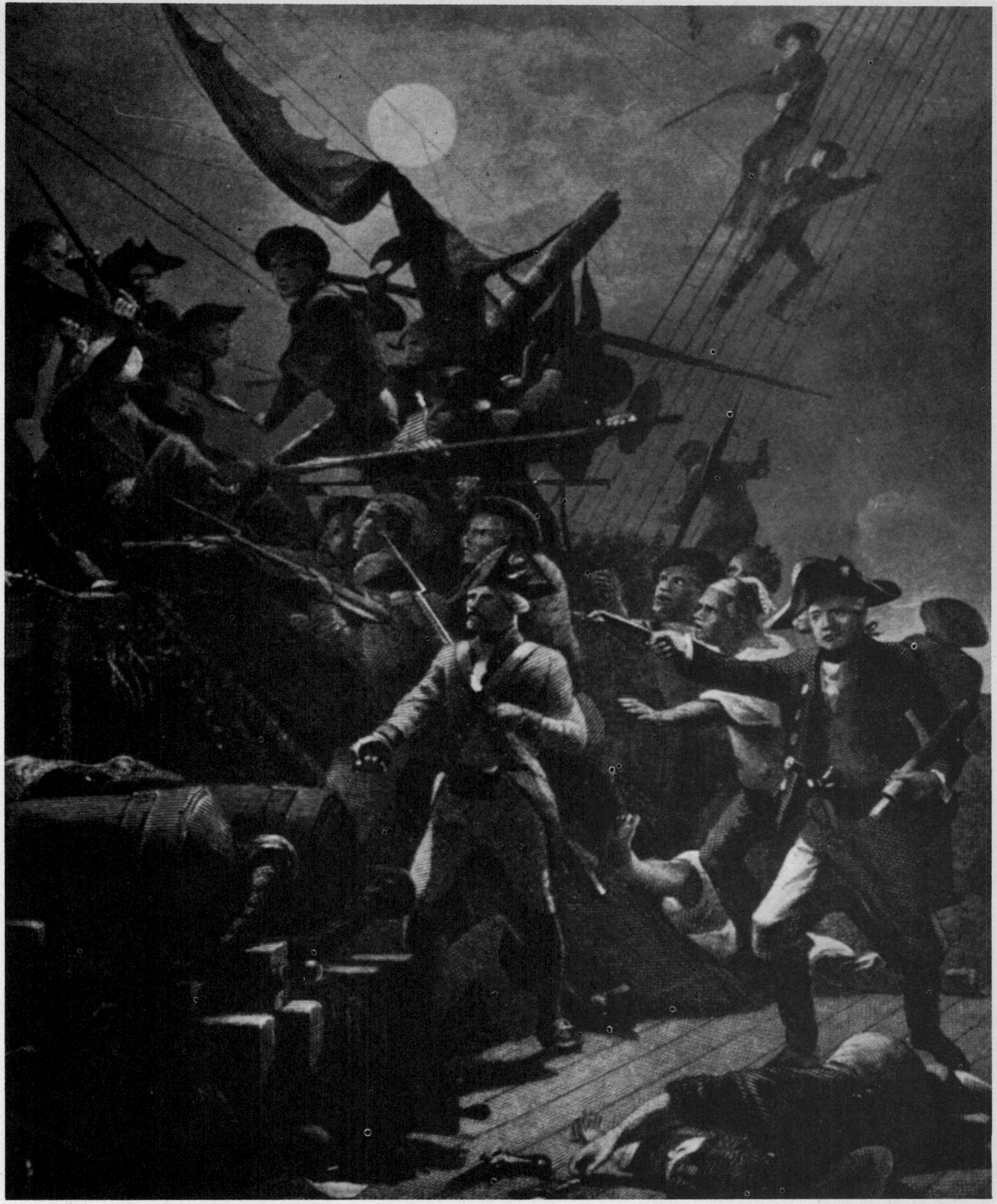

I HAVE NOT YET BEGUN TO FIGHT. —JOHN PAUL JONES

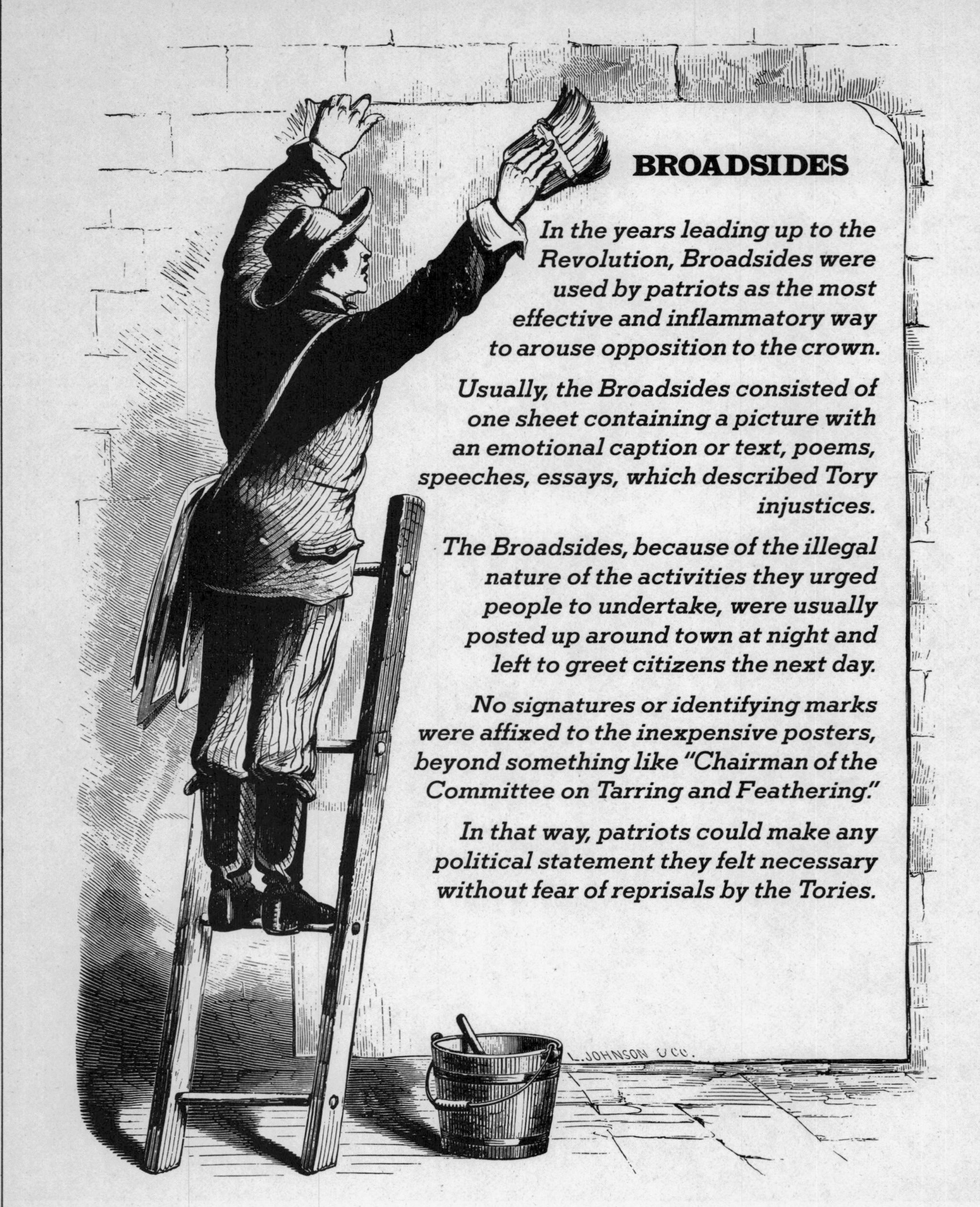
BROADSIDES
In the years leading up to the Revolution, Broadsides were used by patriots as the most effective and inflammatory way to arouse opposition to the crown.
Usually, the Broadsides consisted of one sheet containing a picture with an emotional caption or text, poems, speeches, essays, which described Tory injustices.
The Broadsides, because of the illegal nature of the activities they urged people to undertake, were usually posted up around town at night and left to greet citizens the next day.
No signatures or identifying marks were affixed to the inexpensive posters, beyond something like "Chairman of the Committee on Tarring and Feathering."
In that way, patriots could make any political statement they felt necessary without fear of reprisals by the Tories.
L. JOHNSON & CO.

the worth of your guide—how it gives a true picture of the community, etc. If your efforts are resisted, *demand* equal space in the center; after all, it *is* your community. Threaten pickets, sit-ins or whatever is appropriate. If necessary, mobilize your PBC contacts to carry out your threats. The bureau will give in eventually; the bad publicity will be more than it can take. After all, its main job is public relations!

Conducting Your Own Tours

Once you've done the research into your community and organized it all into a pamphlet, chances are you'll be better versed in your area's history than 99 percent of the folks in town. Certainly you'll be more knowledgeable than the Mayor and the City Council. What better qualifications to designate you as a Peoples Tour Guide?

Start with your friends, relatives and neighbors. Refine your presentation, learn the answers to the commonly asked questions and you're ready for the big time: genuine, out-of-town tourists.

As both a Peoples Bicentennial Commission organizer and a tour guide, you'll naturally want to concentrate on taking *groups* around your community. Get yourself put on the mailing list of the local convention bureau—that way you'll know when large numbers of visitors will be coming into town. Contact local churches, service organizations and youth clubs (YWCA's, Boy Scouts, etc.). Often, groups of these kinds are visited by similar organizations from out of town. In New York City, for instance, youth groups arrive on buses from cities around the country at regular intervals. Once they are in town, New York churches hold workshops and present entertainment for them. A people's tour of Greenwich Village or Wall Street would be perfect in such a situation. Explore similar possibilities in your community.

See America First.